Also by Robert Conquest

**History and Politics**
*Common Sense about Russia*
*Courage of Genius: The Pasternak Affair*
*Power and Policy in the USSR: The Study of Soviet Dynastics*
*Russia after Khrushchev*
*The Great Terror: Stalin's Purge of the Thirties*
*The Nation Killers: The Soviet Deportation of Nationalities*
*Where Marx Went Wrong*
*V. I. Lenin*
*Kolyma: The Arctic Death Camps*
*Present Danger: Towards a Foreign Policy*
*We and They: Civic and Despotic Cultures*
*What to Do When the Russians Come: A Survivor's Guide* (with Jon Manchip White)
*Inside Stalin's Secret Police: NKVD Politics, 1936–1939*
*The Harvest of Sorrow: Soviet Collectivization and the Terror-Famine*
*Stalin and the Kirov Murder*
*Tyrants and Typewriters: Communiqués from the Struggle for Truth*
*The Great Terror: A Reassessment*
*Stalin: Breaker of Nations*
*Reflections on a Ravaged Century*

**Poetry**
*Poems*
*Between Mars and Venus*
*Arias from a Love Opera*
*Coming Across*
*Forays*
*New and Collected Poems*
*Demons Don't*

**Verse Translation**
Aleksandr Solzhenitsyn's *Prussian Nights*

**Fiction**
*The Egyptologists* (with Kingsley Amis)
*A World of Difference*

**Criticism**
*The Abomination of Moab*

# The
# Dragons
## of
# Expectation

*Reality and Delusion in the Course of History*

*Robert Conquest*

*W. W. Norton & Company* | *New York   London*

Illustrations courtesy of John Lucas-Scudamore Collection /
Bridgeman Art Library

For information about permission to reproduce selections from this
book, write to Permissions, W. W. Norton & Company, Inc.,
500 Fifth Avenue, New York, NY 10110

Manufacturing by The Haddon Craftsmen, Inc.
Book design by Blue Shoe Studio
Production manager: Amanda Morrison

Library of Congress Cataloging-in-Publication Data

Conquest, Robert.
The dragons of expectation : reality and delusion in the course of history /
Robert Conquest.— 1st ed.
p. cm.
Includes bibliographical references and index.
**ISBN 0-393-05933-2**
1. Social history. 2. Civilization, Modern. 3. Ideology—History. I. Title.
HN13.C6445 2005
306'.09—dc22

2004019159

W. W. Norton & Company, Inc., 500 Fifth Avenue, New York, N.Y. 10110
www.wwnorton.com

W. W. Norton & Company Ltd.
Castle House, 75/76 Wells Street, London W1T 3QT

1 2 3 4 5 6 7 8 9 0

For my daughters-in-law,
Rosemary and Debra Lou,
and for
Amy B. Desai
and in memory of
Rasik

# Acknowledgments

———∞———

I wish to thank above all Robert Weil, prince of editors (any faults in this book are due to his not having written it himself)—and also to his skilled staff. I am very grateful to Anatol Shmelev and Julia Shmelev for much indispensable research, and in general to the Hoover Institution for its support (notably from my dedicatee Amy Desai). Once again I owe many thanks to Stephen Cohen, for his usual fine purview of Russian sources. And, as ever, or even more than ever, to my wife. Some of the material was first published by the *New Review*, the *New Criterion*, the *Times Literary Supplement*, the *New Republic*, *National Review*, *London Magazine*, the *Los Angeles Times*, the Hoover Press, and The Royal Society of Literature.

From the west I saw fly
the dragons of expectation,
and open the way of the fire-powerful;
they beat their wings,
so that everywhere it appeared to me
that earth and heaven burst.

–from a translation by Thomas Wright (1844)
of the *Poetic* (or *Elder*) *Edda*

# Contents

———❦———

Preface xv

## Part I  Through Reefs and Riptides
**Chapter I**  Heads above Water and Vice Versa  3

**Chapter II**  Lemming Lore  11

**Chapter III**  Harpooning Some Word-Whales  23

**Chapter IV**  Choose Your Enlightenment  37

**Chapter V**  After Utopia  45

**Chapter VI**  Internationalism, Supranationalism  57

**Chapter VII**  Slouching towards Byzantium  71

## Part II  Horrible Examples
**Chapter VIII**  1917: "Revolution" and Reality  87

**Chapter IX**  Revolutionary High Finance:
   Some Notes on a Neglected Theme  95

**Chapter X**  Into the Planned Economy  101

**Chapter XI**  Inside the New Society  111

**Chapter XII**  With and Against Hitler  125

**Chapter XIII**  Cold War: Heated Imaginations  135

**Chapter XIV**  A Gaggle of Misleaders  145

**Chapter XV**  A Collapse of Unreality  165

# Contents

**Part III  Harp Song of the Humanities**

**Chapter XVI**  The Whys of Art  175

**Chapter XVII**  Bureaucracies and Barbarism  191

**Chapter XVIII**  Awake to Affirmation  203


Epilogue  209

*Appendix A* "No One Foresaw the Collapse of the Soviet
    System"  213

*Appendix B* An Anglosphere in the Neosphere (A Political
    Exercise)  221

Select Bibliography  233

Index  241

# Preface

The title of this book is taken from a very unsanguine treatment of human fate—the *Elder Edda,* where the flight of these dragons opens the way to the "fire-powerful," at which point it appears to the bard that "earth and heaven burst."

Some such disaster is indeed among the menaces that have accumulated to threaten our own possible future. But I have been even more struck by the phrase "dragons of expectation" itself. For quite apart from the worst perspective, it seems clear that something in the nature of otherworldly "expectations" has seized the minds of many in the West and elsewhere—with misleading thought about what faces us, much of it bred and projected from unreal obsessions about the still-living past.

Myths and manias have always flourished. Over the generations they have taken new forms: we review their nature and their origins, but also the more general mental atmosphere of less formal concepts and verbalizations from which they emerge, and which also strongly calls for much clarification. And, in that perspective, we go on to consider the current state of the humanities, as well as of the intellectual and evidential sphere.

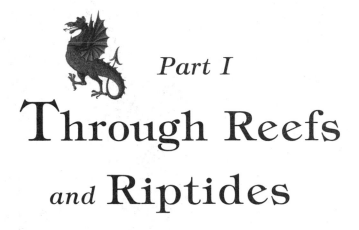

# Part I

# Through Reefs
## *and* Riptides

*offre une brébis noire a la noire tempète*
—André Chénier

. . . for telling men how the was happened and why people must
—foreign student of D. J. Enright's on Milton's motives in writing
*Paradise Lost*, quoted in Enright's *Play Resumed*

*Chapter I*

# Heads above Water and Vice Versa

⤜⤛⤜

1.

We are concerned here to present, rather than to vindicate, arguments and facts. They are accompanied by illustrations and illuminations, rather than "proofs." I have, as far as possible, rid them of excess complexity or coruscation or incrustation. Inevitably, anyone who, as here, covers a wide field must accept and show that in some cases new data can bring fuller understanding. And I suppose it is necessary—though it should not be—to disavow anything like an "ideology." As has been well put by that fine political thinker Maurice Cranston, one can have a worldview in a broad and general sense without falling into such uncivilized frigidities.

2.

The future of the human race? The future of civilization?

Prediction is impossible. Only in an indistinct blur can we see a future, and even then only a short distance into what may seem its immediate probabilities, while never forgetting—as history teaches us—that quite minor events or behaviors may decide between one possibility and a quite different alternative. Can it be taken for granted that the future is now decided irreversibly in our favor? No. We can see some trends or directions, some pressures or potentials building up. There are so many factors, some of which have not yet declared themselves. It may be a near thing or a series of near things.

Still, we can avoid false "expectations." We can, up to a point, have a reasonably sound idea of the unfolding realities ahead and guard against devastating surprise. We can even prepare ourselves to some extent for the unexpected.

3

### 3.

Above all, we can clear up, or begin to clear up, the mind-mists that rob us unnecessarily of any tolerable view of present reality and future possibility. As to the latter, it will be a question of sketches rather than holograms. But at least we can improve our, the human race's, chances.

It is, moreover, largely in apparently sophisticated circles that misunderstandings of alien phenomena, past and future, have been generated. It seems appropriate, in fact urgent, to examine how counterfactual abstractions and generalizations came to preempt reality in much of this mental zone.

For these misconceptions did not come out of nowhere. The psychosphere and the logosphere are permeated by concepts, ideas, verbalizations—a whole apparatus designed in theory to form some sort of mental contact with reality, but often resulting in reality's being blocked off. It can easily be shown that answers from this stratum of thought given two generations ago, or even one generation ago, were distortive and delusive. So in what follows we try to do something towards getting readers to doubt, to get them to think again, and also to question the validity of not only views accepted by habit but also, as will be seen later in this book, supposed historical and other "facts."

### 4.

To grasp the complexities of reality, we do need to use general words and concepts. But these have often, as one might put it, escaped empirical control and grown into obstacles against understanding: "brain blindfolds"—and even mechanisms for stifling, or at least discouraging, real debate. Ideas insufficiently connected to realities have always been part of the human effort to understand.

These ideas are, of course, most troublesome when they present themselves as virtually indisputable: as idols, or at least icons. As Robert Louis Stevenson wrote many years ago, "Man is a creature who lives not upon bread alone, but principally by catchwords." Part of the problem is that the catchwords of current speech or thought are usually supported, offstage, by more complex, superficially impressive wordplay.

Some of the vital information available to us has been distorted—some, indeed, has been actively falsified on a very large scale—by groups, or states, with what by now should be understandable motivations for concealment. But this is only one example, or product, of a broader misuse of the human mind.

### 5.

It has been known for millennia that any understanding of the future is only possible if it includes a reasonable understanding of the past. Thucydides already saw history as, in part, "an aid to the interpretation of the future."

For humanity, as it exists now, is a product of the past—of the intricate, interweaving complexities of recent, and of less recent, history or histories. The psychological, as well as physical, conditions we thus inherited must be considered with as much care and clarity as can be attained. This should, of course, include a proper understanding of backgrounds—so different in different cultures and countries.

Our current confrontations with the enemies of our civilization are in some ways unlike the earlier threats we faced over much of the twentieth century. The West prevailed then but was much hampered by misevaluations of the hostile motivations of the other side, which diverted our citizens' attention from the realities. Writing in the early nineteenth century, Thomas Macaulay expressed the hope that in the future our crises would be handled by people "for whom history has not recorded the long series of human crimes and follies in vain."

Do our countries today meet Macaulay's standard? Alas, no. Both the actions and the intentions of the adversaries and the supporters of a plural society are still being misrepresented by some of those responsible for the transmission of Macaulay's message.

### 6.

One of the factors we can surely improve is the attitudes and assessments guiding our own polities.

We should start by looking at the general state of the Western mind, with both its strengths and its vulnerabilities—and with them, and dependent on them, our prospects over the critical decades ahead. Our aim is not to blame the misinformed strata in the United Kingdom and the United States and elsewhere, but rather to explain, to suggest how to avoid or anticipate similar failings in the future.

The events of September 11, 2001, were, of course, a tremendous shock. And part of the shock was that it brought home to Americans the knowledge that the world is full of immense dangers. Not only the general population but also the politically educated stratum, those concerned with world affairs, were staggered and shaken. They knew in theory that the planet harbors alien and hostile movements and states. But this had always seemed peripheral—psychological rather than physical. They had not really understood the possibilities out there in totally different mentalities, and histories. We need not only to cope with the incendiary powers and movements but also to make sure that our minds, and the minds of all civilized humankind, and especially of its mentally active elements, are brought up to the necessary habits of knowledge and judgment.

When we loosely speak of a "Western" political culture, we should never forget that this culture not long ago produced, and intellectually justified, some of the worst enemies of the plural tradition.

### 7.

No doubt all controversy tends to stress, or overstress, one or the other side of the matter under contention. Nor can we avoid a certain amount of partisan emphasis. All the same, reasonable limits are commonly exceeded. And this is usually from the side, in every debate, that has come to consider its views as unquestionable, so that its adherents react inappropriately to what appears to them to be heresy. So what was originally goodwill or good faith has often been radically degraded. There is always more to be said, more witnesses to be called, before the facts can be faced.

It may seem unarguable that moderation and balance should prevail. But to have much faith in this would be to ignore the historical record. Still, for much of the time, in the United States and United Kingdom at least, opponents of moderation were induced, or shamed, into a pretense of rational discussion, though dogma, nowadays, is often more open and blatant.

There are minds that, having risen beyond primitive, unthinking orthodoxies, often merely turn to a rejection of the traditional. Whoever has made this apparent advance is convinced that he or she has reached a superior condition. Minds that have improved their knowledge and remained open to more have indeed progressed. But we often find those who have achieved a critical attitude to the traditional have also adopted a largely, or wholly, uncritical attitude to untried, or even failed, alternatives whose attraction is verbal rather than real.

"Special interests" are often, and sometimes rightly, indicted for various social and other offenses. But, of course, special interests are not necessarily economic. What may reasonably be called interest groups could equally be emotional or mental factions, that is, insistent minorities in society. Often, what is more, they themselves feel pressure from their own extremer wings—that is to say, a minority within a minority. Greed is only one of the deadly sins.

All this is to say that we should not ignore the fanaticisms and the appeal of fanaticisms within the West, even in the (so far) victoriously defended Anglo-American sphere. Some of this fanaticism is little more than a comfortable anti-Americanism or anti–plural society attitude, which it would be overprecise to call adolescent, as with the teenage appeal of posters, beret at a becoming angle, of Che Guevara. It might be suggested that as one section of the human brain grows, this diverts nutrients from other sections, which are therefore stunted, and perhaps that in adolescence, under a different physiological mechanism, toxins are produced from which recovery is slow and sometimes never takes place.

In much of the supposedly liberal world, there was and is, alas, a sympathy for such critics of the consensual, manifested at its worst in toleration of student-activist actions that silence free speech, disrupt universities, and so on. There are examples almost daily, as informed readers know.

Clearly, one of the mental conditions we can discourage is *righteousness*. This may afflict left wing and right wing alike, as we all know. It is fair to point out that in some cases it emerges only on a particular issue or two—though in others almost the whole mental approach seems warped that way. In certain types of public oratory this is more or less acceptable. But when it is presented as argument, moderate or mature minds simply switch themselves off.

In this context, it is worth noting, as Paul Hollander has done at length in his book *Anti-Americanism*, that some of the churches or their organizations have a terrible record. Seeing the social faults of their own societies, they have—only too often—condoned or denied the sins of the enemies of our order. To take only one example, the World Council of Churches Central Committee, meeting in 1973, passed a resolution deploring oppression in the Middle East, Africa, Latin America, the United States, and elsewhere. An attempt by a Swedish clergyman to add the Communist countries was defeated by 91 to 3, with 26 abstentions. It will be argued, to some extent rightly, that church organizational power, as commonly in other spheres, is often in the hands of an activist minority.

In a plural society we must have plurality. And that means allowing troublesome ideas to be presented. In some cases these are presented by those who are not prepared to listen to argument. Sometimes their ideas have a record of lethal activity. Sometimes they are a mass of demonstrable falsehood. Sometimes they are openly or even ostentatiously aligned with the destructive forces.

What can be done? We must live with the contradictions. Yes, but . . .

## 8.

O ur world can, roughly speaking, be divided into the civilized, the semi-civilized, and the uncivilized (or decivilized) countries. That is to claim superiority, but not anything like perfection, for the first named. None of us, presumably, would see the present state of things in the United States, the United Kingdom, or elsewhere as lacking in faults. On the contrary, there are well-justified complaints, enough to fill volumes, and which indeed have filled volumes. And there is room for argument within our politico-social framework on all sorts of issues—though there often comes a point when dispute is pressed so far as to be destructive of our order's crucial con-sensuality. This amounts, above all, to saying that whatever political feuds or attitudes exist in the democracies, they count for very little compared with the vast and essential conflict between "Western" society and the world-wide fanaticisms facing it. Disagreement will subsist in and between the states of the West and its allies. Two central requirements remain: first, to remain reasonably united in dealing with international dangers; and second, to avoid and discourage mind-sets that (for whatever reason) misevaluate the nature of those dangers.

It is not our province to argue about the details of foreign policy. But it does seem important to establish that the dangers threatening us are the product of human motivations. The mentalities, or rather the particular modes of expression, of those who are enemies of civilization vary. But when it comes to the actualities of terror and aggression, there is a great similarity, a real continuity, among minds closed to tolerance and pluralism. This is obvious enough when we look at Iraq and North Korea—the latter, a product of the Stalin brand of Marxism-Leninism. As we saw, Yugoslav president Slobodan Milosevic was a high Communist official until he looked for different targets. And we are told that a number of members of the Middle Eastern terror groups had originally been in the local Communist movements. The essential is, and was, hatred of the open society. Nor is there much, except for the particular psychological justification, to choose between the Real IRA and the Shining Path, though the latter is, or was, more typical and more "intellectual." The members of these terrorist sects, as with those in Italy or, for example, the Naxalities in India, were almost entirely recruited from student elements who had accepted the abstractions of fashionable academics. And the September 11 bombers were almost all comfortably off young men, some having been to Western universities and there adopted the extreme anti-Western mind-set.

The twentieth century's dangers and disasters were largely attributable in the first place to the specific insane ideas or mind-sets that took control of certain parties and populations. But in the second place, they were the result of the spread or return of this infection into the cultures of law and liberty. And this was part of the reason why, even though finally the then forces of destruction broke down, it was such a difficult and exhausting struggle. The nature of the problem, of the challenge, was imperfectly understood.

Moreover, as we have said, or implied, this contagion was found especially among those who considered themselves to be an intellectual leadership or "educated" class or caste. And these were often minds of high IQ presenting sophisticated fallacies to a wider stratum. This level of misevaluation still persists. The West's herds of saurians still roam our intellectual jungles.

## 9.

It also seems that the spread of general misunderstanding does go with, and provide the matter of, a long-term tendency towards a recognizable form of decadence, accompanied by a type of corporatism, which we also must address.

Are there, in fact, intellectual and, deriving from that, institutional trends within the West downgrading our culture? And culture not merely in the politico-social sense, but in the broadest and fullest meaning? Is there a gradual ossification, if not yet irreversible, of our civilization? A trend that seems to some extent also based on, or justified by, fine-sounding generalities (though it can equally be seen in terms of quasi-organic institutional growth)?

Civilization may, and should, be victorious in the current clash with its declared enemies. But within the West itself there are these downward trends. There is not merely a tendency to what might be called a mentality of conformism but, especially in Europe, an emerging semi-ideological conformist bureaucracy devoted to state control of much of human activity.

These are the themes with which we shall deal.

*Chapter II*

# Lemming Lore

———— ⟨⟩⟨⟩⟨⟩ ————

1.

Vaclav Havel, speaking some years before the collapse of Communism in then Czechoslovakia and other countries, said of Western acceptance of social and political categories:

> *Or the question about socialism and capitalism! I admit that it gives me a sense of emerging from the depths of the last century. It seems to me that these thoroughly ideological and many times mystified categories have long since been beside the point.*

An almost equally prominent dissident of that time, Adam Michnik, in Poland, wrote:

> *The very division "Left-Right" emerged in another epoch, and it is impossible to make meaningful reconstruction of it in present day Poland (and probably also in other countries ruled by Communists). To the vast majority of Poles "Right" and "Left" are abstract divisions from another epoch.*

It was yet another leading dissident, Zhelyu Zhelev, later president of Bulgaria, whose book on Fascism (*Fashizmut*), published and suppressed in the early 1980s, presents the complementary point—the essential similarities between "left" and "right" totalitarianisms.

On the broader theme of human liberty, these three exemplars were united. And they implied that this was not the case among many in the less experienced West. They were of course speaking from inside the monstrosity and had less illusory leeway than those merely threatened, or merely observing, from abroad.

This is not to say that there can be no legitimate divergencies within a consensual society (indeed both Havel and Zhelev were to express some). And in democratic politics such notions as conservative and progressive, or right and left, are of some pragmatic use in covering certain rough attitudes on matters of internal policy. (But much less so, if at all, on the broader themes.) In fact, it might be argued that in the long run it is only by dispute and debate that the democracies can function. Still, the statements of these veterans do imply that there should be a certain level of restraint and, even more important, that domestic dissensions should not be transferred uncritically to alien or international problems—as is perhaps the only plausible explanation for the long-lasting Western misevaluations of the Soviet phenomenon. (Has anyone written a book called *Stalin's Moustache: The Lunatic Fringe*?)

One trouble, a nasty one, is that the more civilized attitudes of both left and right tend to spill over into their totalitarian variants, or at the minimum into one-sided tolerations, a preference for the more appealing totalitarians over opponents within their own culture, with whom they actually have far less real substantive disagreement. If the trouble is largely from a left, it is partly because of a certain reluctance to admit that Communism was not only physically lethal and mentally repressive but also a total failure. (And an example of a yet further spillover into the destructive side of the "progressive" tradition is the blurring of the difference between "activism" and terrorism, at least when the agents of both claim the same theoretical justification.)

But on the whole question of "left" and "right"—and of "activism"—we may note a piece by Walter Laqueur ("What to Read (and Not to Read) about Terrorism," *Partisan Review*, vol. 69, no. 3 [2002]) in which he quotes several of the most extreme right groups in the United States—the American Nazi Party, the White Aryan Resistance, the Missouri Militia, the National Alliance—speaking enthusiastically about the brave Arab bombers of September 11. In Europe, Horst Mahler, once a stalwart of the extreme left Baader-Meinhof Gang but now on the extreme right, congratulated the bombers, as did the most notorious extreme left group in Europe, the Italian Red Brigades.

Zhelev made clear that the extreme or totalitarian left and right had much in common. Moreover, though both are now thoroughly discredited, we can observe a legacy from the total state or the totalist mentality even in an excess of bureaucratization *within* a conformist evolution in the West. One continuing trouble, as ever, is the notion that for all problems there is a "solution," and that when found this can be put into effect by the state (or its opponents).

"Left" and "Right," we should remind ourselves, were only invented in the 1790s, and "Liberal" was coined for Spanish politics less than a generation later. "Liberal" in Britain came to mean something like "progressive but opposed to state power." And we perhaps need reminding that the first humanitarian laws—limiting the working day and ending child labor, in the 1840s, and later providing good cheap housing—were largely the work of conservative reformers. It should be clear that work against social ills does not mean acceptance of what chances to be a "progressive" agenda in other fields.

2.

Let us look at one of Havel's "mystified categories"—Socialism.

Generally, the socialist idea that motivated much political and economic action in the postwar period in Britain and elsewhere no longer appeals to most people in the old way—even as a slogan or emotional belief. But its negative formula, its old banner anticapitalism, survives. Its statist motivation, too, persists, though also less transcendently. And, together with these, we still have the general heritage of radicalism that preceded socialism. Thus if the all-purpose aim and full-time Idea is no longer found in serious politics, this means that what are usually regarded as "left" opinions are a bundle of views or projects no longer presented as part of a single transcendent aim but put forward as often unrelated particulars, each to be judged on its own merit.

The trouble with socialism was its statist version (for there were syndicalist and other variants that more or less died out early on). For if you asked who, after the removal of the capitalists and other excrescences, would run society and the economy, the answer was that it would be done by "society." But who would represent "society"? A simple enough point, but one that has proved refractory. Not the population, by referenda—with the long nineteenth-century and later records. So, not society, but those qualified to run the country. And these were to be, indeed would need to be, free—or comparatively free—from the inevitable accompaniments and attractions of power. But how were they to be identified?

The main general lesson of history, and especially of recent history, is that overriding control of society should not be in the hands of any economic or other stratum, nor in the hands of the state itself. Highly centralized and doctrinaire regimes have time and again proved deeply destructive. To take a single example, Italy took a long time to recover from the despotism of the late sixteenth century. It is hard to remember that a millennium or so ago the Mezzogiorno was the site of the freshest and most intelligent Western thought, and that Salerno had the first modern "university." The form later taken there by society and the state, and the concomitant narrowing of the mind, led to long periods of stultification, even more than did other manifestations of the "old regime" elsewhere.

3.

More generally, in Europe under the eighteenth-century monarchism, we run into the disorganized current of ideas considered progressive, as against the stasis and stupefaction of the old regimes—a current jammed with flotsam and jetsam, and one that yet flows today, even after socialism has steamed on to shipwreck.

So how do we, and did we, identify a general psychological (and not necessarily socialist) "left"? In Britain, as in America, leftist thought now consists of only vaguely associated ideas or aims of the sort the left had attracted even before high socialism. I have previously quoted Eric Hobsbawm on the causes espoused five generations ago, before they got round to socialism, by the consciously progressive: "natural philosophy, phrenology, free thought, spiritualism, temperance, unorthodox medicine, social reform and the transformation of the family." Engels, cofounder of its most influential variant, complained even later that socialism attracted those he thought of as crackpots: "anti-inoculationists," plus vegetarians, antivivisectionists, nature healers, and such. Lenin warned against Bolshevik doctors for similar reasons. What these elements all showed was less a devotion to socialism than an enmity to established thought and its institutions. All these causes are not logically connected, but one can detect a certain mood or mental direction. We are surely reminded of a modern, and not dissimilar, bundle of aims and ideas. Why? How? What can be done about it?

Let us reconsider the phenomenon of "socialism" briefly. Properly speaking, it arose in the early nineteenth century and was put forward as a politico-social program on the lines of, though in many ways different from, Plato's or Sir Thomas More's or all the other fictional concepts of politico-social organization. It derived, too, from what would now be called the "communes"–from Pantisocracy and such, but also, in the case of Robert Owen, from actual and fairly successful cooperatives. It was, its proponents hoped, a blueprint that could be, and might be, applied to modern societies. (Owen, like later socialists, hoped his plans could be forwarded by approaching the British government of the time.)

There was also a revolutionary element, as with Gracchus Babeuf and his "conspiracy of equals", which saw a simple dictatorship as its real aim. But even revolutionary socio-utopianism was not at first linked to the "class struggle." Its milieu and those who believed themselves socialists attracted those of a certain mood and attitude, but it was a late version of socialism that made it a matter of the industrial working class. And as genuine working-class organizations accepted the socialist idea, they began seriously to delete or qualify it and to save most of it mainly for oratory rather than policy. It is a remarkable fact that no socialist movement that was based on organized workers ever went to the logical, verbal, general-idea extremes. Only groupings dominated by theoreticians—or, more correctly, dogmatists—were able to act to impose the full fantasy.

4.

Socialism, and notions associated with it, spread in Britain over the past century or so. In Europe the story is different, and in the United States the comparable "progressive" ideas became influential in something of the same way, but "Socialism" as such was much less in evidence. Given this difference, how did the word or concept of "socialism" become so prevalent in the British psychosphere?

In the late nineteenth century, the English economist and socialist Sidney Webb wrote that to change opinion in England it would only be necessary to win over a few thousand key figures. This may remind us, indirectly, of the new approach to Soviet espionage in England introduced in the mid-1930s by Soviet agent Arnold Deutsch, who recruited the "Cambridge Five"–that spies should be sought in the leading universities, where governmental cadres were "educated."

Sidney and his wife, Beatrice, came to dominate the socialist Fabian Society. Its avowed aim was to "permeate" the political, and thus also the social, realm. (Beatrice Webb, when quite a young woman, is reported to have spoken of herself as "the cleverest member of one of the cleverest families in the cleverest class of the cleverest nation of the world." When she met a woman state senator from Utah who defended polygamy on the grounds that it let women be impregnated by those they felt to be the best potential fathers, Mrs. Webb found the argument valid.)

The Webbs' effect was twofold. First, they wrote a series of exhaustively researched books on various social matters, sometimes with useful suggestions. Second, they had an organizational influence, through sponsoring the great Fabian effort of conferences, seminars, summer schools, pamphlets, and more permanent measures such as the founding of the London School of Economics.

Politically, the Fabians first tried to influence the Conservative Party, then the Liberals, but finally entered the emerging Labour Party. Based on the Trade Unions, Labour allowed various groups to affiliate, giving them access to the party's machine and, indirectly, to its electorate. When Labour was transformed into a full political party after World War I and required a program, an opportunity arose. Though no more than perfunctorily accepted by the Unions, the Fabians succeeded in making the Party's eventual aim "the Nationalisation of the Means of Production, Distribution and Exchange." Nor was the program itself, as phrased, a slogan of mass appeal. A. P. Herbert wrote satirically of an unsympathetic working-class audience listening to a speaker:

> *Comrades! Wage slaves! Ain't it very strange*
> *These 'ere capitalists*
> *Don't want to nationalise*
> *The means of production, distribution and exchange!*

The word "socialism" also proved divisive.

No Labour government went anywhere close to pursuing the formula completely. There were, indeed, as elsewhere in Europe, major nationalizations after World War II. But a decade or two later, during hot debates about the denationalization and renationalization of steel, polls showed that only 10 percent of voters on either side were interested.

On the contrary, what was very popular was a Labour and Conservative (and Liberal) miscalculation, which neither party has yet to handle, and which was not the Webbs' fault, though it is socialist in its way: the National Health Service. Other highly etatist countries, like France, have devised health services that are generally efficient and popular. The British version was based on an absurd assumption. It was calculated that free health care would mean a great improvement in health and therefore less and less demand for the service. But once something is free, people throng to it even when it is not really necessary.

5.

On the other hand, thanks to the Fabians and such, the socialist concept had indeed "permeated" the intelligentsia, including George Orwell, and the educated bureaucracy of the future—foreshadowing the Italian socialist and later Communist Antonio Gramsci's "march through the institutions." Socialism as a general idea or sentiment remained in the minds of many people of goodwill. For Orwell, socialism meant "justice and liberty." What he rejected (like Engels!) was the "prigs" and "cranks" he found in the movement. But what he even more deplored among socialists was their desire to rule and regulate, to "tidy" everything. In effect, what he wanted (though I don't think he ever put it this way) was socialism without socialists (as after the Enron scandal and such, some might feel they want capitalism without capitalists).

But socialism was, even with Orwell, seen as state control of the economy. He, of course, saw that countries and movements calling themselves "socialist" indeed had state-controlled economies but no freedom or justice—and so with his image of the "Party" in *1984*, which "grew out of the earlier Socialist movement and inherited its phraseology."

As to the Webbs, they produced a huge and highly researched book—*Soviet Communism: A New Civilisation?* The two approaches to socialism—Fabian and Stalinist—had merged. This was at just the time when the Fabian effort bore fruit with massive intellectual acceptance and Stalinism became (for a time) a respectable variant. Class war, of which the Webbs had never approved, had reached its aim in Soviet socialism.

At this point it is worth noting, surely, that the Khmer Rouge, the murderous Cambodian regime, was in principle, a socialist, Marxist experiment (its ideas picked up in the West). And that even more devotedly, the North Korean regime still is (I only hope by this time *was*) Marxist, Leninist, and, indeed, seems a parody of Orwell's *1984*. A former Soviet diplomat in Pyongyang told me of his surprise in finding deceptions far more complete than Moscow had ever tried. He had been in large and busy garment stores where, he noticed, no actual purchases were being made.

This may remind one of how the USSR was unable, despite all its oil and other wealth, to provide—even for the dupes it was eager to impress—the mere appearance of decent hotels. Milovan Djilas tells us of how when he was first in Moscow in the Yugoslav Communist delegation in 1944, they were well served at the Metropol by waiters and others dating from before the revolution, while in 1946 in the new Moskva, he and Aleksandar Rankovic asked for a lightbulb to be changed, upon which two workers eventually arrived and one proceeded to stand on the other's shoulders to reach the bulb, since no ladders had been provided. Many later visitors would find comparable examples.

6.

In the United States, and now to a large degree elsewhere in the West, though socialism never prevailed in politics or serious political discourse, the more general left accumulated partisan support—as did the later reinvention of liberalism.

"Liberal" is, indeed, a vague term. Many of us would take a "liberal" position on some issues, a "conservative" one on others—as most of the American or British people in fact do (an attitude shared, too, by the present writer). These two vaguely differentiated attitudes are the poles within the normal development, or balance, of a civic or consensual society. At any rate, a liberal is, by definition, one whose aim is the furtherance of ever greater political liberty, freedom of thought, and social justice.

A number of those who thought of themselves and were thought of as liberals became apologists for the Stalinist or similar regimes whose most notable characteristics were extreme terror, narrow dogmatism, social oppression, and economic failure. They were, in fact, what Orwell called "renegade Liberals." He defines them, with characteristic felicity, in the unused preface to *Animal Farm*, as those who hold that "defending democracy involves destroying all independence of thought." His immediate concern was that "where the USSR and its policies are concerned one cannot expect intelligent criticism or even, in many cases, plain honesty from Liberal writers and journalists who are under no direct pressure to falsify their opinions." Elsewhere (in his "The Prevention of Literature") he comments, "When one sees highly educated men looking on indifferently at oppression and persecution, one wonders which to despise more, their cynicism or their shortsightedness." He felt obliged to add, in his unpublished preface, "it is the liberals who fear liberty and the intellectuals who want to do dirt on the intellect."

Of course, we should say that there were many liberals—and in general many on the "left"—who kept their principles unsullied and were often among the strongest opponents of the Communist despotisms. Nor, indeed, did the bulk of the Labour Party, under Clement Atlee and Ernest Bevin, succumb. On the contrary.

What Orwell's "intellectuals" seem to have ingested was a false idea of social "equality," to which their other principles could be harmlessly sacrificed. We can trace the roots of this aberration a long way back. Even before World War I, the English philosopher and journalist L. T. Hobhouse, in his classic *Liberalism,* had written, "liberty without equality is a name of noble sound and squalid result." But "equality" is a slippery word. In a general sense we may allow that genuine liberals—and others—are committed to a society of equal citizens. A liberal state may have a legitimate role in redressing poverty and making health care available. But after a point we find that the *liberté* and *égalité* that proved incompatible in the 1790s are still awkward companions. And as the liberal attitude became more and more concerned with the use of political power to promote equality, it tended to become less and less concerned with the liberty side until, even domestically, in Thomas Sowell's words, "the grand delusion of contemporary liberals is that they have both the right and the ability to move their fellow creatures around like blocks of wood—and that the end results will be no different than if people had voluntarily chosen the same actions."

### 7.

More basic may be Orwell's idea that most people are in some sense "nationalists," that is, they have and need an emotional allegiance to their country—or against their country. An antipatriotic strain can certainly be noted in one variety of liberalism. Its most frequent symptom is the use of Dr. Johnson's remark "Patriotism is the last refuge of a scoundrel"—commonly employed, even now, as a sort of put-down by critics of the patriotic.

How anyone could imagine that Johnson was against patriotism in its modern sense is most peculiar. If anything, he was almost a chauvinist. In controversy, his main victims were Whigs, about whom he made many offensive remarks. The English poet Winthrop Mackworth Praed writes of a moderate character:

*And much he loathed the patriot's snort,*
*And much he scorned the placeman's snuffle.*

The two factions being in fact the extreme Whigs and Tories. The word "patriotism" for Johnson meant, of course, in its then usage, adherence to the most ostentatious Whiggism, what would now be called "leftism." Macaulay's treatment, in his essay on Horace Walpole, is the most readily available. Himself, of course, a Whig, Macaulay treats the "patriot" faction with contempt. One should surely treat similarly the subliterate misuse of Johnson.

As to the "renegade" left, it might be argued that the true heroes of the long argument were not so much the committed anti-Communist or "patriotic" conservatives. They were of course right, and fully deserve the verdict in their favor as against the pro-Communist liberals. But much of the heat of battle was borne by those within the liberal intelligentsia who not only were not deceived but fought for the truth over years of slander and discouragement. We might, in fact, say that there are two sorts of liberal, as there are two sorts of cholesterol, one good and one bad. The difficulty is, or has been, that good liberalism implies a good deal of mental self-control.

8.

In Britain, it might be said that by 1984 the Webbite side had won. But this was only part of the old left-wing appeal. The "cranks" had at least not been, or not yet been, dictatorship material. But the utopian or sub-utopian mind-set pervaded or indoctrinated part of the intellectual semi-educated class. Over the past half century, Western minds that were diverted by the socialist idea largely abandoned it as a serious program. However, the minds of a generation of the educated are not restructured as easily and completely as that. The thought patterns are, often enough, still set in the direction of central state control, though to represent this with anything like the old sublimity is a hard challenge.

Socialism has thus largely petered out, except as the decorative phrasing of more or less kleptocratic states. But the cluster of social and other ideas that accompanied socialism persists. And the idea of using state power to impose them has, of course, flourished and more than flourished both as a mental habit and as a political reality. Its adherents are now no longer socialists but, as we have said, remain implacably hostile to "capitalism" without seriously advancing any real alternative.

It seems that the usual course of the trend to mental unreality is not, to start with, so much the use or abuse of general ideas so much as an at first barely formulated inhaling of an atmosphere of hostility to envisaged unrighteousness and to those seen as its perpetrators. These feelings are then traditionally deployed in terms of abstract, or semiabstract, words and phraseology, whether in approval or condemnation.

## Chapter III

# Harpooning Some Word-Whales

〰〰〰

### 1.

That is putting it a little strongly. But some of the biggest words we are accustomed to use need, let us say, to be pinned down. Paul Valéry, in his introduction to Leo Ferrero's 1929 *Léonard de Vinci*, speaks of how some human activity cannot "be simplified and reduced to a simple and abstract thought, for its origin and effect is held in an inextricable system of independent conditions." In spite of this, general concepts are unavoidable. So we need to demystify key words used in political speech—"democracy," and its awkward relationship with "liberty" and "progress"; "Fascism," as an almost equally misapplied term.

### 2.

The common addiction to general words or concepts tends to produce mind blockers or reality distorters. As Clive James has put it, "verbal cleverness, unless its limitations are clearly and continuously seen by its possessors, is an unbeatable way of blurring reality until nothing can be seen at all."

"Democracy" is high on the list of blur-begetters—not a weasel word so much as a huge rampaging Kodiak bear of a word. The conception is, of course, Greek. Athenian democracy commonly gets high prestige in the sense that the idea, and to some degree the practice, later became widespread—or widely proclaimed—in the West. Pericles, praising the Athenian system, is especially proud of the fact that policies are argued about and debated before being put into action, thus, he says, avoiding "the worst thing in the world," which is to rush into action without considering the consequences. And, indeed, the Athenians did debate and discuss, often sensibly. One trouble was, and presumably is, that debate can be influenced by plausible but misleading rhetoric.

It was a matter of the free vote by the public (though confined to males and citizens). This has been compared to the early New England town meetings or those of Swiss rural cantons. And clearly there are limits to the number of possible participants.

Its faults are almost as obvious as its virtues. And examples are many—for instance, the sentencing of Socrates (who lost votes because of his politically incorrect speech in his own defense). Or the Athenian assembly voting for the death of all the adult males and the enslavement of all the women and children of Mytilene, then regretting the decision and sending a second boat to intercept, just in time, the one carrying the order. Democracy had the even more grievous result of procuring the ruin of Athens, by voting for the disastrous and pointless expedition to Syracuse against the advice of the more sensible, on being bamboozled by the attractive promises of the destructive demagogue Alcibiades.

Even in failure, the thought-fires it set off went on burning. But the views it posed did not really return to Europe and elsewhere until a quarter of a millennium ago. Thus it was not its example but its theory that hit the inexperienced thinkers of the European Enlightenment. Unfortunately, the inheritance was less about the Periclean need for debate than about the need to harness the People (to a succession of rulers). And though the broader forces of real consensual rule began to penetrate, from England and elsewhere, they had to compete in the struggle for the vote with inexperienced populations and "philosophical" elites.

The revival of the *concept* of democracy on the European continent saw this huge stress on the demos, the people. They could not in fact match the direct participation of the Athenian demos, but they could be "represented" in principle by any revolutionary regime claiming to do so—often concerned, above all, to repress "*enemies* of the people." Also, the people, or those of military age, could be conscripted in bulk—the *levée en masse* that long defeated more conventional armies. As the nineteenth century continued, the people could be polled in plebiscites and thus democratically authenticated. Napoleon III, of course, relied on this, and it is clear that he actually had high majority support. Marx himself wrote that in the Second Empire, the rulers had to some degree a certain autonomy from any economic class. The peasant majority endorsed them; the state machine was theirs. In any case, the new orders, democratic or not, now had to seek, or claim, authentication by the people, the masses, the population.

3.

Another aspect of premature "democracy," is the adulation of what used to be and still might be called "the city mob" (noted by Aristotle as "ochlocracy"). Even Britain had a city mob experience in the late eighteenth century—the Gordon riots of 1780 in London, in which such mobs were unleashed for days in anti-Catholic destructions. In France, of course, in the 1790s, a spate of ideologues turned to the Paris mob, in riot after riot, until the 18th Brumaire, Napoleon's coup of 1799. The ploy was that, as A. E. Housman put it, a capital city with far fewer inhabitants could decide the fate of the country's millions. (As he says, in 1871, Paris was down to the lesser aim of seeking its own effective independence from the majority, and this time was denied even that.)

Certainly, the French majority was itself not what could be called politically mature. But at least they were the majority. . . .

That democracy is not the only, or inevitable, criterion of social progress is obvious. If "free elections" give power to a repression of consensuality, they are worse than useless. We will presumably not forget that Hitler came to power in 1933 by election, with mass and militant support. The Communist coup in Czechoslovakia in 1948 was effected by constitutional intrigues backed by "mass demonstrations." We need hardly mention the "people's democracies" and the 90+ percent votes they always received. They were compared with, and declared superior to, "bourgeois democracy." (The protocols of the secret trial of the July 1944 plotters against Hitler have lately been published in Moscow, having fallen into Russian hands at the end of World War II; the official Nazi comments on the document complain that one of the defending lawyers had behaved as such in a "bourgeois" fashion— that is, presumably trying, in some way, to help his allotted client.)

Indeed, if they felt like it, the Nazis and the Fascists spoke of their own style of democracy. Mussolini called the Fascist state "organised centralised, state democracy." Joseph Goebbels said that "in Germany there is true democracy, in which the whole nation can freely express its will." Hitler too, in 1940, said that the British "so-called democracy" was much inferior to the German version.

Clearly, if a military coup in 1933, projected by a few at the time, had prevented the election of Hitler, the German people, and all other peoples, would have benefited.

As to later elections, a few years ago there was a fairly authentic one in

Algeria. If its results had been honored it would have replaced the established military rulers with an Islamist political order. On the record, this was something like the choice facing Pakistan in 2002. At any rate, it is not a matter on which the simple concepts of democracy and free elections provide us with clear criteria.

"Democracy" is often given as the essential definition of Western political culture. At the same time, it is applied to other areas of the world in a formal and misleading way. So that we are told to regard more or less uncritically the legitimacy of any regime in which a majority has thus won an election. But "democracy" did not develop or become viable in the West until quite a time after a law-and-liberty polity had emerged. Habeas corpus, the jury system, the rule of law were not the products of "democracy" but of a long effort, from medieval times, to curb the power of the English executive. And democracy can only be seen in any positive or laudable sense if it emerges from and is an aspect of the law-and-liberty tradition.

Again, the problem with "democratic" socialism was always that if the country remained democratic its electorate might reject or dilute or hamstring socialism—and what then?

What we define as Western constitutional arrangements vary a good deal in their institutions. Now, it is perfectly clear that some possible structures are nonviable—that of eighteenth-century Poland, for example. But institutions that differ in the United States and the United Kingdom have worked (though forms created in some other countries that were theoretically much the same have often collapsed). That is to say, at least two formally different sets of institutions have generally flourished. It seems that the main thing they share is not so much the institutions as the habits of mind, which are far more crucial, and above all the acceptance of the traditional rules of the political game. A country commonly called "democratic" has the following set of characteristics:

1. The state is able to operate.
2. The plural views in the polity are represented and allowed expression.
3. All opinion within the polity accepts the mechanisms, the public rules, over at least a period.

More broadly, in the West it has been *tradition* that has been generally determinant of public policy. Habituation is more central to a viable constitution than any other factor.

Even the Western "democracies" are not exactly models of societies generated by the word, the abstract idea. Still, they, or some of them, are roughly within the concept as we know it, and at least are basically consensual and plural—the product of at best a long evolution.

The countries without at least a particle of that background, or evolution, cannot be expected—even at that level—to become instant "democracies"; and if they do not live up to it, they will unavoidably be, with their Western sponsors, denounced as failures. Democracy in any Western sense is not easily constructed or imposed. The experience of Haiti should be enough comment.

What we can hope for, and work for, is the emergence, in former rogue or ideomaniac states, of a beginning, a minimum. The new orders must be nonmilitant, nonexpansionist, nonfanatical. And that goes with, or tends to go with, some level of internal tolerance, of a plural order, with some real prospect of settling into habit or tradition. And though it is true that it is hard to read too much from a particular case, there may be positive elements even in what look like hopeless disaster areas, awaiting possible development.

Democracy cannot work without a fair level of political and social stability. This implies a certain amount of political apathy. Anything resembling fanaticism, a domination of the normal internal debate by "activists" is plainly to be deplored. And it must accept anomalies. As John Paul Jones, the American naval hero, sensibly put it in 1775, "True as may be the political principles for which we are now contending . . . the ships themselves must be ruled under a system of absolute despotism." The navy, indeed, is an extreme case. This is a matter of expediency and compromise, but no democratization in any real degree makes sense, any more than it does in, let us say, a university, at the other end of the spectrum.

Democratization of undemocratizable institutions is sometimes, doubtless, the expression of a genuine utopian ideal, as when the Jacobins by these means destroyed the French navy. But more often it is (in the minds of the leading activists, at least) a conscious attempt to ruin the institutions in question, as when the Bolsheviks used the idea to destroy the old Russian army. When this, among other things, enabled them to take power themselves, they were, of course, the first to insist on a discipline even more rigorous than before.

When the Provisional Government took over in Russia in March 1917, the country had been run by a fairly efficient political and administrative machinery, and the discipline in the army was satisfactory. (It is a myth that "war weariness" was among the major causes of the February Revolution: it was, on the contrary, carried out with the idea that the tsar and his milieu were insufficiently committed to the fight against Germany, and the program of the new government, at first enthusiastically accepted by the soldiery, was designed to make the war a more national one.) But the "liberals" who now took over in the capital and the localities changed all this. In the name of "freedom," they destroyed the local administrative machinery and replaced it with amateurs; they destroyed the police force and replaced it with nothing; and in the army they permitted "democratic rights" incompatible with discipline.

The advantages of a strong executive have always included the maintenance of legal order. The Venerable Bede tells us that in the days of Edwin, king of Northumbria, in the seventh century, "If a woman with a new-born babe then wished to walk across the land from sea to sea, she would come to no harm. . . . King Edwin so considered his subjects' comfort that when he saw clear springs by the highway, he had posts set up with bronze cups attached for the refreshments of travelers, and no man dared . . . or wished . . . to touch them beyond his need." For that, an effectual state power was essential.

4.

There is a hierarchy of types among the social animals. On the lowest rung are the colonial invertebrates: polyp buds off from polyp but remains connected by filaments of tissue; each polyp fulfills various specialized functions such as tentacles or stomachs, almost as if forming a single animal, with no individual sphere of action at all. The social insects are not physically connected but are linked by communication (mainly odors) and have very limited individual flexibility, though the individual can survive for a time in isolation. The social mammals, like baboons, have far more individuality, recognize each other as individuals, and can play a variety of roles, sometimes in rotation. Human beings go further still in the same direction in various obvious ways. One may similarly note the hierarchy of human societies, in which the lowest give the least scope to individual action, allow the least variation in attitudes, and impose the narrowest limits on opinion.

In its most important aspect, civic order is that which has created a strong state while still maintaining the principle of consensus that existed in primitive society. Such an aim involves the articulation of a complex political and social order. The strains cannot be eliminated but can be continually adjusted. Political civilization is thus not primarily a matter of the goodwill of leaderships or of ideal constitutions. It is, above all, a matter of time and custom.

All the major troubles we have had in the last half century have been caused by people who have let politics become a mania. The politician should be a servant and should play a limited role. For what our political culture has stood for (as against the principles of total theorists and abstractionists) is the view of society as a developing and broadening of established liberties and responsibilities, and the belief, founded on experience, that in political and social matters long-term predictions, however exciting and visionary, seldom work out.

Nor is an abstract "libertarian" principle of much use in real life. Since a political order of a consensual type depends on the maintenance of a strong mediating state, since liberty and law are mutually dependent, it follows that when state and law are threatened by immediate danger, they have the duty to defend themselves, even at the cost of a temporary suspension of particular rights.

Moreover, while democracy can be made to seem, however illogically, to amount to a claim to complete libertarianism, civic culture cannot. Democracy is almost invariably criticized by revolutionaries for the blemishes found in any real example, as compared with the grand abstraction of the mere word. With a civic culture it is more clearly a matter of a basis on which improvements can be made. For a civic society is a society in which the various elements can express themselves politically, in which an articulation exists between these elements at the political level: not a perfect social order, which is in any case unobtainable, but a society that hears, considers, and reforms grievances. It is not necessarily democratic, but it contains the possibility of democracy.

Meanwhile, as we have seen, there are those who, often without knowing it, become apologists and finally accomplices of the closing of society. They often start by imagining that people who have no monetary interest in a political stance, who urge changes apparently of no benefit to themselves, are thereby proved to be of pure motive, and their cause a deserving one. This is to forget the attractions of power, of revenge, of all the nonprofit nastinesses that have afflicted the world. As Alexander Hamilton wrote in *The Federalist Papers*, no. 1, "a dangerous ambition more often lurks behind the specious mask of zeal for the rights of the people, than under the forbidding appearance of zeal for the firmness and efficiency of government. History will teach us, that the former has been found a much more certain road to the introduction of despotism, than the latter."

5.

A s to Fascism, Zhelyu Zhelev's thorough and excellent *Fashizmut*, referred to earlier, came out in Sofia in 1983 from the People's Youth publishing house of the Central Committee of the Democratic Youth Union, in ten thousand copies. The book soon became well known even among Russian and other dissidents. In Sofia, bold students would ask at the bookstore, "Do you have Zhelev's book *Kommunismut?*" "You mean *Fashizmut?*" "Yes, of course, slip of the tongue."

Zhelev's thoroughly illuminating theme is developed in clearly delineated sections. First, "the structure of the Fascist State." He goes through the whole "Fascist" totalitarian phenomenon, covering in chapter after chapter the importance of indoctrinating the "masses," the need to keep out foreign influences, the role of farcical elections and a powerless "parliament", the necessity for fanaticism, the view that Western "academic freedom" was false. But above all, the single party and that party's control of the state, of mass organizations, of all opinion, of literature and the arts, of the police, of the courts.

Zhelev then covers the structure of the one-party state, the unification of the whole of public life, the authoritarian way of thought and the cult of the national leaders, concentration camps, total espionage, incessant propaganda, the need to isolate the country, and the difference between the "Fascist" state and military dictatorship.

The last section, *"On the Fall of the Fascist State,"* must have been particularly troublesome to the regime. It develops the Spanish model, where the (rather shaky) "party" was eased out of power in favor of a "reactionary" authoritarian regime—a step "towards Liberalism."

The book was soon suppressed.

I have quoted elsewhere Orwell's list of people and things he had heard referred to as "Fascist." The mere recitation of it is always a hit with students—that is, with those supposed to be susceptible to the nonsense. Orwell had heard "Fascist" applied to a list of targets including "farmers, shopkeepers, Social Credit, corporal punishment, fox-hunting, bull-fighting, . . . Kipling, Gandhi, Chiang Kai-Shek, homosexuality, . . . Youth Hostels, astrology, women, dogs . . ." Perhaps one could devise a cell phone or similar device that on hearing the word in a domestic context would interrupt the speaker with a warning buzz.

It was in the 1970s that I first heard the word "Fascist" used with that sort of meaning. Giving some talks in Norway, I asked a professor, one of my hosts, why he and three others were listed as Fascists in a student hand-out. What had they done in Nazi times? Another host told me: one had been in a concentration camp; two others had been in the underground, one of them having helped the British raiders sabotage the Nazi heavy water project; the fourth had escaped to England and joined the Norwegian democratic armed forces. They had all, however, prevented or deplored a more recent student disruption.

Nowadays, in fact, the use of the word "Fascist," and pressure to outlaw unprogressive parties, is based on their reversion, or supposed reversion, to unacceptable nationalism or racism or whatever. We do not seem to find any similar objection to more obvious Fascist actions, like the public disruption of legal and legitimate (and nonracist and so on) activities with which "activists" disagree.

It is remarkable, too, that the word "Fascist" has become usual in the West as the description of a foreign "right-wing" tyranny or movement (indeed, in some cases of any "right-wing" phenomenon). "Fascist," for some reason, is so employed more often than, say, "Nazi" or "National Socialist." This is odd, in the sense that the original Italian model was a good deal less oppressive than the German (or, of course, the Soviet) parallel. One can see why "National Socialism" raises queries, while "totalitarianism" mixes a whole order of rule, right *and* left.

The word and idea of Fascism indeed arose in Italy, and Mussolini's Fascist Party produced imitators elsewhere. Nevertheless, Italian fascism was a mild form of the affliction compared with the other totalisms, though it was itself a would-be (and self-proclaimed) totalitarian regime.

Again, you can be a racist without being a Fascist. Ian Smith, last ruler of white Rhodesia, for example, could certainly be called the first but not the second. More strikingly, you can be a Fascist without being a racist. Mussolini's regime, until the early 1930s, had no racial program, and when it came, it was milder than that applied in Hitler's Europe (until 1943, when Mussolini's Social Republic was thoroughly Nazified). In its first decade, it was oppressive and maltreated its political opponents, but this hardly approached the Hitler-Stalin level. A recent book on concentration camps, *Le siécle des camps* by Joel Kotek and Pierre Rigoulot (the former is the author of an earlier study of the Warsaw Ghetto), deals with concentration camps everywhere but finds the Italian example small—a few thousand and in general not very inhuman; a common measure taken against hostile politicians was to exile them to a distant village, rather as Lenin was dealt with in pre-revolutionary Russia.

On a different but relevant point, Maxim Gorky, the revolutionary writer incarnate, lived for years in Sorrento and was lured back to Russia only in 1932. It is hard to imagine the opposite.

### 6.

As to real Fascists in the West, the oddest were the British Union of Fascists, known as Blackshirts, with Sir Oswald Mosley as Leader. Mosley had been successively a Conservative MP and a Labour MP, then briefly led the New Party, with four MPs (including Harold Nicholson and John Strachey). How anyone could have thought that a movement identified as "Fascist" and whose members used the sobriquet "Blackshirts," all an import from Italy, could be presented as a British "nationalist" movement passes belief. But Mosley had been considered a possible future Prime Minister by both leading parties: Politicians!

The Irish Fascists were at least Blueshirts.

Then there are various various odd usages: for example "Monarcho-Fascist" was the term applied to the Greek government whose overthrow by Communist partisans was prevented by British troops in 1944. It was indeed under a King—as with the restored governments of the Netherlands, Norway, and the others—though at first it was headed by a regency under Archbishop Damaskinos, Head of the Greek Church (whose chief of staff was the poet George Seferis). Nor should we omit the usage "Social-Fascist," used of the Western Socialist and Social Democratic parties by the Comintern and Moscow agencies in general, in the period up to 1935.

A New York song of the time was in part meant as an attack on the American Socialist Party ("The third capitalist party / By the boss") but mostly was aimed at the Cloak Makers Union:

*They preach Socialism*
*But they practice Fascism*
*To keep Capitalism*
*By the Boss*

Then again, later on, when Nikolay Bukharin confessed to plotting against Stalin's regime in favor of bourgeois democracy, Andrey Vyshinsky several times commented with, for example, "In short you relapsed into outright rabid fascism." Local Communist leaders, like Panas Lyubchenko, First Secretary of the Ukraine, were called "National-Fascists."

A Marxist application of the concept of Fascism, well worth our attention, is to be found in the minutes of the Third Conference of the Cominform (see *The Cominform: Minutes of the Three Conferences, 1947/1948/1949*, edited by Giuliano Procacci):

> *As a result of the counter-revolutionary policy of the Tito-Rankovic clique which usurped power in the Party and in the state, an anti-Communist police state, a fascist-type regime, has been installed in Yugoslavia. The social basis of this regime consists of the kulaks in the countryside and the capitalist elements in the towns. Power in Yugoslavia is, in fact, in the hands of anti-popular, reactionary elements. Active members of the old bourgeois parties, kulaks and enemies of people's democracy are at work in central and local government bodies. The fascist ruling group is supported by an inordinately swollen military-and-police apparatus, by means of which they oppress the peoples of Yugoslavia, which they have turned into a armed camp, wiping out all the democratic rights of the working people and trampling on any free expression of opinions. . . . The policy pursued by the Yugoslav rulers in the countryside is kulak-capitalistic in character. The pseudo-cooperatives forcibly established in the countryside are in the hands of kulaks and their agents and serve as an instrument for exploitation of the broad masses of the working peasantry. . . .*

A remarkable class analysis.

### 7.

"Totalitarian" is often (no doubt unconsciously) rejected as implying the essential similarity between the "left" and the "right" versions, as noted by Zhelev.

The Soviet system and its various offspring were, if anything, the furthest advanced into what we call totalitarianism. The parallel with Nazi Germany is inexact. The Nazis were, of course, a criminal regime, whose atrocities and human destructions are understandably felt by most of us to be in important ways even worse than those of the Communist rulers.

But this should not prevent us from examining the different manners in which the systems worked. First, we note that the Nazis did not carry out, or did not have the time to carry out, the full totalitarianization of their regime and its mechanisms. In fact, as totalitarianism goes, Stalin's regime developed it more deeply than Hitler's. In part this was due to Hitler's need to purge, rather than create, a state machine. But in part it was surely due to the unpleasant fact that Hitlerism in Germany was more popular than Stalinism in Russia. At any rate, on all the criteria Zhelev puts forward as characteristic of "Fascism," the USSR's was much more highly developed than the German version.

In Germany itself, the Nazis did not attempt to crush any but their political enemies; and the non-Jewish population at least, in general, well into the war, had not suffered in their ordinary lives at the hands of the state—indeed, actively or passively, most accepted it—and in their turn were not regarded by that state as a potential source of hostility. This obvious point is well illustrated by a comparison of the smaller number of informers employed by the Gestapo compared to those employed by the postwar East German Stasi, and over a much smaller population.

A further comparison of this sort arises if we look at the—peacetime—reaction to foreign visitors. I first went to Germany, for a few days, as a student backpacking around Europe, in 1937. My co-backpacker, John Blakeway, took me to stay with friends in Munich, where he had spent a year at the University. There were no problems with visas or any other harassment of foreigners. In 1938, John Willett, the expert on Brecht, and I drove an old truck round Central Europe, sleeping each night in the back. Again, no trouble. We arrived from Berlin at the Czechoslovak border late at night, after it had closed. We parked, had a late drink at the neighborhood pub, and went through the next morning—and this was on the eve of Munich.

Of "totalitarian" Italy, it is hardly necessary to write. Many English and other foreigners (such as Gorky!) lived there and had summer villas or whatever. As children we lived in the south of France and now and then crossed the border to visit old friends of my father, who had lived there as a child in San Remo. The only thing that had struck my mind was that British residents found it tactful to refer to Mussolini as Mr. Smith.

The differences are doubtless due in part to a Russian tradition of bureaucratic intrusion. I have the passport of my mother's grandfather, who spent much time around 1848 going around Europe in a couple of coaches with his family. It contains an accumulation of stamps from half the little states of Europe from Spain to Russia, including the Kingdom of Sardinia, where my grandfather was born (in Nice, then Nizza) in 1849. Only on the pages from his Russian diversion—from Stettin to St. Petersburg—do we find a page of police-check comments.

Later on, a century or so ago, passports for Westerners were only required for travel to Russia or Turkey—so that even under conditions of considerable international hostility, movement elsewhere was fine. The Soviet regime developed far beyond that, and even reintroduced the internal passport system that Lenin had, earlier in the century, denounced as a sign of tsarist oppression.

Even in the USSR at the time of my trip, where the backpacker was very much under Intourist control, things were far easier than they became later. At Odessa in 1937, I was simply put on a local train, from which I had to change, on the track to the Romanian border, to another peasant-packed local (I had no Russian or Ukrainian). The diaries of British and other consuls, a few years earlier, give a yet more open feeling—though most of the consulates were soon closed.

The ideal totalitarian state should control the mental as well as the physical lives of its population. Real life is not quite up to this. But if we consider the Stalin and other similar regimes, we see that they had progressed a long way towards it. The most obvious and critical point is the degree to which all channels of information were blocked, and the extent to which a radically false picture was forced on Russian minds. For the Stalinist regime did not merely deny reality; it substituted for it a fully ideologized world fantasy.

Even *1984* presented a whole section of the population—the proles—as at once subject to an otherwise complete totalitarianism and yet to some degree outside the totality. There was no such stratum under Stalinism.

### 8.

A regime or rule can be revoltingly murderous and despotic without being totalitarian. Or, to put it another way, there are various levels of despotism, and they can be distinguished one from another by several different criteria, of which the degree they attain totalitarianism is one.

The element of totalitarianism most neglected is its large reliance on the idea of the "people" and the "masses." Zhelev notes that the Nazis also abused the word "people's" in, for example, People's Court (*Volksgericht*), People's Youth (*Volksjugend*), People's News (*Völkischer Beobachter*).

Hitler is quoted as saying that the Communists and socialists thought they had a "monopoly of the masses," but he had proved them wrong. The masses were indeed much appealed to by Communist regimes. In the 1940 Soviet *Brief Philosophical Dictionary*, we are told, "the corner stone of Marxism is the mass, the liberation of which is the main condition for the liberation of the individual."

The opposite of the Western view.

"Imperialism"? We'll postpone that to another chapter.

Meanwhile, let us consider another variety of commonly employed generalities, applied with less vacuity than is common with "Fascism" but often seen as merely valid, though noisy, terms of abuse. "Anti-Semite" is an example, since it will not be denied that such an attitude has existed, and exists, in virulent form. Orwell, reviewing Jean-Paul Sartre's book *Anti-Semite and Jew*, comments that using the phrase as a complete identification deprives it of reality. For in most cases, Orwell points out, anti-Semitism is part time and of variable intensity. So it is misleading to say, in most cases, "He is an anti-Semite," or that he can be identified as "*the* anti-Semite." It is thus a misleading—and often a consciously and demagogically misleading—label. Allen Tate quotes W. H. Auden as saying he has made, and is ashamed of having made, the odd Jewish joke—and Tate himself says he has done the same. So, under the principle of calling a dog a bad name, they automatically figure on the list. Offenders vary even at this level: T. S. Eliot, it is true, actually put crude 1920s saloon Jewish stereotypes into poems, certainly earning a negative score. But even this is pettifogging on the Hitler scale.

The point, of course, applies to all the other stereotype labels, such as "racist" or "sexist," even "homophobe": these are often, like "anti-Semite," merely incitements to stupefaction. "Is" is a main problem, as I recall being heavily stressed in first-year philosophy, or perhaps earlier. But the effective designation can be produced in languages without the use of "is"—referring to someone as "he Fascist," for example.

We must avoid prejudice. And we must avoid the unthinking attribution of prejudice to others.

*Chapter IV*

# Choose Your Enlightenment

⎯⎯⎯⎯⎯⎯ ⎯⎯⎯⎯⎯⎯

1.

In his play *The Coast of Utopia*, Tom Stoppard has the Russian nineteenth-century liberal Alexander Herzen say of the English, "They invented personal liberty, and they know it, and they did it without any theories about it."

On the Continent the early part of the sixteenth century saw what appeared to be, or foreshadow, the rise of a tolerant human order. Names like Erasmus and Montaigne gave a strong impression of the advancing of thought. Their work survived and kept these attitudes richly in existence. But it was not they who prevailed over the following years. Dogmatists of various types kept most of Europe on a downward track, with internecine wars as devastating as any since. In many cases, the contrary ideas or attitudes condensed into various verbal concepts, theories, and slogans that were formulated and became powerful over the last couple of centuries.

2.

The United States and the United Kingdom have nothing to learn from that Europe?

Of course we have much to learn, and not only from Europe but from (at random) Confucius and Ibn Batuta on other continents, and from Russians (a people not in the EU) like Pushkin and Dostoyevsky and Chekhov, and from the pre-European West, the contribution of the Athenian sponsors of freedom of speech, the great humanists of the Renaissance, the splendid literatures. But do the United States and the United Kingdom have anything much to learn from the European political or politico-academic theories and practices of the last three hundred years? I think not.

37

We are often told to look back at the eighteenth-century Enlightenment. But there were two different Enlightenments—the British and the Continental (the latter at first often muddleheadedly generalizing from what it thought to be the lessons of the former: the initial period of the French Revolution has been described as an unsuccessful attempt to become England). The British Enlightenment was concerned with the rule of law and particular political liberties, the Continental with intoxicating generalizations. British principles did not arise out of nothing or from abstract philosophy. They emerged gradually (and with interruptions) from the Middle Ages. (Habeas corpus, which evolved over centuries, is still not practiced on the Continent.)

In the eighteenth century, the English enlighteners, if you wish to call them that, debated in pubs and clubs and homes, the French in châteaux and salons and academies. In politics, there could scarcely be two "activists" more different than John Wilkes and say, Condorcet.

Earlier, Voltaire and others had validated the British experience, but in the long run it was the theorists and emotionalists who triumphed mentally in Paris.

The French, and European, Enlightenment thus emerged not on the basis of a political class or political institutions, but from minds more or less bombinating in a vacuum.

The two cultures can accept a measure of spillover from each other, as with parts of the U.S. Constitution. So if we speak of the two traditions as mutually exclusive we are only generalizing. Still, the historical or historico-cultural difference stands.

Those fully subjected to the Continental Enlightenment lost by it, from the time when the best poet of France and her best scientist went to the guillotine. (But Parisian creativity was not extinct, if we include the new calendar of Cuspidor, Frigidaire, etc.)

From quite early on in the French Revolution the abstract general principles were regarded as truths applicable to the whole of humanity. Thomas Carlyle's classic description tells of how the strange group of Anacharsis Clootz, who headed a delegation of foreigners as an "Embassy of the Human Race," with a broad range of nationalities represented, was welcomed by the National Assembly. His speech was warmly applauded and he and his colleagues were "admitted to the honors" of the assembly's session and called on to tell their peoples of their experience, though their reply, given by a non-European, was not comprehensible to the "senators." Clootz was perhaps, in a sense, qualified to speak, if not for the world, for the Continent—a Prussian aristocrat of Dutch origins, he obtained French nationality in 1793, just in time to follow (or precede) his betters to the guillotine.

3.

In brief, from the French Enlightenment we got
1. Exciting generalities
2. The *levée en masse*, and the subsequent validation of regimes and movements by mass plebiscites
3. The People and the Nation (it is often forgotten that its heritage produced not only the Marxist disruption of liberty but also the extreme nationalist equivalent)

The loud abstractions arising in France before the Revolution and propagated in and by that Revolution were historically dominant over much of the politically inexperienced parts of the Continent—that is to say, almost everywhere except Switzerland—so that over the forthcoming century, theorists and committed academics took much of the lead, in the revolutionary current's People but also in the chauvinist current's Nation. As Hugh Seton-Watson writes in his *Decline of the West?* in the late nineteenth century international crises were largely contained by surviving general traditions and commonsense, and had been manageable by statesmen like Bismarck but then became entirely unmanageable. He continues,

> *And that process was due to the appearance of an arrogant state of mind in a large section of the German public (it was symbolised by the Kaiser, though by no means created by him). If you look for one social class which was more to blame for this rising arrogance than any other, it was my own class—academics, gymnasium teachers, and university lecturers. German spokesmen, led by the Emperor, were beating their fists on the table whenever there was a minor international crisis: "Germany will be heard . . . Germany is a* Weltmacht *. . . we will make ourselves felt everywhere."*

Sounds very much like Russia in the post-Brezhnev period, more dangerous in many ways than with Stalin.

## 4.

The German intellectual experience brings to mind Hegel, who befuddled minds over six or seven generations—including, of course, the Marxists and post-Marxists.

We go on, alas, from Hegel to Heidegger. In his recent book *The Dream of Reason*, Anthony Gottlieb, in an otherwise restrained passage, writes, "Any subject that is responsible for producing Heidegger, for example, owes the world an apology."

Hegel—described by Schopenhauer as a charlatan—gave up on real phenomena (after predicting that no minor planets would be found, not long before the discovery of Ceres). Then he was the hyperacademic, the dominator of university appointments, the agent of the Prussian state, and, in connection with that, the purveyor of massive, "sophisticated," complex, impressive verbiage. And the demand for this has never abated—the current version being mainly a matter of academic logobabble at a lower level, in fact what a distinguished professor of philosophy has called English Department philosophy (while congratulating the great John Searle for relieving his fear of any obligation to read it). So let us note, and dismiss to the sphere of the unreadable, the silly-clever corners of academe, the surviving freak fashions—Derrida, Foucault, etc.

## 5.

Having looked, perhaps not briefly enough, at the French and German mental experiences, let us compare factual Britain to the others in that nineteenth-century period. Misapplied Marxist, and sub-Marxist, writing on the British Industrial Revolution is still found among both the Continental and the Anglo-American politico-intelligentsia. So we should look at the real record, which does not rebut the social distortions and sufferings but which gives the progress of humanitarian reform undertaken through the traditional institutions without the utopian-cum-revolutionary drive—in many cases, in fact, pressed effectively by ideologically reactionary activists.

In Britain progress came, erratically and against opposition, through Parliament, and expert evidence given to parliamentary committees, as with John Howard, the prison reformer, in the late eighteenth century, and more especially in the mid-nineteenth, with Shaftesbury and his devoted colleagues (mainly of nonliberal views) piloting a whole cycle of industrial reforms—a large subject we will not develop. With it came, for instance, what came to be known as the Great Sanitary Awakening—see, for example, *The Conquest of Epidemic Disease,* by C. E. A. Winthrop—when British, and later other, health was improved radically as a result of work in the free society and through its institutions.

Engels, the leading source of the Marxist view, was using the results of official documentation, whose mere cumulative existence was due to the reform drive in official circles. Elie Halévy, in his *History of the English People in the Nineteenth Century*, makes it clear that Engels's description of the human cost of the Industrial Revolution in Britain is flawed (indeed, as the historian Gertrude Himmelfarb has shown, his private letters to Germany are milder than his published account). For instance, it was not the factory "proletarian" employees who suffered most, but home weavers. Nor were the cotton towns "typical."

A striking thing about the whole of that period of Chartist activity is that it really was a movement of the masses, of the working class. There were huge demonstrations backed by the trade unions. But though there were a few localized riots (even the odd still more local armed clash), its nationwide mass movement was peaceable, in spite of the intellectual extremists among its leadership. The conclusion seems to be that the British "proletariat," given its way, even when in a mood generally very hostile to the government, kept itself comparatively free of extraneous enthusiasm and ideological manipulation and remained paradoxically attached to the traditional institutions. (It is also true that Chartists sometimes joined the Tories against the Liberals—a phenomenon not unknown in later years.)

The veteran Marxist scholar E. P. Thompson, long dismissive of dogmatism, wrote on the period's history at some length in "The Peculiarities of the English" (in his *The Poverty of Theory and Other Essays*). He is concerned with the weaknesses of Marxist, as well as of other, social theoreticising. When he develops the historical data, he is clear and unanswerable on the developments of Chartism. He notes (as others did even at the time) that there was no armed force in Britain that could have put down any serious mass rising. (The French had used overwhelming armed force to suppress trouble in Lyon.) And he shows, from contemporary sources, that in the suffering industrial areas the economic crises had, far from leading to class struggle, brought workers and employers closer together, from their mutual interest in the "factory system." As to friction within society, he and others have noted that the cultures of the "people" and the "patricians" were indeed different but that both were conservative and rooted in Common Law and "fair play." Thompson notes that in a famous case, "Royalty was defeated in open court" (on the preservation of Richmond Park), which would have been "unthinkable in Russia, Spain, Prussia, France or Naples."

The "masses" could be recruited to fanaticism even in other countries only if their own organizations were penetrated by an ideological intelligentsia with its own agenda. Even in Russia, Lenin, early in the twentieth century, found that the real *worker* element among the Social Democrats supported the "Economists" concerned with immediate and real interests, as against the Bolsheviks or the Mensheviks. In 1917 Petrograd, as we shall see, it was very much a matter of the institutional penetration of marginal workers' committees, with military-style organization. In a slightly different way, it was Hitler's method of recruiting followers into a totally centralized, semi-militarized movement that enabled him to deploy his "masses."

Engels, of course, rode to hounds—and it was thought remarkable that this odd foreigner had been accepted by the Hunt. One wonders how he would feel about his House of Commons descendants voting for the abolition of his sport but not for socialism.

6.

In a disordered pluralist society, enough energy is released into humanly profitable fields for that society to progress and prevail. A recent study shows that the great majority of the past century's innovations were made in the United States and, to a lesser degree, in Britain, and that, generally speaking, those from elsewhere of great intellectual capacity who are trained in the United States and then return to their own countries' research institutes still do not generate innovations in the way they arise in theoretically similar environments here.

This technological lead has always included the military side. Something similar can be said over the earlier centuries too, at least as far back as when in Elizabethan times the *Revenge* "justified her designers" in that extraordinary last fight. It remained true over the following centuries that the British were, leaving aside a few minor engagements, never defeated at sea—except by the Dutch, inhabitants of another pluralist order, indeed the most intellectually tolerant of all seventeenth-century societies. As Kipling wrote,

*For, now De Ruyter's topsails*
  *Off naked Chatham show,*
*We dare not meet him with our fleet. . . .*

The failure of the English side was due to neglect by the political authorities.

In later times another trouble arose, or became technologically more troublesome—the prevalence of bureaucracy (civil and military). It is said that of ten important changes in naval matters, nine were resisted by the British Admiralty. (And of course later the experience of the United States' development of naval aircraft is even more striking and notorious.) But the bureaucracies eventually conceded.

Over the whole of the past century and a half, while there were major confrontations and strikes, including the British General Strike of 1926, and what seemed to be intense frictions, these were nothing compared to those of their Continental contemporaries. In general, the political class and the public attitude remained unshaken. Engels himself complained that the English working class had "disgraced itself" by voting Conservative in the election of 1867.

This is not a history of this evolution, of this nonrevolution. But we may note such details as the Conservative victory in a pre–World War I bye-election, in a working-class constituency, under a slogan calling for more dreadnoughts to face the expanding German fleet:

*We want eight*
*We won't wait . . .*

This energized the government accordingly. The point being that the country's attitudes were not those of the nonempirical clerisy.

### 7.

None of the points we have put forward here or earlier are meant to deny any of the positive Continental, French, or German contributions to the Western or world mind. Goethe, a supreme humanist in every sense, wrote of German philosophy that he wondered how English or French people would understand it, when Germans couldn't. And the great Kant was, of course, German, as I remember thinking when I saw his monument in the bombed cathedral in what is now Kaliningrad. Even Nietzsche is not to be blamed, as he sometimes is, for the decivilization of his country, from which recovery has been remarkable, though not yet irrevocable, according to some Germans and some indicators.

As to France: there I have many ties. My father, serving with the French army, won the Croix de Guerre at Verdun in 1916. Later we lived for years in France. After World War II he settled down, often visited, with our cousin Elizabeth de Vilmorin, in Vence.

I have debated live on Paris TV, and often spoken at French conferences; I have written on Stendhal and Chateaubriand, have translated Lamartine and Rimbaud. But perhaps an even stronger memory is that my first book, *Poems* (1955), was dedicated to the memory of my dear friend Maurice Langlois, who died, as my dedication puts it, "in the hands of the secret police of the occupying power." (And who has a poem dedicated to me in his short collection, *Les Passagers Clandestins*.) Or my other friends, such as the fine political writer Alain Besançon, who named me as épée for his highest academic ceremony, or my close friend from earlier days, Léon Levine, whose family died in the Holocaust but whom I met again later when he was an *avocat au court* and took me in his robes to the Palais de Justice to see the French courts in action. No, it was the French political and bureaucratic intelligentsia, against whom some of the best French work of our time was written, that prevailed and, as Besançon pointed out, infected the Anglosphere: the Sartres of this world, followed by the Derridas, helping to undermine our academe, our thought.

Socialism, in Britain indeed, came and went. It was, as Marxists and others complained, a shaky and incomplete and nonauthoritarian socialism: liberty and law survived. Yet it left in its wake a ferment of alien abstraction, of flat generalization, of program and formula as against memory and experience. It swept into Britain largely from the outside, from the heirs of the etatist variant of the Enlightenment. And it brought with it, to some extent as a substitute for Socialism, the Idea of Europe.

# Chapter V

# After Utopia

⎯⎯⎯∞⎯⎯⎯

*Ow! A great acorn just fell on my head!*
*Cut down that oak. Plant a upas instead!*

### 1.

Such, in effect, was the socialist view. When the upas option proved worse than useless, one would expect that its sponsors might return to the—fairly good—old oak. But, as the Anglo-Australian political thinker Kenneth Minogue has noted, this is not what happened. Though a full and consistent ideology no longer served, the anti-Western, anticapitalist, antipluralist assault took on a more extreme sharpness, recalling, the American scholar Kenneth Jowett points out, the nihilism of the most violent section of the Russian intelligentsia a century and a half ago. Socialism's unconscious offspring were thus seemingly regressing to roots older than their later Leninisms and such.

We now face, in fact, an increasingly irrational conformism, often no longer open to, or even cognizant of, argument. The socialists—at first anyway—had at least known of other attitudes and opinions and sought to counter them in one way or another. The new antis seem to have sunk to an alarmingly lower mental level.

It had long been clear that much of the emotional drive had not come so much from a devotion to the proclaimed social transformation as from a hatred for the actual. As Albert Camus said, French intellectuals did not adore Stalinism as much as they "heartily detest part of the French." In a more or less similar way, though the collapse of actual alternatives to a pluralist order is now generally accepted, detestation of it persists—as does (often enough) the lack of, indeed rejection of, any serious attempt to examine the probable defects any feasible alternative might, or would, produce. And the most vocal have, as before but in a broader and more effective fashion, been able to impress, or even partly silence, a more moderately inclined stratum.

Negative utopianism is perhaps the best way to describe this current Western anti-Western mind-set. To the extent that current attacks on the Anglo-American culture of law and liberty consist of this high-emotion hostility and "activism," they nowadays often fail to advance *anything* in the way of positive alternatives, however doctrinaire or even debatable. "Capitalism," "globalism"—bad. But what is a *good* nonutopia?

We are told that Ideology has gone (though we note major residues and resonances). As Jean-François Revel has put it, all real social and political orders are imperfect. And no one should resist genuine criticism and reforms. Yet we should not countenance the inflation of its real defects into rejection of the three-quarters open society and its proposed replacement by a phantom, untried and untrue.

One might imagine that our unpromising consensual polities has failed, and in particular that they have lost the support of the truly aware. No, what support they have lost is among the half aware, who are conscious of its faults and blunders but ignorant of the real alternatives. These faults are set, as others are not set, against a vaguely utopian criterion.

Real politics is full of what it would be charitable to call imperfections. Political parties in the United States, the United Kingdom, and other Western states are often highly off-putting to any sensitive voters. So are politicians, even among their own followers. Of the great English diarist Thomas Creevey, himself a Whig MP and supporter of the 1832 Reform Bill, Lytton Strachey wrote, "The Tories were villains of course. . . . But all that was obvious and hardly worth recording; what was really too exacerbating was the folly and vileness of the Whigs." Such virulence is to be found even today, not merely within consensual politics but even within the constitutionally competing parties. And clearly those more radically rejecting, or almost rejecting, the accepted order are more intolerant yet. A common feature of "committed" partisans of either, of any, view is that aura of righteousness found almost as much among the so-called Christian Right as among the Red-Green side on the left. Perhaps commoner in America than elsewhere.

2.

How did the mental distortions arise? How did the aversion to and alienation from reality come about? How did the destructive intellectual epidemic strike?

We should turn our attention to the evidential side, properly speaking, and consider how such a phenomenon has arisen and how similar phenomena have arisen in the past. It is not an intellectual question at all, but a question of the mental habits of one element in the intelligentsia. Once refuted it is no more a subject for debate than are the beliefs of the Fifth Monarchy Men.

In every literate society from far back, there has been an accumulation of temporally parochial thought or argument about the main issues of the period. Where there are minds and time to spare, there seems no way of avoiding it. We can envisage the scribes who worked on the *Book of the Dead*, the documentation of the Byzantine synods, the volumes of pretentious drivel that so aroused Erasmus. In our day, the tradition persists (though it is a bit much to go on finding sub-Marxism and such still thumping away). More generally, as always, one has to run over the reasons that doctrinairism-cum-scholasticism is such an obvious intellectual disaster. So, with a sigh.

That a more or less institutional hostility or alienation grows between the intelligentsia and the less progressive, more ordinary strata of society is clear. Czeslaw Milosz, who became one of the great witnesses to reality, describes how in postwar Warsaw even more or less disillusioned intellectuals felt at home in the left-wing cafés and never thought to consort with the reactionary peasants and colonels or their representatives. This divide was to be found in the West as well—less in Britain, more in America, most in France.

George Orwell says that the man in the street is at once too sane and too stupid to fall for the fads of the intelligentsia. We might note that the opposite of sane and stupid is insane and intelligent. But insanity is itself a denial of intelligence.

The crux is less intelligence than a failure to confront that intelligence with reality—and even a drive to use that intelligence to deny or pervert reality. None calling himself an intellectual is intellectually (or morally) entitled to sponsor opinions who does not first accept his duty to clear the ground of false witness. It has seemed appropriate (later in this book) to consider some examples of the actively misleading efforts of some highly influential intellectual Goliaths of the West.

Meanwhile, what in general were, and are, the distortive mechanisms? We all know what, roughly speaking, constitutes the "progressive" agenda and who its implementers are—an "educated" stratum accepting an attitude and voicing it but always basing the fashionable opinion on odd theories or impressive-sounding general words and usually treating their realization as state responsibility.

In the West, it is sometimes said, coherent and comprehensible political standpoints have largely evaporated. What are seen as left-wing or right-wing views are, except at the periphery, little more than batches of vague or superficial attitudes. One trouble is that such orthodoxies or conventionalities are widespread in the written and taught (and televized) subworld. We may recall that the Taliban were largely recruited from students and village teachers.

### 3.

One would think that the purpose of education was to get people to listen to the arguments and the evidence—especially before making an intellectual commitment. What one finds too often is an "educated" class—particularly but not only in Europe—which is simply *not aware* of any general attitudes but its own. There is a tendency to take the current package for granted. For example, in *Singled Out,* Simon Brett has Laura, his main character, listening to a student and being "riled by the girl's habit of making statements as though no alternative opinion was possible," the views churned out being all from the package.

A recognizable type? And at the other end of the academic world, I note the writer Anthony Powell, in his *Journals* for 1982, describing his getting an honorary doctorate at Bristol University: Its chancellor was the Nobel Prize biologist Dorothy Hodgkin, who made a speech urging that spending on education should exceed that for defense. Afterwards, Powell felt he had to tell her that he disagreed; if the country was not safe there would be no education to protect. His point in telling the story, though, was "I have never seen anyone so surprised."

One is reminded that a verse of Philip Larkin's "When the Russian tanks roll westward" takes the same view as Powell and is preceded by a hostile epigraph (not printed in *Collected Poems*) to the effect that spending on education had now surpassed that in defense.

Sometimes one can see the earlier physical signs of someone trying to reconcile his strongly felt opinions with experience of the realities. That fine observer of the tsarist scene (and elsewhere) Ronald Hingley wrote of the deceiving and self-deceiving phenomena there in full swing, with their accompaniment of "expansive gestures, a piercing glance, a swelling neck, an empurpled face and that curious constricted voice which suggests that the speaker is on the point of choking."

4.

How does this affect the advance, or decay, of civilization (apart from how it can affect the way in which we understand and cope with the immediate threats to civilization's existence or extension)?

First, of course, that we have an educated class which has historically misunderstood and misevaluated history. When there is a conformist atmosphere, it is well to keep remembering that their equally or more intelligent educated predecessors were to a large degree similarly drawn into fearful misjudgment. But also now, more even than in earlier times, this class permeates the media and lower-middle academe. (Though we should say that some in the media—apart from writing more comprehensibly—have shown themselves quicker to adjust to the facts than much of academe.) We sometimes get a formal tolerance of other views, but these views are comparatively excluded from any but marginal media and educational products. That itself may be thought a recipe for the long-term decline of pluralist civilization. When one adds that the bureaucratic elites and subelites and sub-subelites are largely inclined to the uncritical acceptance of, not indeed an ideology, but still a package of old and new Ideas, the prospect looks yet worse.

So, we have a clerisy that has scarcely heard of opinions other than those appearing to be (if sometimes really being) the acceptable expression of concern for humanity. More important, the bureaucracy, having in no way diminished, has turned much of its activity to different social channels, such as the regulation of activities seen as morally subversive.

5.

One trouble, as always, is that, as we have said, some at least of the component Ideas are taken up by mental or "moral" (emotional) "interest groups," which bring pressure to bear on the political and other institutions far more strongly than their numbers or their popular or even media influence would justify. To take an example from the late 1990s, the relevant lobby put pressure on the U.S. Defense Department to admit women to various infantry and other military activities from which not only custom but also the fact that almost none could pass certain physical tests had excluded them. The leading generals gave in when even the liberal secretary of defense opposed their admission. Plainly, the generals were not willing to risk political obloquy. This is one example of these pressures.

The activists in that and other fields may not be numerically very impressive. But they may represent or seem to represent swing voters in marginal constituencies. Or, if not that, they may have the ability to bring a measure of disrepute to those opposing or critical of their agenda. Nor should one forget what might be called psychobribery: there are various much touted experts who started off as sensible but neglected and who won fame by converting to fashionable silliness.

The worst of this is, of course, that there is a strong tendency to silence those who disagree with one or another of the accepted beliefs, so that colleagues or others unwilling to face all the fuss and abuse can hardly even raise their objections. Thus more broadly, throughout the West—to a great extent in Europe, to a lesser extent in Britain, and to a much lesser extent in the United States—there are various mental threats to the further evolution of the law-and-liberty culture, threats that tend to render the Western world vulnerable to its enemies.

Capitalism and etatism have in many countries been melded into, or become two elements of, a bureaucratized and closed order. In the long run, this implies a more or less rapid decline into a closure of vitality and thought. Part of the current ideational fashions are in themselves, in one way or another, signs of intellectual decadence (though, in some of the cases we shall examine, doing no more immediate harm than an excess of limpets on a yacht's hull).

## 6.

But there is, of course, a further element—the organizational, sectarian, personal connections set up over the years. The works of the Guild Socialists, a century ago, were probably difficult to keep in print. The works of Marx and Engels, in contrast, were financed by politically subsidized publishers. And the penetration of Marxist sects was far more complete. Their movement was, moreover, manned by long-established veterans, whose critical minds had been taken over in early years and never returned.

And though nothing is left of Marxism as scientific prediction (that is, nothing left of its substantive claim to attention), there remains the vague notion that it for the first time opened up various historical perspectives—or some such rather vaguer pretension. But it can easily be shown that those who accepted this were proved completely mistaken about almost everything that has happened within the past century.

There seems little point in going through the argument—if only because, as we've seen, the holders of certain opinions, at a certain level of conviction, are both argument-proof and fact-proof, as was the case with their grandparents on the USSR. It is, unfortunately, only too easy to show that many of the then intelligentsia in the United States, the United Kingdom, and elsewhere were deceived into accepting and supporting a huge fabric of lies. The Soviet Union, despite its horrors, remained acceptable or even praiseworthy, until Khrushchev's "secret speech" of February 1956, and even after that with some.

But how was it possible? The truth, though not provided by the Soviet authorities, was available in scores or hundreds of firsthand accounts. It was clear, too, that foreign correspondents were not admitted to vast areas from which hostile evidence was available. It might even have been thought consequential that dozens of the highest leadership under Stalin simply ceased to be mentioned. The census figures, even as given in 1939, after the public denunciation of a 1937 census as the work of enemy agents, must have been seen as inexplicably low (though in fact even the 1939 census was exaggerated by some three million). Where had the still-missing millions cited seven or eight years earlier got to? And so on, and so on. There were even Westerners who believed that Trotsky was an agent of Hitler. In the second section of this book, we examine the Communist order and all the falsifications that took in the Webbs—not only the Webbs, but a whole mob of others, and this in spite not only of a mass of contrary evidence but even of apparently direct observation. They would often reject these data as irrelevant, or excuse them as, at the worst, superficial defects of a regime heading in the right direction. The USSR also managed to Potemkinize its future—which no evidence, or sense data, could refute.

### 7.

As to politics in general, the level of understanding in academe has long been kept low by a series of theories and methodologies. Not only does Marxism, or at any rate a sort of sub-Marxism, still put out shoots in academic spheres that have been inadequately unweeded, but even non-utopian theorizing, attempts to inject rigor into the political–systems analysis, rational choice theory, path dependence—all tend to remove realities from academic work or, in many cases, to make real research and thought acceptable to academe only if provided with an attached theoretical view (all well covered by Alan Wolfe, in the *New Republic,* October 14, 2002). If a political theory is taken as thoroughly correct, it follows first that your critics are "wrong." (This is a recipe for taking over university departments.) Worse still, at least in extreme cases, it follows that you can formulate policy and even largely predict results. But we *are* seeing the rise of a generation of scholars whose work is free of (or makes only a formal bow to) the theory-thumpers.

Without giving an assessment of problems or a philosophy, let us insist, at least, that there is nothing new (nor of course convincing) in the attempt to substitute theory for the complexities of reality. A classical scholar wrote, "Greek philosophy sought for uniformity in the multiplicity of phenomena, and the desire to find this uniformity led to guess-work and neglect of fact in the attempt to frame a comprehensive theory" (W. H. S. Jones quoted in H. D. F. Kitto's *The Greeks*).

Both of the greatest writers on politics, Aristotle and Machiavelli, had experience of, or immediate access to, a large number of variously ruled states. It is perhaps not to be wondered at that a professor, separated by thousands of miles of space (or reams of paper) from any but the most indirect and misinterpreted notions of other types of polity, should come to shallower conclusions.

It is for the most part evident to serious students that except in a very short-range sense, predictability in the political and social fields is both in principle and in practice unattainable, at any rate with the aid of the weak and fallible general theories at present in existence. The urge to promote premature and inadequately supported generalities, far from being a higher development, is a sure sign of primitivism.

What is more, the delusion that problems are susceptible, in principle, to being solved by political decision has led many backward countries further and further into the grip of incompetent autocrats. Each time a solution imposed by force has, after all, failed to improve matters, it is thought that the fault is merely that insufficient power has been put behind it. If one more refractory social group is liquidated, if party discipline is tightened and all shirkers and compromisers adequately dealt with, then next time all will be well. We should have learned by now from these unfortunate "social experiments" that there are problems that cannot be dealt with even by the maximum application of political power.

In the hard sciences, all the more interesting papers are those that seek to test a theory by finding exceptions or apparent exceptions to its operation. "An Anomalous Case of . . ." is a typical paper title in a scientific journal. In the quasi-sciences, the opposite is generally true. The concern there is only too often to prove what is already believed. Nor, in most cases, are there factual or experimental data which the propounders of the theory would admit as casting doubt on their belief if they went one way rather than another. It is true that the adherents of rival theories reject each other's proofs, but the arguments they use are seldom those of the hard sciences.

Insofar as these do retain the element of intellectual rigor that makes them liable to refutation on empirical and evidential grounds, they are invariably so refuted. Insofar as they are irrefutable, it is precisely because they are so general and flexible as to convey no real information. In that case, why do they emerge? We are plainly in the presence of not an intellectual but a psychological phenomenon. This is, at any rate, an astonishing tribute to the power and persistence of the desire for tidiness and certitude.

As the Italian philosopher Nicola Chiaromonte put it, the most perverse of all modern ideas (though similar notions go back a long way) is that "the course of things must have a single meaning, or that events can be contained in a single system."

At the same time, judgments in political matters may be made in simple terms and be none the worse for that. Churchill understood the Nazis better than Chamberlain did not because he had a vast vocabulary of political science terms to analyze it by but because he had some knowledge of history and of evil. I remember after the 1956 Hungarian revolution that the distinguished scholar Professor Peter Wiles, who had chanced to be in Budapest at the time, was interviewed on television. Asked what, in his view, were the causes of that revolution, he answered simply, "They were fed up with telling lies."

## 8.

That may, in a slightly different context, remind us that Marx wrote of, indeed based his whole political theory on, the Idea of "surplus value." The profits accruing to capital he attributed to what was withheld from the working class, constituting exploitation. This mere assertion is the part of Marxism still accepted by some. It is interesting to note that in the 1968 Czechoslovak liberalization, it was revealed that in the great nationalized factories like Bata, workers' pay was proportionately less than it had been under capitalism, while managerial bureaucrats were getting a bigger share than the capitalists had (and the shoes Bata produced were worse). After the demise of the Soviet Union, it similarly emerged that the workers' proportion of a factory's finance was the lowest in the industrial world, running at about 30 percent.

If we look at the West today (without bothering to distinguish between "information" and "production" workers), we see that an equivalent noncapitalist "surplus" evidently goes to the state, including education. The state is of course an important necessity. And education is also a major component of a free society. There are, indeed, many other state posts that play a positive role. Social workers, when well trained and careful to avoid gross intrusiveness, are a positive element (though in one South London borough where the "good" social worker went back to her home in Essex in the evening, locals organized a volunteer group to cover their woes more fully). Someone has to issue the drivers' licenses. Someone has to put down crime—though the efforts of the police (in Britain anyway) are often diverted to other matters.

But, as we shall argue, the state often exceeds its legitimate purposes. And an ever larger section of society is put through "higher" education. One element of this is educated in scientific and other specialized disciplines, though often unaccompanied by much in the way of "education" proper. The other element is given a (shrinking) slice of the "humanist" training that used to be the crux of learning, but a growing proportion of them have no option afterwards but to go on into an increasingly large and less-educated academe or to seek jobs in the bureaucracy (or in the bureaucratic section of academe itself) or, of course, to enter the media or such spheres as advertising. At any rate, the state is to some extent creating a nonproductive class and providing nonproductive work for them.

This class contains thousands of admirable, thought-provoking, fact-deploying professionals. The problem is among the other thousands and among the politically, or semipolitically, activist stratum and the "idealist" undergraduates whose disruptive behavior is their support. The playing of the sex card or the race card is currently the most obvious and most deplorable aspect of this problem. But if we take a longer view, we see a whole anti-intellectual tendency. As we have said, the evolution of a supposedly educated class has unfortunately usually included a stratum alienated not only from its own society's values but also from reason and fact. Of course, it is not only a matter of politics.

At a lower level, there is bound to be a partly educated stratum pervaded by the ideas of a more intellectual, or at least more publicized, level, and that is given the impression that certain views on political, cultural, and such matters are generally accepted by the knowledgeable. Versions of what might be called the progressive packet are seen in all the food for the mind now offered to a larger element in society—that is, those who are deemed qualified to man the institutions forming, or tending to form, a barrier to reality. The atmosphere is thick with their suppositions, though their record is one of failure when the verbalizations are compared with reality.

It seems important that these circles are made fully aware of the errors to which educated—indeed, educating—minds are prone; that the record is rubbed in as firmly as possible; that we make as sure as may be that the lesson of earlier errors, the susceptibility to falsifications, is taken to heart.

Of course, there are considerable overlaps. But we can distinguish several different mind-sets in society: unpretentious ignorance and pretentious ignorance, good sense and idiocy, superficial knowledge combined with dogmatic views, achievement in special fields not matched with even minimally tolerable judgment in others, claims to a higher moral attitude together with ambition and intolerance. All this serves to keep the muddle going. Society can be marred and mangled by addicts of misconceived ideas of social and political life, unless the mental atmosphere is greatly detoxified.

We must remember that repression, intellectual persecution, and stultification have always been accompanied by complex and highbrow paperwork. In the Middle Ages, the crushing of the heretics of the Languedoc, later the Inquisition's burnings at the stake, were justified by well-educated academics, with whom even later the voices of sanity, like Erasmus, Montaigne, Rabelais, contended against odds.

We may forget that those who seem to us to have been the winners of intellectual debates were often opposed by what then seemed to many to be just as sophisticated opponents—and who often, in political *practice,* lost the debate (as with Pascal and the Jesuits). It is also perhaps relevant that the complexity and sophistication of a view is not necessarily decisive. Eratosthenes' solar system was truer than Ptolemy's epicycles, but it lost out for centuries. As for the compilation of massive "evidence," the Baconians are notoriously more knowledgeable than most of us.

The psychosphere, the logosphere, is permeated by concepts, ideas, verbalizations, a whole apparatus devised, or rather evolved, to form some sort of mental contact with reality—or to block it off. That is, a large circle of the "thinking," "educated" class take *ideas* as more veridical than facts.

## 9.

Given that record and that mental motivation, is argument possible? One can only hope so. But this is a fairly Herculean task. There are other problems besides war and terrorism. There is a mind-set to unscramble.

*Chapter VI*

# Internationalism, Supranationalism

————— ⊗⊗⊗ —————

1.

The urge to international understanding is an admirable one. But it runs into problems when we look at the realities. The world that Americans, and other Westerners full of goodwill, want to mount and ride, feed and pat, is not a sweet-tempered little pony but a huge vile-tempered mule.

The words "United Nations" have a splendid sound. The United Nations has been offered to the world over and over again as the highest representation of humanity.

Not so fast. It is a "union," of course, not of nations but of states. And many UN states exist—even not counting ones recognized as "rogue"—that in no sense embody a civilized past, present, or future for the world or for themselves. Its members include governments largely or totally opposed to their own citizens' liberty and, of course, to Western culture in general. It lost some prestige when, for example, the UN Commission on Human Rights elected Libya as its chairman. Sudan is also a member, but the United States was dropped in 2001. Israel is in effect permanently barred. Meanwhile, Syria was elected to the presidency of the Security Council.

It is not, therefore, a body whose powers can be allowed to include rulings contrary to our principles. It is a forum for discussion, compromise, adjustment, and possible agreement on certain general issues. Of course, even apart from the UN, states that "recognize" each other and exchange diplomats have to observe certain amenities. The UN itself is an arena in which views are publicized and interests pushed and a venue for negotiation. At best, it is more like a stock exchange or a hockey field than a nice family picnic.

For a short time in 1950 I was a first secretary at the U.K. delegation to the United Nations. I was at a number of sessions of the Security Council—you can see on TV (or could) behind each top delegate two or three of us ready to take his messages, bring his materials. In the breaks, we would be briefed in taking on and getting the support of various groups in the General Assembly.

In those days, it was usual, though not habitual, for the "democracies" to get their views accepted, even if toned down. But a major difference between then and now is that there were then many fewer states represented, so that they could be approached more or less individually. It was more like a town meeting than a football crowd. And now?

The major trouble, from the point of view of the civilized world's addressing the real problems, is that the unreal, high-flown, old Continental vocabulary now dominates. It is not merely that some European states or political classes tend to push these verbalisms but that these have become the main language of their and other representatives—in fact of most of the world's diplomats, and especially those sent to UN-sponsored organizations and conferences.

If the UN is regarded as having the potential to become a world government, one can only say that this potential is very weak and could only develop when the majority of states become politically civilized—in reality rather than rhetoric. But the UN has tended to develop a concept of international action based on the necessity for compromise and peace even with aggressors. Unfortunately, it still claims to be supreme "arbiter." The UN record in Bosnia, Rwanda, Sierra Leone, and elsewhere has been useless or worse—and always because the use of force against the guilty party was denied or mishandled. But, as Michael Ignatieff has put it (of Sierra Leone), "to be neutral here is to be an accomplice in crime." As to Iraq, we shall see.

Then there are the treaties and the international organizations that have been associated with them: if one starts with a general statement of human rights, one is led willy-nilly into a set of particulars that are supposed to follow or interpret the high generalities. On the other hand, if one starts with a true legal attitude that concerns itself with particular real abuses, they can be settled as they arise, rather than adduced or invented and added to by anonymous regulationists.

In a rather different, though also politically driven, context, we may note that the United Kingdom is now suffering from its subscription to those sections of the Maastricht Treaty that gave intrusive regulatory powers to a political and judicial "international" bureaucracy in Brussels. Even at that level, treaties are affected by laws being obeyed by some signatories and not others. Robert D. Putnam's classic *Making Democracy Work* shows how this cultural difference in attitudes to law persists even between different provinces in Italy. How much more so between different countries and different legal traditions.

It is even maintained that binding the United States or the United Kingdom by signatures to a treaty is automatically a Good Thing. The obvious objections don't seem to register in some critical minds—not only do some of the states putting ink to paper fail to carry out anything like their obligations in the real world, but permitting international bodies to intrude into the law-and-liberty countries also involves the institutionalization, on purely abstract grounds, of an, as yet, primitive apparat. A very important trouble with international arrangements of all types has also been that Western governments sign on to policies that have not been properly (or at all) argued or debated by their publics or legislatures. Thus these arrangements are a means of giving more power to their own executive branches and, of course, more power to the international bureaucracies and permanent staff, whose interests are so deeply involved.

2.

The signing of international treaties and the acceptance of international tribunals appeals to a certain internationalist idealism—a worthy enough sentiment in itself, but one that needs to be carefully deployed, especially in this sort of context.

But the question of international courts and tribunals must arouse various qualms. Who sits on them? By whom are they appointed? What are the laws—if "laws" is the right word—that they administer? When it comes to the International Criminal Court and similar bodies, Madeleine Albright said (of the Yugoslav war crimes tribunal), "The Nuremberg principles have been reaffirmed." An unfortunate comparison. Even at the time, my (late) friend the philosopher Sidney Hook objected to Nuremberg, not, of course, because he had any sympathy whatever for the accused. In the same way, few would defend Milosevic. And it is natural enough for us to seek penalties. That the National Socialist leadership was guilty of loathsome crimes is clear. Few, unless unusually opposed to the death penalty, would not happily have sat on a court-martial and had them shot for any number of atrocious offenses.

The Nuremberg trial, however, had a number of disqualifying defects, if considered as a legal operation. The accused were not allowed to address any facts that impugned the attitudes or records of any of the attorneys or appointed judges. On trial for, amongst other things, wars of aggression, they were thus unable to make the point that one of the Allies—the USSR—had been expelled from the League of Nations a few years previously on just those grounds or that, indeed, it had colluded with the Nazis in the first aggression of World War II, against Poland. The appearance of Iona Nikitchenko as the Soviet-appointed judge should also have raised questions and provoked objections. He had been one of the "judges" in the notorious Zinoviev trial of 1936—which was widely believed, even then, to have been a gigantic fraud. Now, of course, this is indisputable, and we know of other, more secret fake trials in which he took part. So even if not proved at the time, we might agree that, at least retrospectively, Nuremberg can be pronounced defective on this basis alone.

On the Soviet prosecutorial side we find not only Nikitchenko but Lev Sheinin, who had also already been associated in public print as having the prosecutor's role in various faked trials, together with several others on the panel. (And we now know that the secret Soviet commission for manipulating the trial consisted of Andrey Vyshinsky, lead prosecutor in the show trials, three civilians, plus three leading secret police officers—the latter all shot later—while their organization was represented at Nuremberg by the later notorious interrogator and torturer Colonel M. T. Likachev, also eventually shot.)

The indictment included a charge that the Nazis had murdered the Polish officers found in 1943 in the mass graves at Katyn. The documents fully proving Soviet culpability were released in Gorbachev's time. But even in the 1940s, there was considerable evidence casting much doubt on the Soviet story. Meanwhile, the Soviets produced to the court much evidence—faked, of course—to prove the Nazis' responsibility. If Katyn was indeed to be regarded as a crime within the competence of the court, it should have been properly examined and other witnesses presumably called. In fact, the accusation against the Germans was simply dropped from the verdict—an unconscionable anomaly.

It is worth adding that Moscow had under arrest and was about to "try" a group of leaders of the Polish political and military underground, that is, a group of leaders of another Allied state. They had been promised safe conduct. . . . This gross offense to justice and to democratic politicians was thus an immediate background to Nuremberg.

There are other faults to be found with Nuremberg, for example in the selection of the accused, who included Julius Streicher: an appalling villain certainly, but one with little status as a war criminal (he was chosen presumably because his earlier record was widely known to the Allied public). But the selection of defendants is doubtless not to be regarded as a point against the court itself.

The Soviet participation is, however, crucial. It can be justified on political but scarcely on legal grounds. But this means that nonjudicial considerations—indeed considerations incompatible with the judicial—affected even the most respectable of Western judges and lawyers who participated. That this point should be to some extent neglected today is a disturbing sign.

Nuremberg was a single operation. But over the period that followed there were several international agreements reached binding on their signatories in the longer term. In the 1970s, for example, the USSR signed the Helsinki Agreement on human rights. The agreement's key clauses were not implemented (to put it mildly).

3.

We still need to be critical indeed about what may have the appearance of high internationalism, especially when the appeal is humane and the objections are more recondite, less simply expressible. At any rate, it is surely right to note that the acceptance of international obligations, and nowadays especially those affecting the policies, interests, and traditional rights and powers of the states of established law and liberty, must be preceded by, at the least, negotiation that is careful, skeptical, and unaffected by superficial generalities, however attractive at first sight.

The current International Criminal Court is not subject to defects as grave as Nuremberg's. Nevertheless, it is absurd for countries with established courts and the rule of the law to give so shakily based a tribunal any sort of seniority over domestic or other actions by the law-and-liberty state.

The UN, like the EU, approaches "human rights" on the basis of the general high-mindedness of the Continental Enlightenment. Declarations are made, agreements are reached. It is taken for granted that many states— about half the membership of the UN—will not in fact conform. And in the regions where liberty largely prevails, the signatories find their own countries denounced, often by their own citizens. As the late Raymond Aron, who spent so much of his life trying to educate the French intelligentsia, put it, "every known regime is blameworthy if one holds it to an abstract idea of equality over liberty." Which is to say that under abstract human rights definitions, every state in the West that submits to treaties of the human rights sort lays itself open to aggressive litigation.

4.

We can all see that today there are social and environmental as well as political problems. But that discussion and action on them has been distorted first by exaggerating them and second by blaming them on capitalism, and the United States in particular.

It is clear that the problem of global warming was taken over by, let us say, "enthusiasts"; but it is also clear that there is indeed, as the senior researchers concluded, a general global warming, "partly due to human activity," and nothing like all of it industrial (the recent highly smoked skies of the Indian Ocean were the product of wood-burning for fuel). There is, of course, much to be done. And there is much already in hand that will greatly help: fuel cells, the new-technology, nuclear power projects, etc.

The one thing that should not be done on this is to grant decision-making power to the international, intellectually demagogic bureaucracy. As ever, there are politicians who do not really follow the much-proclaimed hype. One high State Department figure urged the acceptance by the United States of the Kyoto Protocol on the ground that it was merely verbiage and could do no harm. And this was clearly the feeling of many in the countries that did sign on. Whatever the faults of Kyoto, it may be argued that the United States should have taken part—though of course it may be argued that few bona fide participants gained much.

All the same, the American boycott of the Kyoto discussions was regarded, and understandably so, as a clumsy and quite unnecessary gesture to a more or less isolationist trend in U.S. politics. Whether or not any sort of tolerable result was to be extracted from the Kyoto project, this is not the way to handle America's public image, either at home or abroad. The international forum, however unpromising, can be turned to advantage. When my friend Daniel Patrick Moynihan was sent to the UN, he took a harder line than had hitherto been seen there—and had more success in arguing down the hostile, or muddleheaded, representatives of less-friendly states. In a similar vein, we may note the American withdrawal from UNESCO, which has now resulted in a much-improved organization. It all depends on how the particular issues are handled; but merely being right is in itself useless.

If, as appears, we are in for a warm cycle regardless, or almost regardless, of human input, our world will have to cope. I have been reading a book on the Paleolithic Lascaux Cave—only fifteen thousand years ago. It includes tables on climatic changes and large-scale variations in animal and tree species throughout Europe through little warm ages and little ice ages. (Indeed, these are recorded even in the past millennium.) There is certainly a problem, or problems, but it is one the international treaties have not, so far, properly addressed.

5.

P overty throughout the world, like pollution, is commonly blamed on the West.

This comes in two variants: first, imperialism is put forward as the supreme sin of the past century; then, it is argued that it now persists in a different but also deplorable form. One of the major mind blockers is, of course, that word "empire," and the whole concept of "imperialism." Even in the absence of American or Western armed interventions, the terms are used to criticize the West, since nowadays they are often applied to "globalization." But more deep-seated is probably the false idea that empires—particularly the British one—were mere oppressors.

As to traditional British imperialism, I have argued elsewhere that though in the long run untenable, it contained and transmitted much that was positive. (And that empires and their heritages differed: I quoted Joseph Conrad as saying that "liberty can only be found under the British flag all over the world." I will add another East European observer, Karel Čapek: "Wherever on this planet ideals of personal freedom and dignity apply, there you will find the cultural inheritance of England.")

In any case, when cultures spread into others with very different customs, the adaptation is not merely political. Let us look at a meld or compromise reached over a century ago between a Western and an Asian conception of "morality." Victorian legislation in India shows something of the problem of satisfying different, indeed contradictory, habits of mind. Section 292 of the Indian Penal Code (Calcutta, 1895) provides penalties for "whoever sells or distributes, imports or prints for sale or hire, or willfully exhibits to public view, any obscene book, drawing, painting, representation or figure [etc.]."

But then it provides an *"Exception.—*This section does not extend to any representation sculptured, engraved, painted or otherwise represented, on or

*63*

in any temple, or on any car used for the conveyance of idols, or kept or used for any religious purpose."

This is a trivial-sounding example, though one showing that intercultural compromises are possible, if concern with compromise is given priority. But we should not forget that such issues may be psychologically as divisive as or more divisive than the overtly political.

It may remind us too that people take time to adjust to what may broadly be thought of as deep-seated cultural differences. There is no reason to regard the Islamic countries as immovably resistant to what we would regard as progress. The eleventh- and twelfth-century Avicenna and Averroës are known to all concerned with the history of thought as serious philosophers and above all for transmitting the earlier work of the Greeks to a mentally barbarized Europe. They were both given trouble by more fanatical coreligionists but were protected by Muslim rulers, with varying success. But in our context, on the confrontation between Moors and Christians in Spain, it is good to note that in spite of severe fighting and differences of religion, there was at first much less institutionalized fanaticism than what arose in the late fifteenth or early sixteenth centuries. When Pedro the Cruel was negotiating peace while Grenada remained Muslim, he treated Ibn Khaldun in Seville with great courtesy and even offered him a place at court.

At any rate, it seems that war, as such, did not breed the mentality found later in the Inquisition and a far narrower and more atavistic Spanish power at home and abroad. And the Muslim culture of Spain, at its highest development, can be judged as superior in many ways to the order that succeeded it. In a not very different context, much the same might be said of the early thirteenth-century Albigensian Crusade, in which a higher and tolerant civilization was brought down by more fanatical invaders from the north.

With that in mind, we should note that most Christian European countries took centuries to reach their present imperfect level. There seems no reason why Islamic countries should not evolve similarly. (The one pluralist country of the Middle East, Lebanon, was both a civic and an economic success until crushed by Syria.)

### 6.

The economic globalization that took place in the nineteenth century and whose essentials had been created earlier brought various changes.

But where experience was not long enough or was not deeply planted enough, the export of political and intellectual institutions did not match the other, and worse, Western inputs.

But many, while no longer retaining a belief in the large alternatives, still fall back on scenarios that depict the market economies as guilty of offenses against the environment and/or against the underdeveloped countries (known in the latter context as "imperialist").

Ironically, the destructive effect of some of the more "progressive" ideas exported from the West—or even imposed by the West—is clear enough. The then Undersecretary for the Colonies, Dingle Foot, actually wrote against encouraging the Ghanian "kulak"; and there was the disastrous "ground nut" scheme that was inflicted on what was then Tanganyika. That is, on any scale, independence was, or might be, better than subordination to a Western intellectual stratum at least as misled as any local variety.

We must recall that products of the West included, in the twentieth century, socialism, on the one hand, as an idea or program, and Leninism, on the other, as a method of rule. One result of the encouragement of uncompromising anti-imperialism was that this created a huge obstacle to progress—the obstacle being that the tightly centralized "democratic centralism" parties in the developing world were often able to take over or eliminate the looser (and usually more moderate) organizations. At the same time, the old idea that the West could be caught up with (by even partial assimilation to its cultures of law and liberty and by the development of at least legislatures with limited power) was trumped, in the eyes of a younger intelligentsia, by the long-fashionable wave of the future seen in the theoretical perspective.

Even when not specifically of that sort, political organizations often accepted the centralized type of organization and party discipline Lenin and Hitler pioneered. This, coupled with the whole idea of complete state control, resulted in what the Marxist historian George Lichtheim noted of the Third World: the proliferation of regimes best described as "National Socialist," with the obvious negative effects even if in incomplete form. And as so often with one-party states, there are two long-term results. First, it more or less inevitably, or at any rate almost invariably, becomes highly corrupt. Second, where feasible, it inclines to aggression against neighbors (and is often in that context oppressive of sections of its own citizenry). That is, unmoderated nationalism, like any dogmatic belief, inherently provokes threats to peace (including, where attainable, the nuclear threat).

It is in this context that we may return to the question of terrorism—though terrorism may arise from any extremism: national, political, or religious. The motivation, the feeling behind it, was demonstratively seen in the "reactionary" German writer August von Kotzebue's assassin's famous comment, "A Christ thou shalt become," referring not to his victim but to himself. We should note, in terrorism's development, that there has, generally speaking, been a moral deterioration even within the whole terror apparat. The Russian "People's Will" terrorists condemned the assassination of the American President James Garfield in 1881. In a free society, they argued, terrorism was inappropriate: they only practiced it themselves in the absence of any alternative. Whether this was completely sincere is another question. But more important, terrorists in general even a century ago saw themselves as stalking particular targets, human and physical. We can distinguish these from the terror groups whose admitted aim is maximum destruction.

Thus the IRA in its later form did not, of course, meet even the most modest civilized criterion. And it was, equally of course, pro-Nazi in World War II—though the most striking demonstration of anti-Allied attitudes was the condolence call paid at the German embassy in Dublin on the death of Chancellor Hitler by Irish prime minister Eamon de Valera.

Still, history gives us many good, as well as less good, examples of fierce nationalisms being, after all, contained. One that seems to be helpful in modern times is that of Hungary following the national revolution of 1848, which was put down by the Austrian Hapsburg monarchy largely through Russian intervention. You might have thought that this bloodstained confrontation would have led to deep and permanent Austro-Hungarian estrangement. But moderates on both sides had, by 1867, negotiated the *Ausgleich,* by which Hungary became an equal participant in the "Dual Monarchy." It is even quite probable that other Hapsburg territories, such as Czech Bohemia, might have evolved similarly but for World War I. At any rate, the experience shows that fierce nationalism can be abated and avoided.

### 7.

In the twentieth century, the world saw a generation of nontotalitarian "nationalist" political leaders educated in the economic fallacies then dominant in the academic intelligentsia of Britain and elsewhere—that is to say, regulationism.

India itself produced clear-minded economic and social thinkers, like Gujarat University Professor B. R. Shenoy, who right from the start of the country's Second Five-Year Plan was able vigorously to point out the destructive effects of the whole approach. But the winds of dogma were then blowing too strongly, and for over half a century what he called the "Permit Raj" entrenched itself.

It is now largely accepted that the British economist Peter Bauer was right on the best approach to "Third World" poverty—as far as possible to give aid or assistance never to local governments or officials but to other recipients, in states needing them. And the world's advanced nations can indeed help, even in present conditions. The huge area in which Bauer has proved right is the major world issue of trade and investment in the developing countries, where the old formulae are still afflicting many minds. As Jagdish Bhagwati of Columbia University notes, "the use of tradable permits to pursue environmental objectives exactly illustrates what the reformers were doing in using the market to improve environmental policy, not to eliminate it."

But worldwide, the problem is deeper. As Professor Deepak Lal pointed out in his *Times Literary Supplement* review of Bauer's last book, almost all of the long-advanced reasons for world poverty and most of the alleged cures for it are simply false. What we still see is aid that fails to reach the world's poor or else turns them into dependents, combined with a blaming of imperialism, colonialism, or neocolonialism for what can be improved by more sensible methods. Here is a major defect in the minds of much of the Western, and other, intelligentsia—even if economists may now accept Bauer's view of the past half century as the era of "Disregard of Reality," there are many laymen who have not.

On "globalization," Bhagwati has powerfully argued that economic globalization, when not blocked by local politicians, has always benefited the population, reduced poverty, and abated social evils. That is by no means to justify, for example, IMF mistakes over "capital account liberalization," let alone the errors of the Russian and other governments. But he shows that globalization, as such, does not warrant any of the moral or material criticism to be found among the doubtless well-meaning but uncomprehending demonstrationers.

## 8.

The European, or Euro-American, dominance of the greater part of the world was in part the product of trade, of Euro-centered globalism.

But it was only effective in the best, as well as the worst, examples because of a great superiority in military technology, which was not itself decisive but was successful in connection with, usually, a reasonably flexible political engagement.

At any rate, a liberal, or survivalist, world today must also clearly be based on just such a military-technological superiority; without it, the world is perhaps doomed. As the very experienced David Rieff concludes in his *A Bed for the Night*, the international humanitarian effort, admirable in intention, has not come up to the expectations of its sponsors and volunteers. Rieff points out, in regard to photographs of sick children being saved by American nurses, that this admirable effort does not show the more lethal context (in Sudan, for instance) of political or ethnic slaughter. Devoted work has of course not been fruitless, but the major background of massacres is beyond the scope of the humanitarian workers. He shows how those efforts of devoted Western organizations to give aid to the populations suffering from hunger and disease are often negated on the spot. Rieff reluctantly concludes that only military action could help the major sufferers. And he is driven to a conclusion—that "liberal imperialism" is the better choice against the common alternative of barbarism.

All this is to say that the disaster areas of the world cannot be revived without Western help, as is widely recognized and warmly urged when it comes to the fight against disease and poverty (and much more can be done in these areas), and that the deeper and more deadly phenomena can only be overcome by what amounts to direct intervention on the part of the more developed states.

That is, intervention includes armed intervention.

This will be called "imperialism."

Now, first the obloquy attached to the word must be decontaminated. It is clear that much of Africa was far better off under British, perhaps even French, rule than it is today. And even now, it has only been (belated) British troop intervention in Sierra Leone that has restored sanity, let alone humanity and order. That unarguably humanitarian Michael Ignatieff has covered the pros and cons of what he takes to be in effect a new, American empire in the making, with U.S. troops already intervening, regime-changing, state-building. And, as he has to remind his readers, the United Nations is not "the world community" and is in itself unable to act effectively.

We have to ask, why America? The European countries alone have just as much in the way of resources. But between them they amount to incomparably less militarily. Even so, a largely American "imperialism" could be broadened and—as it were—enhanced by a real internationalizing. That is, not the spurious and unreliable supranationalizing of the UN, but a genuine joint effort by states already in profound agreement, not states that are balky or need to be wheedled, but full contributors to and beneficiaries of a better world. But Europe today? Obviously not unless its electorates and its political intelligentsia can be made to abandon their obstructive mode—a struggle not all that different from, though subsidiary to, the larger challenge.

And one question Ignatieff poses is, will the American—let alone any other—public support the burden? It goes without saying that it will be opposed by the anticapitalist, antiglobal, and anti-Western fringe, and that they will be heard from, as in Britain and Europe.

NATO itself, while at least keeping a transatlantic community out of the hands of Brussels, still contains European members that block effective international action. The countries of Eastern Europe were, for obvious reasons, intent on joining it—as a protection against a potential Russian threat. But the NATO sphere does not extend beyond its original area. The Russian threat is, at least for now, virtually extinct. So, while NATO should be maintained, there is a case for a new Western alliance. It would consist of the states that supported the United States and the United Kingdom in 2003—that is, most countries in Europe outside France and Germany (and Belgium). That is, it could not be sabotaged from within (and another Rwanda-type disaster could be avoided). I envisage the bloc or world alliance as including what one might call the Outer Europe, and, of course, the Europes Overseas and others.

Meanwhile, political feeling in Washington and elsewhere includes isolationism on both the far left and the far right. Taking the key decisions will be hard—though the United States has suffered more from apparent weakness than from strong action. Osama bin Laden's original argument against the United States was not only that it deserved ruthless assault but also that it was losing its willpower. He cited, in particular, the debacle in Somalia—and the decisions taken then do indeed appear to have been deleterious in both the short and the long run.

There are obvious and heavy difficulties. The British Empire came into being when nationalism, to say nothing of totalitarian ideology, was hardly to be found in the countries we have to deal with today. These drives or motivations are now much more powerful (though, even so, they are declining to some extent in some areas). And to train anything like a colonial civil service would be hard to do from scratch. Nor is it clear that obsolete thinking is extinct among American military and political professionals—nor fresh but fallacious thinking either, come to that.

Perhaps the best perspective, to sketch it roughly, would be (after, or instead of, military reduction of the worst suppurations) a support for successor regimes, with an American or NATO watching brief from "sovereign bases" such as already exist, ready to provide immediate protection to nations in torment.

However looked at, the difficulties are enormous. But what if all the alternatives are even more dangerous?

# Chapter VII

# Slouching towards Byzantium

———— ⊶∞⊷ ————

1.

Assuming the defeat or containment of the immediate enemies of the Western political order and its longer-term penetration and pacification of the world, are there other signs of a negative future? Is there nowadays any particular tendency to that which can be seen as disturbingly retrogressive? That is, do we face the possibility of a politically and intellectually, though not necessarily technologically, static society, or worse?

The answer, unfortunately, is yes. As we have noted earlier, we face, so far more in Europe than in Britain, more in Britain than in the United States, strong tendencies that, if they continue, must lead to a society in mental (though not only mental) decline.

The pioneer masters of sociology have taken a skeptical view of state action. Weber, Durkheim, Tönnies, Simmel, more recently Robert Nisbet—all saw the disadvantages as well as the advantages of the change from the accepted community sense of traditional premodern society to what they felt to be the individualism and "rationality" marking modern progress. Nisbet, following Tocqueville, sees as the main trouble the weakening of all communal ties except that provided by the state. He points out that the whole tradition of the "liberation" of the individual, from Rousseau on, has been to make individuals independent of each other and of society but more dependent on the state. As he says, this is based on an error: "Centrality of sovereignty does not lead logically to the centralization of administration in public affairs. . . . Decentralization of administration is not merely feasible technically; it is a prime necessity of free culture."

It would perhaps be generally admitted that the civic order in Western countries is now more at odds with the centralizing bureaucratic element than has been the case for a century. We now have, and especially in Brussels, a large stratum for whom only "hyper-bureaucrat" seems adequate.

71

They might be called "regulationists," which sounds like an early-seventeenth-century sect. The civic, consensual culture has always had to cope with attempts by the executive to increase its power as against the powers of the individual, the locality, the community. Recent troubles may, in one respect, be viewed as galloping elephantiasis of the executive as it usurps new areas of decision—and this is true not merely of those theoretically committed to state socialism but also of the managerialist, "technocratic" conservatives. The growth of "corporationism" was brilliantly described and discussed a generation ago by that fine British scholar Samuel Brittan.

The downward movement in the United States differs from its equivalents in Britain and Europe. The progress of mental and political conformism, and the trend against the law-and-liberty civilization, is conducted in America rather more by activists' penetration into, or blackmail of, the governing apparatus—by pressure rather than seduction. And on the whole it is less successful—so far.

2.

There have been instances in the past when an ever more rigid bureaucracy and an ever more constricted mentality have developed. One thinks of the classical world's decline into Byzantium—and, for example, the closing of the Academy in Athens in 529 A.D. and the earlier abolition of the Olympic Games. It is doubtless unfair to take this well-known instance. And Byzantium was better than most other polities of its time. But the mind, outside internecine theology, had by earlier standards fallen low, become desiccated. Instead of Aristotle, for example, we find synodic records described by Edward Gibbon as a mass of "nonsense and falsehood." Nor was this mental decline offset by the exemplary codification of the law that accompanied it.

In addition to the current international changes and challenges, there is a tendency in the West (also to a large degree based on "educated" assumptions) to move in the direction of a nontotalitarian but nevertheless single-minded corporatism—stultifying and intrusive on law and liberty.

Though disagreeing with James Burnham as to its desirability or inevitability, Orwell saw the future corporate state as a real possibility: "it is quite easy to imagine a world-society, economically collectivist . . . but with all political, military, and educational power in the hands of a small caste of rulers and their bravos."

Orwell also gives us an interesting analysis of a sort of prototype of state-entrepreneur cooperation, in this case of "re-housing from the public funds" in Liverpool, which he calls "in effect socialist legislation" put into practice by the city's corporation, which was "almost entirely Conservative" but said to be "entirely ruthless towards private ownership." The "actual work" was done by contractors, who tended to be friends or relations of those on the city corporation. "Beyond a certain point, Socialism and Capitalism are not easy to distinguish, the State and Capitalist tending to merge into one." And this was in the late 1930s!

Given modern circumstances, in which the state has abandoned even in principle its hostility to capitalists as such, this perspective involves a high-level working relationship, even if with some points of friction (indeed a unity still in the nature of a pantomime horse), between capitalism and etatism, each strengthening and using the other's power and both accepting a dominant establishmentarianism. The music-hall song comes to mind:

*Don't tell my mother I'm half a horse in a pantomime*
*Don't let her know that I'm a sham*
*But if you have in due course*
*To tell her I'm half a horse . . .*
*Don't tell her which half I am*

Though our problem is not so clear-cut.

The long-term prospect, in fact, is what a French commentator has called "pink Fascism." There is no need of a monolithic party if the effective apparat is in general agreement, makes the same assumptions. The totalitarian attempt to control all aspects of life was untenable in the long run. A far greater leeway on small matters, even disagreement on tactics, is much more viable.

This dilute corporatism does not exclude a contest of political parties. But these parties become more and more alike, differing only on what would have been thought peripheral issues in earlier days. Nor are voices of ideological dissent stifled. In Byzantium, there was still much theoretical debate, but unlike that between Stoics and Epicureans, this was the trivial though incendiary dispute between iconoclasts and iconodules (the question being should icons be worshipped; the level being that of Constantine V being known in history as Copronymus, having allegedly soiled the font at his baptism).

3.

A South American scholar once told me that revolutionary movements on most of his continent were due to the countries' having an educated class twice as large as was needed to man their institutions. Those excluded became revolutionaries because of their drives to take over power—the views and ideologies issuing from them being little more than what Marx himself saw, in rather different circumstances, as products of the "false consciousness" emanating from real economic and power motivations.

This is doubtless an oversimplification. All the same, it is true that nowadays a much larger "educated" stratum is out there seeking nonphysical employment. And, of course, there is a simple non-"revolutionary" answer to my South American friend's problem: double the number of state institution employees.

4.

James Madison's great argument for the American constitutional settlement was that under it, "ambition must be made to counteract ambition," and similarly with interests, so that the community could take due account of, but prevail over, the diverse elements of the social, political, and economic order. In fact, it was the tensions between the institutions—and between the social and other elements represented in them—that gave us our early pluralism.

In principle, there are spheres in which private enterprise is now everywhere granted to be superior to state control. But what if the higher capitalist stratum can permeate and be permeated by the state bureaucracy? Too great a rapprochement, let alone merger, between the two would break Madison's view of the state and the community.

And even apart from that, the large-scale capitalist elements that thrive best in such a context are, often enough, less those that provide the "private" drive than those that know best how to placate and cohabit with the inhabitants of the state machine.

Some sort of accommodation has always existed and will always be needed. But beyond a certain point, a merger of state and capitalist hierarchies is to be deplored, apart from anything else because it tends to form a barrier against "small businesses," on which (as the *Economist* points out) much economic progress depends.

5.

Meanwhile, a large stratum constitutes a quasi-monopoly that excludes—or bribes—the rest of society. Thus we still face powerful forces, over the longer run, leading us towards the ossification and decay of our culture. For, in addition to current international dangers and challenges, this tendency flourishes in the West itself.

Of the matters that need the cooperation of the state and large businesses, we must register, largely on the positive side, the development of defense and associated technologies. Here both strata are under considerable pressure to create success (as was true to some extent in the Soviet case, where the air force could demand real airplanes from what was otherwise a kleptocratic industrial base).

The other, basically more fundamental hope of our order is that "small" entrepreneurs will be able, to a great extent, to avoid etatization and bureaucratization. There are hundreds of such small firms in Los Angeles that avoided the effects of the slump. They had two advantages. First, they were not absorbed into state and corporation. Second, if threatened with intrusive action by the local authorities, they could move, or threaten to move, to another county, having no vast concrete palaces to quit—in which context, one should note that the California counties are large (whereas those in Texas are small and not economically hospitable and competitive). One is reminded of C. Northcote Parkinson's first work, on Malaya: Chinese farmers would pay 10 percent of their profits to a local bandit. But if the bandits attempted to charge more, the farmers would move. In this way, a balance of sorts was maintained.

The subject is a large one. And we should remember that too great a diversion into local power is not in itself a positive (there is more corruption in France than Britain because of greater local power and thus easier illegal fixes); that is, to be effective, the power of the law needs to be centralized, while the power to resist local or other regulations should be citizenized.

6.

A declining educational system affects the leading capitalists, and at the same time they are not only less educated in but also less experienced in political realities.

A paradoxical point distinguishing the Anglo-West today from the viable consensual polities of a century, or half a century, ago is that the financial power no longer overlaps the political sphere. There used to be a common experience and social connection, a broad mutual understanding among these supposed elites, the political and the financial. Now we get, instead of, say, the Rothschilds, such people as, say, the Ted Turners. And not only are the new rich liable to involve themselves in political absurdities. It seems also that even those of the rich with more common sense are often uneducated.

Such points are indeed true of a large swathe of all economic strata, but with the rich, it means that they are no longer involved, in the old way, in a more or less serious political life. It also means that, as has been to a lesser extent true for quite a time, some of them are easily duped by overseas political con men (Castro and the like).

In somewhat of the same way that the new corporatism has brought together the capitalist and socialist, state and private, enterprises, it has tended to cool down the other potential friction that might be expected to arise outside the social and economic order proper—the role of the intellectual rebels who had given trouble to earlier establishments. These were now, one could see, increasingly deradicalized for most purposes through their assimilation to the new order, including heavy financing of their supposedly irreconcilably independent mental and artistic output. The paternalist state began to be seen as Dada.

In Parkinson's *The Law and the Profits*, published in 1960, he describes successive ways of staffing the British civil service. Two centuries ago, a candidate facing the selection committee had to establish his relationship to one or another peer (except in the Admiralty, where a naval connection was the requirement). This, Parkinson tells us, often had excellent results.

It was followed by a period when the questions were which public school the candidate had attended and what games he played. This too "produced good results."

In the 1850s, this system was replaced by a written examination in classical, that is, Latin and Greek, literature and in ability to write. This was a "moderate success."

It was replaced in more modern times by "the intelligence test and the psychological interview." This had the worst results by far: staff members chosen from hundreds of candidates had to be sacked for incompetence within months.

We shall go further into this in a later chapter.

We are in the presence of a general diffusion of power, and the largest and most intrusive and expanding element is, of course, the new bureaucracy—not only as an instrument of others but in itself even, at its lower levels, as what might be called a petit buroisie. That alone may be thought a recipe for the long-term decline of pluralist civilization. When one adds that the bureaucratic elites and subelites and sub-subelites are largely inclined to the uncritical acceptance not indeed of ideology, but of a package of old and new Ideas, the prospect looks yet worse.

Even the Mafia had a justification code. In general, the distinction between an ideological adherent and a partner in crime is often a false one, as we note, for example, of the Stalin leadership.

## 7.

The concepts and programs that rose in the nineteenth century (and sometimes earlier) have had their day and are fading from the political scene. State control of the economy, and not only in the Communist version, has failed. Yet, if no longer driven by theory, the instinctive urge to impose values or opinions remains. And the urge towards using the state for those purposes is still common in the West, and with it a tendency to accept uncritically the currently prevalent ideological fashion or dogma.

The promise of the future fulfillment of socialism validated for many of its adherents their drive to power, at least in their own eyes. This, in itself, should make us wary of the whole psychological tilt engendered by such Ideas. We should remember that the urge to interfere, to gain some element of power, is not confined to the Communist and National Socialist extremes. Most people will have come across, and many novelists have written about, the types who seek power in a village, or a college, or a business, and often with a high level of self-justification. In a statewide, or continentwide, bureaucracy, there is a great deal of room for this unfortunate temperament.

In America, large firms and the state have to employ bureaucracies to cope with and satisfy each other. One major result, everywhere, is the continual increase, in numbers as well as power, of a new largish cadre educated with this in mind. Indeed, institutions such as universities are now bureaucratized past belief, only in part by the new information technologies, with their ever-increasing demand for new recruits.

## 8.

Even apart from such needs, bureaucracy has always emerged. A Russian friend, something of an expert on Dostoyevsky, once took me walking towards the writer's house and the apartment depicted in *Crime and Punishment* as Raskolnikov's. The long street we first went through had a long line of identical little dwellings, built for the myriad clerks who had had to produce copies of imperial decrees in the nineteenth century.

Nor is the current expansion of the state in the United Kingdom a new thing. Unless actively prevented, London's bureaucracy increases regardless of actual duties. Parkinson's famous analysis of the British Admiralty, over half a century ago, shows that the number of officials continually increased as the number of ships and of dockworkers shrank. He similarly noted that after World War II, as the number of British colonies fell, the number of Colonial Office bureaucrats increased.

Back to "pink Fascism." "Fascism" is an overstatement. But what about "pink"? It means that this new corporatism is based on and is largely staffed and directed by people accepting the postsocialist "progressive" set of ideas, a vocally predominant stratum using the state institutions to impose these. If they prevail, the "pink"—even the "green"—may leave an unorganized area around, that is, allow a certain freedom of thought, as the "red" and the "brown" did not (since it is now understood that the total anti-consensual society doesn't work). This is some sort of consolation.

## 9.

Bureaucracy nevertheless brings with it what may legitimately be called "bureausophy," providing a high-minded justification for the whole phenomenon—not merely for the results but for the existence (and enlargement) of the institutions themselves. To support the transition from the aim of efficient administration to that of major agendas of state-enforced change, it inevitably follows that transcendent justifications are needed. There is a great emotional difference between "I am doing a useful service" and "I am fulfilling a sublime mission." And then the indoctrinated meet those who have not joined for any particular purpose, but rather to gain employment, like any other job. These in turn begin to feel they are fulfilling a high purpose—or, even if themselves privately cynical, go along with attitudes that provide increasing power and prestige.

As we have noted earlier, Antonio Gramsci, now often quoted as an alternative to his Communist past, spoke in favor of his comrades "marching through the institutions," and such has indeed been the attitude of many who are called "progressive theorists." Sidney Webb and other Fabians took this route. One trouble is, of course, that those directly involved do not just "march through" the institutions; they stay in them.

It is the purpose of this book not to develop these immediate themes but to examine the mind-sets, or cerebral jellies, that produce them. And—as indeed in Byzantium—the power, the conformism, the mind blockages are to be found not merely in the bureaucracy properly speaking but in all the peripheral institutions—above all, perhaps, in the educational stratum and among the organized media (such as the BBC).

10.

A culture different even in origin from the law-and-liberty tradition of the Anglosphere naturally has anyway, among its other deficiencies, a much stronger addiction to etatism. The most striking current example of bureaucratic extravagance and decadence is, of course, the EU. Not that it appears to be viable in the longer run. Brussels is not Byzantium.

But for now the European Union is the supreme attempt to build a regulationist superstate. And it figures, above all, as a supposed focus of mental glamour, socialism having petered out but the psychological thirst for a higher aim remaining—like a movie cartoon figure (Mr. Magoo or Sylvester) still walking on air for a while after his girder has collapsed. They are impelled to grab whatever alternative may appear plausible.

I have written elsewhere of the main defects of the European Union:

*It is an attempt, by a stratum that needs, and no longer has, a justificatory "Idea" like "Socialism," to synthesize one.*

*It is an attempt to build a state from populations that have none of the qualifications for nationhood, neither historical nor ethnic.*

*It is an extravagantly expensive bureaucratic nightmare. In pursuit of a supposed high and even transcendent aim, it pursues a vast over-regulation of human life.*

*It is a project imposed from above, and maintained by misrepresentation.*

*It is divisive of the European culture, omitting the Europes overseas.*

The latest European subsanity, as I write, is to make the expression of xeno-phobic views illegal. This is the simple notion that a thing is bad, so can be made illegal—logically and empirically a view that has been the basis of trouble and, often, of tyranny. (But, of course, xenophobia does not extend to anti-Americanism. And to liken George W. Bush to Hitler is, at worst, a little slip.)

A minor example: a European Children's Rights agreement the U.K. government signed and found themselves stuck with all but forbids spank-ing or, presumably, such acts as I heard threatened the other day by a much-loved grandmother to a four-year-old, "Drop that at once or I'll bop you one," to stop him doing something dangerous to himself and others. This (and a mass of other Brussels intrusions) needs a law to be passed in Westminster to the effect, "Any rule or regulation affecting the citizens of the United Kingdom, brought in by treaty without the approval of parlia-ment or people, is hereby declared invalid."

At best, we find bureaucracy sprinkled with a few particles of general words or paragraphs signed by a few delegates or by a handful of inattentive politi-cians, after which the regulationists take over and start trying to decree the straightness of bananas (a true example, which should in itself have provoked a mass dismissal and a total restructuring, being as it was only one of a whole series of the combination of idiocy and paranoia found all over Brussels).

In fact, the most profound and most disturbing piece of Eurocracy is, of course, the increasing subordination of English common law to the Roman, or Napoleonic, legal arrangements of Europe. This even goes so far as to pro-pose that Britons will not be covered by habeas corpus. It was urged that this measure should be accepted by the U.K. parliament with the understanding that Britons could be arrested under its provision and deported to the Continent under European warrants—contrary to traditional British law—without evidence being provided if suspicion is established. One of the Laws Lords rightly queried this.

The English and American common law, especially in its protection from the executive, is central to our culture. And it is, in this, better than, different from, and incompatible with the Continental model.

I have recorded further objections to the EU in my *Reflections on a Ravaged Century*. And others have done it in depth and in detail—including journalists, television editors, experts, and others brought to Brussels to pro-vide favorable publicity, which they found themselves unable to give, and even members of the EU apparat itself who are equally, or more, disillu-sioned. Here I will merely note the substantial objections: above all that the whole basis for the European superstate is absent. There is no "European" nation; instead there is a muddle of intellectuals and interest groups who seem to think that one could be created from above. There cannot be a democracy where there is no demos.

Instead of the real protection of rights found in England, Europe provides the usual generalities, with supposedly relevant detailed deductions arising from them. As a result, Britain finds itself sinking in a swamp of regulations it unknowingly accepted in treaty form, which is to say without any sort of popular or democratic approval. The whole European venture has the same defect. In the countries where the law requires a referendum—as in Ireland and Denmark—a vote is taken again and again until a yes vote is secured, and it is then pronounced irrevocable.

It is only as I finish this book that a full account of the earlier phases of the EU has emerged, with documents hitherto unavailable showing the concealed maneuvers that accompanied it from the beginning (see Christopher Booker's 2003 book *The Great Deception*).

But even apart from the new "Constitution," there is not much to add to David Pryce-Jones's interim description:

> *In Brussels, its capital, the EU today has a bewildering structure in which there is no link between its institutions and the freedom they are supposed to ensure. At the apex are a president and twenty commissioners, appointed to office by national governments in a process invisible to the public. Not elected, they cannot be dismissed. The commission, and its subordinate councils of ministers drawn from national countries, have executive and legislative powers, and some judicial ones as well. These politicians are accountable to nobody but themselves. Here is the only legislative body in the democratic world that meets in secret.*

He adds that

> *A European court of justice was established, with the political mission of granting legal force to the commission's work; its members are also appointed and may not be removed; there is no right of appeal. A variety of instruments are available, including regulations that are binding, directives open to interpretation, recommendations, opinions, and resolutions.*

Nearly thirty-thousand civil servants, spread over two-hundred buildings, with about seven-hundred standing committees, form the body of this

Leviathan. While regulating its unfortunate victims, it is unable to regulate itself. In spite of huge and tax-free salaries, allowances, and air expenses, corruption is everywhere. Every year up to several billion dollars are unaccounted for. A few top officials have, indeed, been prosecuted—including the head of the French Constitutional Court. The new order, even without the United Kingdom, seems to combine bureaucracy with Aristotle's concept of ochlocracy—mob rule. Corporatist officialdom enforces its rules and uses the state to disseminate its opinions. At the same time, it permits indoctrinated "mobs" to silence and disrupt. An absurd example was the demand of French demonstrators against a recent international conference for free railway passes to reach their target; the authorities settled for half fares.

The current tolerance for street violence and other extralegal but less-destructive activities is not confined to the undereducated left. Indeed, its great exemplars in the Germany of the 1920s and early 1930s were the National Socialists and the Communists; even in Britain, it was Mosley's Fascists who were prominent in this sphere. And in Germany, as has been shown, after the Hitlerite victory in 1933, the Communist street fighters largely went over to their old opponents, doubtless partly by habit.

## 11.

In a more general way, Britain is exceptionally unamenable to the Eurocracy. A poll printed in the *Economist* shows increasingly large majorities hostile to the whole EU project.

When it comes to issues, large-scale immigration to the West is due, naturally enough, to economic attractions. These may come in two categories. First, there are those who come to find unskilled jobs left open or newly created for various reasons. But in addition, as has been pointed out, there is the attraction of the welfare state, which in principle pays adequate life support to all who come. That there is a limit to this is obvious. And it depends in part on our helping the countries of origin, in which we have not done enough, or rather have done the wrong things. But admission on the ground of "asylum" is another, and often absurd, category. The number seeking asylum in Britain trebled in a couple of decades. And even more striking, while 5 percent of asylum seekers *from Algeria* were granted asylum in France, in Britain the figure was about 80 percent.

London's reactions were based on inadequate experience of un-British attitudes, on concepts and customs and verbalisms, produced by abstractionists and in circumstances alien to the evolution of the Anglo-American culture of law and liberty. In part this due to a bureaucratic xenophobia—the "xen" in this case being the United States.

## 12.

But it is the downgrading of the mind, the advance of political stultification implied, that is the more basic trouble, of which the EU is only part, though a potential disaster not only locally but on a world scale. At any rate, if these trends continue in the West, it is downhill, into a citizenry appeased by entertainment, thought narrowed to a meager spectrum.

William Tenn, the science fiction writer, has a story in which one of the American parties, by a stroke of genius, runs as a presidential candidate the man discovered by polls to have exactly the average view on every subject. He wins overwhelmingly and is followed by his sons, grandsons, etc. After centuries of dumbing down, the country is taken over by a species that has evolved from a group of dogs long ago shipwrecked on an Arctic island. Humans are bred for their proficiency in throwing sticks, but once this skill is mechanized, they die out. A fantasy, indeed, and one that is merely provocative. Woof! Woof!

A more plausible way in which a country can be ruined is to be seen in the history of Argentina. A rich country, with an economically well-heeled citizenry, lost it all for a simple reason: rulers who became or remained popular by giving their subjects more than the country could afford. That is, the electorate was seduced by promises that it should not have accepted. It is not hard to see that elsewhere, for instance in Germany, tendencies the same way are to be found.

Beyond a certain point, the larger the section dependent on the state, the more difficult it is for an elected government to keep its economy balanced, or to save it from disaster. And this is as true of an excessive bureaucracy as it is of a vote-rich underclass.

The downward slope, unless interrupted, can scarcely lead to anything but corporatism. The only probable interruption would be due to the buildup of resentment against the system. That is to say, this etatism may itself produce the catastrophe from which it purports to save us. Let us hope we survive.

*Part II*

# Horrible

# Examples

. . . the conscience may slumber in a mixed and middle state
between self-illusion and voluntary fraud.

–Edward Gibbon

*. . . le spectre en plein jour raccroche le passant!*

–Charles Baudelaire

# Chapter VIII

# 1917: "Revolution" and Reality

---

### 1.

The chapters that follow are not presented as a broad or general history or even as full accounts of their particular subjects. They are more concerned with still current errors and distortions. And, at the same time, they add some of the newest material that specially illuminates their themes.

Thomas Jefferson wrote that education should be "chiefly historical," on the grounds that we should learn the lessons of the past. In his day, "history" may have been partial or have been seen in a rather local perspective, but it was not falsified, and the themes of actuality were generally understood.

We shall be dealing with the history of our recent and relevant past, but particularly with major and still not fully abreacted distortions and even falsifications, and their acceptance by inadequately skeptical Western intellectuals. Many of these were, in the main, deluded by clumsy and implausible cover stories, but they had often already been seduced by a barrage of fine-sounding general words, some of which still exercize their quasi-hypnotic powers even today. One of them was, and is, of course, "Revolutionary"—especially referring to the cycle that started in Russia in October 1917.

The Bolshevik Revolution brought an atavistic ideocracy, with a narrowly sectarian mind-set, and a total, and indeed self-admitted, amorality of action. And its long-term effects have been overwhelmingly negative. Its real nature was understood by many even at the time. But its myth, especially among the ideas-and-ideals thirsty of the West, still vaguely survived. Let us deal, on a less broad basis, with some of its evidential reality. We may begin by looking at the radically fictionalized story still given it by historians who have had a broad influence, or at any rate a broad seepage.

One, Eric Hobsbawm, is still active as I write, and his approach is the general and "persuasive." Another, E. H. Carr, relied on a vast apparatus of detail, supposed, in turn, to prove broad generalities. Both have been called great, or at any rate good, historians. And each, which is much more my point, was regarded as, to an important degree, the voice of a powerful section of the establishment. Carr, though inconsistent on this, described the October Revolution as "proletarian" and thus, unlike a "bourgeois revolution," able to proceed with a "planned economy." His main theme, based on that view of the more developed Soviet period, we shall refer to later.

Hobsbawm writes agreeably, and often with an air of having judiciously presented the data—abilities that are fairly uncommon these days. And the omission of clotted evidential material would matter little if the main themes were sustainable. At his best, especially in his earlier books, his views are "controversial," and presented in terms of Marxist conceptions that still vaguely exist elsewhere. But I am concerned not with these, but with his more recent work on the Soviet phenomenon. And here we find not merely the controversial but the counterfactual.

Hobsbawm (unlike, for example, that other Marxist historian E. P. Thompson) was a member of the Communist Party of Great Britain until it collapsed under him, though it can rightly be pleaded that he wore his Communism with a somewhat loose straitjacket. But even years later, he was explaining his long support of Stalinism on television, in terms of Communism's having been the "only hope" and so on. And his much praised *The Age of Extremes* is marred by what continues to be massive reality denial.

This would matter less if Hobsbawm had not won a reputation with establishment and media circles. In this context, it is not so much his views, or even his errors, we may deplore, so much as the fact that a politico-corporate British stratum has so taken to him—thus, presumably, identifying itself as a field for the acceptance of a factually and intellectually disorienting account of the modern world.

Hobsbawm no longer represents the October Revolution as wholly benign. But he takes it as the best option available—which is, to say the least, disputable. And he holds it to be the crucial and critical event of the twentieth century. For this there is a good case. And it is certainly of real importance that it should be understood, and understood correctly.

2.

Hobsbawm presents the October Revolution as "made by the masses": "the radicalised groundswell of their followers pushed the Bolsheviks inevitably towards the seizure of power."

So let us look at the actual record.

During 1917, the Bolsheviks had (by the type of maneuver that was to become traditional in Communist movements) gained a measure of control over working-class organizations, and especially in St. Petersburg. This did not mean that the organizations, let alone the workers they represented, pressed for a Leninist revolution. In fact, Lenin had great difficulty in getting a majority even of his own Central Committee to support the seizure of power, and reports from its own agents in the city districts spoke in most cases of a lack of enthusiasm for the coming revolution—as has been clear since the publication in Moscow of these reports in 1928.

After the seizure of power, almost all such "proletarian" circles pressed for socialist rather than Bolshevik rule. But even if it were true that these "masses" were keen on Leninism, we should note that the Petrograd "proletarians" were most inexperienced politically and in the main fairly fresh out of the villages (to which many of them would return when the new regime brought in a collapse of the economy). No "mature" proletariat anywhere ever so succumbed; and indeed the more settled section of the Russian working class—the railwaymen, the printers—were totally opposed to the Bolsheviks.

Nor were even most of the Bolsheviks themselves committed to their own dictatorship. On November 11, 1917, the Bolshevik Central Committee, with Lenin and Trotsky absent, unanimously voted in favor of a coalition government. Negotiations were immediately undertaken, with Lev Kamenev as the leading Bolshevik delegate. On November 14, Lenin, after failing to get a majority vote in the Central Committee for suspending the talks, fell back on a negotiating position clearly unacceptable to the other parties, and on November 18, Kamenev, Aleksey Rykov, and three others resigned from the Central Committee and from the Council of People's Commissars (together with eight People's Commissars who were not also members of the CC) on the grounds that all working-class parties—that is, all parties represented in the Soviets—should be brought into the government: "Other than this there is only one policy: the preservation of a purely Bolshevik government by means of political terror," or, in Yemelian Yaroslavsky's words, Lenin's "regime of the bayonet and the sabre."

Lenin played for time. By the end of the month, the threat to his rule had faded away and the erring Bolsheviks had submitted.

All these points are thoroughly established, and in cumulative and decisive detail, in all veridical accounts or analyses of the period.

3.

B ut even if the opposite view were taken, if it were held that the Bolsheviks momentarily represented "the masses," we still find them, only a month or so later, with power in their hands, only getting a quarter of the vote in the Constituent Assembly elections, even failing to get a majority in Petrograd itself, and, when it met, dissolving the assembly by force and ruthlessly putting down worker demonstrations against this.

Within weeks of the seizure of power, Lenin was telling workers that they should be concerned not to "improve their position" but to strengthen labor discipline and their "attitude to work." Later he complained that they "stubbornly maintain the traditions [formed under capitalism and continued with the Soviet government] as of old to give him less work and, even worse—to pay him more. Perhaps there are few of these villains, but they are among the Soviet typographical compositors, among the Sormov and Putilov factory works, etc." (As a Russian historian in *Voprosy istorii*, 1998, no. 5, points out, these last two were the strongholds of Lenin's proletariat.)

After Lenin's consolidation of power, our documentation naturally became thinner. We learned of the massive worker opposition to the Bolsheviks from individual accounts, and since these contradicted official evidence they were, by some, disregarded.

But we now have, from Russia, a remarkable collection of hitherto unpublished documents on the worker unrest that emerged almost at once. Putting the final, decisive touches to the whole myth, this recent research in St. Petersburg has produced material long consigned to official oblivion. In *Petrograd Workers and the Dictatorship of the Proletariat, October 1917–1923*, V. Ju. Chernayev and his colleagues have assembled reports of meeting after meeting of the key factory workers, which show them often enthusiastically endorsing speeches and voting for resolutions of the Social Revolutionaries and the Mensheviks and others and often being put down by force. Throughout 1918 there were strikes, which Lenin ordered to be suppressed "mercilessly."

As to the army, in July 1918, Lenin was almost overthrown by a ham-handed Social Revolutionary coup and was only saved by Latvian regiments, the Russian troops in effect remaining neutral. And no masses turned out to help the regime.

As for the degree to which the Soviets were in any case proletarian organs, Lenin put it in 1920 that

*So far, we have not achieved the state where the working masses could partici-
pate in government—except on paper; there is still the cultural level, which you
will never render subject to legislation. This low cultural level has the effect of
making the Soviets, which according to their programme are organs of government by the working people, actually into organs of government for the working
people, by the advanced elements of the proletariat, but not by the working
masses.*

But even at a higher level the whole of the Leninist approach to the proletariat was subject to the obvious comment made by the Russian anarchist
Mikhail Bakunin about the Marxist concept in general: "Those previous
workers having just become rulers or representatives of the people will cease
to be workers; they will look at the workers from their heights, they will represent not the people but themselves. . . . He who doubts this does not know
human nature." And so it turned out.

Again, it was always a difficulty for Soviet historians, for example, that
the "workers' army" formed at the new industrial center of Izhevsk was
strongly anti-Bolshevik and finally, having to choose, went over to the
Whites. (So it was determined that they weren't "real" proletarians; they
were peasants who happened to live round the factories; and so on.)

Meanwhile, as the Menshevik leader L. Martov was surprised to note,
the victorious Bolsheviks, with a few exceptions (Martov records Bukharin
as one), settled into a comfortable or even luxurious life in the newly confiscated apartments and villas. The same, indeed, was noted of the partisans
entering Belgrade in the 1940s and later of the Sandinistas in Managua.

4.

We may pause here to ask, what, in any case, is the status of the
"masses" or the "proletariat" in modern Western conceptions (and
not only of the October Revolution)? The whole concept of the "proletariat"—an industrial working class defined in the ancient Roman fashion as
a stratum with no property but their offspring—is obviously skewed from the
start. And then we may ask ourselves why, in any case, the supposed class
should embody the future. The answer is mere theorizing.

The take bourgeois intellectuals had on the workers was often ludicrous.
The workers as such are no better or worse than any other stratum. One
American professor who thought otherwise spent a year or two among them

as a research project and of course found as much good and bad, the latter unexpected, as elsewhere.

In the earlier revolutionary epoch of 1791, the "people" was the form this idolatry took. These were seen as the urban poor, the sansculottes, taken as a sort of supernal mass entity—often gaining prestige not so much from their social side as from their addiction to terrorism in the service of their usually well-heeled leaders.

The "people," at least notionally, was a general representation, if not a realistic one, of the city poor, even of the oppressed overall. The Jacobins and their successors had mobilized the urban mobs. (And urban mobs have often followed a variety of different inciters—as in eighteenth-century London or the successful revolutionaries in Tehran.)

In the Russia of the Civil War period, the party sought the proletarians in the provinces wherever it could find them. A skeptical view is given in *Doctor Zhivago* (in the text submitted to the authorities by Boris Pasternak with a view to publication):

> *In the first days, people like the soldier Panfil Palykh, who without any agitation hated intellectuals, gentry and officers brutally and rabidly, like deadly poison, seemed to be rare finds to the elated left-wing intellectuals and were greatly esteemed. Their total lack of humanity seemed to be a miracle of class-consciousness and their barbarism seemed an example of proletarian firmness and revolutionary instinct. This was what Panfil was famous for. He was in the good books of the partisan chiefs and the party leaders.*

Lenin, of course, not only made use of just such characters but, with his usual clarity, justified the action: "Party members should not be measured by the narrow standard of petty bourgeois snobbery. Sometimes a scoundrel is useful to our party, precisely because he is a scoundrel."

Pasternak's notably hostile experience raises a much broader question: How did the idea of a socially or politically transcendent proletarian class, having arisen in the mid-nineteenth century, present itself as the utopian revolution incarnate—and not only at the time but even now in some minds?

### 5.

Despite the evidence to the contrary, there are Western academics still presenting assertions that not only the workers but even the peasants took the Bolshevik side for want of better leaders. A typically counterfactual comment is that in the early 1920s the peasantry "tolerated Bolshevik grain requisition" as the "alternative to the old regime," a view massively refuted by a vast array of facts.

One reads, to this day, in books published by reputable university presses, such things as "the Bolshevik Party was a product of idealistic, egalitarian, and socially progressive strands in the Russian intelligentsia and working class." Something missing here, you may think—for example fanatical hostility to and finally total suppression of other groups with the same ostensible aims.

We are similarly told of Lenin, though it is not denied that the regime he imposed on Russia led to tyranny, that he nevertheless had humanitarian motives. This appears in the companion book to the 1999 CNN documentary *Cold War* (*Cold War: An Illustrated History, 1945–1991*, by Jeremy Isaacs and Taylor Downing), which we shall return to later: "His socialist principles were meant to ensure decent education, free health care, common ownership of the land, and fairness for all under the tough guidance of the Bolsheviks." Lenin's real attitude to humanity, except in the abstract, is well illustrated by his comment on the 1891–92 famine in Russia, when students and others threw themselves into relief work, that "psychologically, this talk of feeding the starving masses is nothing but the expression of saccharine-sweet sentimentality characteristic of the intelligentsia." Maxim Gorky was to note that "Lenin has no pity for the mass of the people," and even that "the working class are to Lenin what minerals are to a metallurgist." There are now many documents available in which Lenin insists on mass shootings and hangings. And Bertrand Russell, who met him when he was in power, reports that "his guffaw at the thought of those massacred made my blood run cold."

## 6.

The recruitment of proletarians into the Communist Party had left few Communists among the factory and other working strata. The party had, by now, no real social basis but its own membership. With the abandonment of the socially and demographically disastrous policies of 1917–21, and following Lenin's death in 1924, the party was enlarged and recruited in the "Lenin intake," supposedly giving it a larger and stronger proletarian base. More recent evidence shows that the party's new rank and file in or attached to the reviving factories was largely not made up of the industrial workers proper, who had little time to spare for politics, but of those who had taken up economically peripheral or propagandist jobs.

The Soviet regime right up to the eve of collapse in 1991 continued to describe itself as "proletarian." This was required by Marxist mythology—though any genuine "class analysis" would have noted the emergence of the New Class, or caste, already complained of by Communist veterans such as Khristian Rakovsky in the 1920s.

It is hard to say how much and at what psychological level the party leadership still believed in the concept. One way of looking at it is that as the country approached the 1930s, the new quasi-proletarian cadres embodied an important real advantage. They had come up through, and had no distracting experience other than, the party machine and its commitments and ideology.

It was from this narrow pool of veterans and recruits that the authoritarian mechanism of the regime was manned. Even so, it had to face more and more challenges, be further hardened and coarsened by endless "struggle," and be purged again and again of remnants, or suspected remnants, of notions of compromise with different ideas or loyalties. Meanwhile, the mere existence of other regimes in the outer world was seen as in principle unacceptable; and these apparent challenges had to be met out there as well as at home.

# Chapter IX

# Revolutionary High Finance:
# Some Notes on a Neglected Theme

---⸙⸙⸙---

### 1.

I am not sure if the origins and spread of Marxism-Leninism have ever been explored in terms suited to the Materialist Conception of History—in other words, in terms of the primacy of economics.

### 2.

L enin, of course, was not unschooled in the influence of economics, and he saw the need for economic support early in his movement's history. From the beginning, his conception of the Bolshevik faction of the Social Democratic Party had centered on creating a cadre of "professional revolutionaries." But, by definition, a professional needs to be paid, and Lenin saw this and sought fundings unthinkable to other socialists. He was, in fact, able to use some money from donors like Mrs. A. M. Kalmykova (referred to as "the Bucket" in confidential documents). But he also had recourse to every possible target, such as by marrying two Bolsheviks to the Schmidt heiresses.

Then there was the simpler expedient of bank robberies—the most notable organized by the young Georgian later known as Stalin. This, along with Lenin's diversion of money intended for the Social Democrats as a whole, led, in 1910, to a rebuke (later made public) by the Second International.

In the years that followed, much Bolshevik funding followed a similar dubious path, as in the work of party members diverting workers' insurance funds, and so forth. In one way or another, the Bolsheviks were able to sustain a paid party cadre, giving them one essential element in their seizure of power in 1917—a lesson never forgotten in Communist circles.

3.

Their establishment of a state inherently hostile to all others in a country as large and powerful as Russia was a main factor in destabilizing the world: it started in Lenin's time—but went on long after what a frivolous historian might call the elimination of Germany in the semifinals.

When Lenin took power over Russia, large sums became available. Whoever controls a state, however poor it may be, can wring money out of it—as various ex-dictators of Third or Fourth World countries have more recently demonstrated. At any rate, Soviet foreign policy and influence required massive funding. The Soviet regime now began to employ a vast and increasingly experienced apparatus of propaganda and persuasion. Ideas do not merely seep into the "intellectual" consciousness; this sort of general penetration must be materially assisted and was.

From 1921, with the formation of the Comintern, funding became a very important consideration. What has been neglected, or denied, until recently, is the huge advantage over left-wing rivals that the continuous financial support from Moscow (up until the late 1980s) gave the world's Communist parties. A party or organization that can afford a network of paid officials, newspapers, book publishing companies, and so on has a very big edge over one that cannot.

One of the complaints that quickly arose among Russian workers in the early Soviet years was that funds from their meager subsistence went into foreign revolutionary activity. But, of course, at that time the Bolsheviks believed that the regime could not survive without revolution in the West (which they knew would provide even more funds). This was true, and crucial, even when Lenin reluctantly allowed American humanitarian aid to overcome devastating famine at the beginning of the 1920s. America, often represented as, above all, anti-Bolshevik, nonetheless provided Herbert Hoover with the needed help, and the United States, despite being in the throes of a Red Scare, had Congress vote millions of dollars in aid. As a result, U.S. volunteers worked effectively inside Russia, in spite of difficulties both objective and inflicted by the apparat.

It was at this time, too, that Lenin ordered the seizure of church valuables, specifically on the grounds that the hungry populace would welcome it. In fact, the Patriarch Tikhon had already offered all but the sacred vessels to help alleviate the famine. And we now learn, I suppose ironically, that the organization and propaganda of the seizure cost more than the value of the loot.

Yet while Russia internally suffered, funds went to Western and other Leninists. John Reed, Lenin's supporter and popularizer (and later something of a myth in progressive American circles, though it's hard to see why) was, for example, given large sums. The Communist Party of Great Britain was getting £55,000 as early as 1921, at a time when its own income was around £100 per annum, as the party leader, Albert Inkpin, reported to Moscow. But after adequate financing, its actual political expenditure was almost as high as that of the Labour Party (see John McIlroy, "Rehabilitating Communist History," *Revolutionary History*, vol. 8, no. 1 [2001]).

The obvious, and even now often neglected, result was, let us reemphasize, that the Communist parties could afford large permanent staffs both centrally and locally, and above all could publish propaganda and versions of Soviet falsifications in a major way. The general wave of Western intellectual leftism was given a disciplined, single-minded center (and a vast output of Moscow's media products). Leninism not only provided the funds, it also did so on condition that foreign Communist parties organize on the basis of the Leninist conception of "democratic centralism"—that is, on rigorous internal discipline. It took some time before all those who thought of themselves as Communists were reduced to proper obedience. But eventually, as we know, they proved able to switch from anti-Fascism to anti-anti-Fascism overnight.

### 4.

It is only recently that the extent of Soviet financing of Communist parties has become known—though mostly through documents dating from the early 1950s to the late 1980s, and in particular in *Oro da Mosca*, by Valerio Riva (and also in such Russian documentation as Fond 89 at the Hoover Institution Archives). Riva's is a thorough and, more important, a richly documented account of the Soviet funding of the world's Communist parties, based on information found in the Russian Federation's archives. While there are gaps, there is an overwhelming amount of key evidence. There are many odd records from the 1920s of sums paid through the Foreign Commissariat. But a full account has now been given of the years 1953 to 1984, if not yet of the whole Soviet period. In 1959, for example, forty-three listed Communist parties received a total of $8,759,700; by 1963, it was c. $15,750,000 covering eighty-three Communist parties and a few others. You wouldn't think there were so many CPs, but they go as far down as the CPs of Réunion and San Marino.

Over the period the CPUSA received $42,102,000, almost as much as the French Communist Party ($50,004,000) and the Italian ($47,233,000). The British Communist Party, which was never quite as well financed after the late 1950s, only received $292,000, at least through this fund. Another subsidy was the payment of royalties on books by Western Communists and sympathizers published in the USSR, which normally printed foreign materials without payment, Moscow not having signed the international copyright agreements until much later on. We find royalties awarded to Harry Pollitt, the head of the Communist Party of Great Britain, and in general books by foreign Communist leaders, virtually unsellable at home, were given decent editions in Moscow.

There were, of course, other perks, such as free holidays given by all the Soviet bloc countries. In 1950, Czechoslovak president Klement Gottwald, speaking for his country's Communist Party, which had, with others, been required to contribute to the main funds, complained that his party had already given the French Communist Party a hundred thousand dollars and was now giving free holidays to fifty of their officials (and to five to seven from the CPGB) and was running a party school for the Italian Communist Party. The documents record in detail payments to "foreign guests" at the 20th Party Congress: totaling 3,500,000 rubles, they included outlays for travel, hotels, theater tickets, and "personal hygiene" (scent, toothpaste, soap, etc.).

These data are not complete. There were other fundings—of Communist newspapers and publishers, for example. Moneys were provided as late as 1991 to the U.K. productions *Morning Star, Seven Days,* and *Marxism Today* ($173,000). And there were other odd payments: an (earlier) citation Riva lists is $600,000 "personally" given to the Italian Communist leader Pietro Secchia on his visit to Moscow on December 14, 1947. And what are payments to "Morris Cornford, England (8,300 dollars)" and "Comrade Rothstein (2,789 dollars)," and a few others doing on a long list of parties funded?

5.

We must not conclude without looking, as a postscript, at another of Stalin's material investments in the struggle for foreign support. Moscow did not depend only on the direct financing of foreign Communist parties. A quite important example of other financing was the diversion into the hands of the American ambassador to Russia Joseph Davies and his collector wife of important artistic treasures free, or at nominal prices, from the Tretyakov Gallery and various nationalized monasteries and other collections. Davies became a keen adulator of and misinformer on the USSR.

In general, this is a neglected field. So are most others. Why people didn't, and still don't, understand the Communist regimes has to do with their concentration on reputable, or reputable-sounding, phenomena. This is what amounts to an attempt to tame the data or, perhaps more correctly, a mental or psychological bent towards blocking the real essentials, the real meaning.

## Chapter X

# Into the Planned Economy

⸻⸿⸻

### 1.

With the Soviet Union taking on its final form after 1929, the country now appeared to certain minds in the West as a great social experiment, with the creation of a planned economy.

The realities of the Stalin period have been comprehensively covered in my earlier books. As to what we have learned more recently, the most striking thing is that, in almost every respect, the history, including the history of Stalin's postwar foreign policy, turns out to be even worse than we had envisaged.

The initial "dekulakization" and the collectivization of the remainder of the peasantry into state-controlled farms need little further analysis. But there is much useful and decisive information about the even more devastating "terror-famine" of 1932–33. Here we find evidence of what we could only reach earlier by deduction. My *The Harvest of Sorrow*, first published in 1986, had an entire page of individual reports of Ukrainians going north into Russia in 1930–33 to seek bread and being arrested or sent back. Now we have the secret telegram, dated January 21, 1933, from Stalin and Molotov to the party and police chiefs of the provinces affected. It orders the blocking of peasants trying to enter Russia from the Ukraine or Kuban; they are to be sent back and the ringleaders arrested. This is followed by a report from Genrikh Yagoda, at the OGPU, that over two hundred thousand have been sent back and several thousand arrested. The Stalin-Molotov telegram blames the influx of peasants on Social Revolutionaries and Polish agents wishing to start a famine scare—not an evidential point but one revelatory of the Stalinist mind-set. More substantially, we have been able to conclude from various sources that the leadership knew famine would follow if their plans were met (though this was long dismissed by various Western academics). We now have a document that records the decision of the Politburo in July 1932, when Molotov, just back from the Ukraine, reported, "We definitely face the spectre of famine, especially in the rich bread areas," after which a Politburo decision ordered that "Whatever the cost, the confirmed plan for grain requisition must be fulfilled." Further such evidence appears in a letter written by Dnepropetrovsk party secretary Mikhail Khatayevich in November 1932, which states that in order to ensure the state's production future, "we must take into account the minimum needs of the kolkhozniks, for otherwise there will be no one left to sow and ensure production." Molotov's answer was, "Your position is profoundly incorrect, unBolshevik. We Bolsheviks cannot put the needs of the state—needs precisely defined in party resolutions—in the tenth or even the second place."

The newer material also gives a number of minor insights. For example, on the basis of previous evidence, I was able, from the odd report, to note that the registration of death had been largely suspended in the Ukraine after October 1932. From the newly available documents, we now have direct analyses. In the Kiev Medical Inspectorate, 9,472 corpses were noted, only 3,997 of which were registered, and similar things were reported from other districts. On another point, a report to the Central Committee from the deputy head of the North Caucasus Political Section of the Machine Tractor Stations alleged that kulak bodies were being left near the railways to "simulate famine" (see E. N. Oskolkov, *Golod 1932–1933*).

To gain some general idea of the extent of the transformation that took place in Soviet agriculture, it is useful to remember that before World War I, Russia was by far the most important grain-exporting country in the world: its grain exports were well more than double those of the United States and constituted nearly one-third of the total world grain market. Collectivization was, right from the start, carried out in a thoroughly irrational manner. Yet it is possible to finance industrialization out of the productivity of the peasantry, if handled properly. In nineteenth-century Meiji Japan, despite having the disadvantage of a far smaller existing industrial base than twentieth-century Russia, incentives were provided which improved agricultural production, and productivity in fact doubled between 1885 and 1915, in complete contrast to the results obtained in the USSR.

Yet the enserfment or dispersal or deaths of the free peasantry were designed not merely to destroy any independent economic forces but also to finance socialist industry—so that millions of tons of grain were exported to pay for foreign machines while the famine raged.

2.

The Soviet regime had been forced in the beginning to use "bourgeois specialists" in many fields, and in the minds of the leadership, their uncritical loyalty could scarcely be relied on. They could now—from the late 1920s—be replaced and repressed. The degree to which the new cadres, even in engineering, were inadequately trained is sometimes forgotten. But this "cultural revolution," sometimes neglected within the more striking context of collectivization and terror, was a crucial part of the totalitarian program.

Economically, the plan consisted of an unintegrated array of crash programs. The results were falsified on a big scale. It is now generally recognized that the level of new industrialization that actually took place could have been achieved, without the human or other losses, by a more balanced approach, and that the increases actually produced were no greater than those in other European countries at the same period.

The crux on this economic side, as on the political, demographic, and intellectual fronts, was the contrast between facts and the falsifications. Even the production of steel, the Soviet favorite item, did not increase significantly faster under Stalin than during the period of Russia's pre–World War I industrialization (nor faster than in Japan or elsewhere at comparable economic periods).

Local officials in charge of any industry or region were under both ideological and administrative pressure to produce the maximum output at all costs. As a result, the highest conceivable plan figure was the one regarded as most in accord with revolutionary principles and least damnable as evidence of right-wing or bourgeois timidity (or even sabotage—a phenomenon seen in Cuba, for example, as much as in Russia). In this atmosphere, the administrator had no choice but to sacrifice everything to the immediate target, even if this meant destroying resources necessary for the following years, and could certainly not concern himself with a mere bagatelle like pollution. As Aleksandr Solzhenitsyn puts it, in *The First Circle*:

> *It was more than flesh and blood could bear to be hopelessly caught up in impossible, grotesque, crippling schedules. You were trapped and held in a deadly grip. The system crushed you, driving you harder and faster all the time, demanding more and more, setting inhuman time-limits. This was why buildings and bridges collapsed, why crops rotted in the fields or never came up at all.*

3.

So far, these are minor additions to our grasp of the Soviet order established in the early 1930s. But before we go on to an equally brief run over of further insights into the crucial period of accomplished Stalinism taken from newly available evidence, we may examine important high-level Western delusions about what we have already considered.

*The Harvest of Sorrow* gave many contemporary examples of this. Still, in a way even more peculiar than misevaluations is the almost dismissive attitude sometimes found: A recent American History of Russia gives a mere half a page to a demographic disaster that killed almost as many as were killed in all countries in World War I.

The "planned economy" appealed not only to revolutionaries but also to foreign scholars and others seeking a rational society—though it may be thought disillusioningly disqualificatory to find, for example, that the State Planning Commission had estimated that the Soviet population in 1937 would be larger by some fourteen or fifteen million more than turned out to be the case, hardly a minor statistical matter even for the economy.

Indeed, it would be otiose to bother further about the scholarly delusions of the 1930s—even of the ludicrous *Soviet Communism: A New Civilisation?* by those deans of Western social science Sidney and Beatrice Webb, who earlier, in another context, we discussed as among the main progenitors of the Fabian Society and the rise of etatist socialism in the United Kingdom. The present writer once held the Sidney and Beatrice Webb Fellowship at the London School of Economics, of which they were founders, but took a view unlike theirs. In fact, though immensely influential in the 1930s, their main fault was the acceptance of facts and figures supplied by Stalin's apparat. And they are now, in this field at least, rightly forgotten.

4.

The work of E. H. Carr, though, is still influential, and his academic standing still powerful even now. Carr's first political book, *The Twenty Years' Crisis*, was a major exercise in the application of political "realism" to the European scene in the late 1930s. It came out just as war was declared in 1939. His error in advocating appeasement of Hitler was at the profoundest level. Superficially, in the rational terms in which he argued, the problem was tractable. What was missing from his calculations was the key fact that Hitler was unappeasable. This misunderstanding of such motivations was, and in different contexts continued to be, one of the fatal defects of Carr's historical and political work.

Carr's next public incarnation, over the war period, was as a leader writer for the London *Times*. In those days, the anonymous pronouncements of that newspaper were regarded as truly the voice of the establishment and even, up to a point, of official government thinking. The tone, of which Carr was a paragon, might be called magisterial or condescending, depending on one's taste.

Over a short period of time, he grew increasingly favorable to the Soviet Union: his biographer, Jonathan Haslam, describes a *Times* editorial he wrote in 1944 as showing "a degree of optimism that in retrospect seems hopelessly extravagant." His editorial on the fighting in Greece the same year, when British troops prevented a Communist takeover, showed a complete absence of Carrite "realism." On that principle, the West's entitlement to hegemony in Greece was indisputable—and on this issue Stalin himself was, or became, a better Carrite than Carr himself. Carr was hotly opposing the policy of his own all-party government, from a platform widely regarded as the voice of sane and solid Britain.

His argument was that EAM, the Communist partisan force, "appeared to exercise almost unchallengible authority" over most of Greece and was "the largest organised party, or group of parties, in Greece." Haslam takes it that he was "initially unaware of the extent to which it was merely a Communist front." That is, he was pontificating on the basis of false data. Much of the London press, represented in Athens by much the same correspondents who had misreported the fighting in Barcelona seven years earlier, had swallowed the Communist line. It is true that EAM had seized control over wide areas and crushed, or almost crushed, the other, non-Communist partisan forces. But that they were widely popular was in any case negated by, first, their refusal to face elections and, later, their performance in such elections.

But even if Carr had been right on these points, his position was in total contrast to his attitude to the almost simultaneous events in Poland, where the *anti*-Communist resistance really was uniquely well organized and broadly based and which he denounced for its reluctance to accept Soviet control.

After the war, he started on his monumental, in its literal sense of the word, *A History of Soviet Russia*, that in the end ran to fourteen volumes, of which the last six come under the heading "Foundations of a Planned Economy," taking us up to the end of the 1920s. This is usually regarded as his masterpiece. The *History* is, in fact, overwhelmingly centered on the "planned economy" he saw as emerging in the USSR and he believed represented the direction of the world's future. We may take him as an exemplar of such views.

5.

As even scholars more or less in Carr's camp on the political issue have pointed out, Soviet economic problems of the mid- and late 1920s were misunderstood by the Communist leadership and, in any case, were based on thoroughly unreliable statistics. As to the Five-Year Plan now produced, it was not a comprehensive plan at all but merely a set of targets for various industries. These targets were then increased time and again. And there was huge pressure to "overfulfill" the plan—for which where would the raw materials be available except from other "sectors"? (Indeed, the successive Five-Year Plans never achieved the sought-after economic balances even on paper, let alone in reality.)

The professional Soviet economists were mostly shot in the early 1930s, in two batches—first, those who had urged smaller figures and, then, those who had accepted the higher figures. The targets of neither were ever in fact achieved. Recent Russian and Western scholars have shown that the real industrial increase in the USSR over the 1930s was about the same as in Germany—though much less efficient. In any case, as one of the best analysts of the matter, the late Professor Stanislaw Swianiewicz, put it back in the 1960s, the whole method "was an outcome of the irrational forces which have been released and are not easily to be mastered."

Carr was later to object to the historian Stephen Cohen's favorable presentation of Bukharin, on whom Carr took and expressed an extremely negative stand. He wrote of him, in oddly Stalinist phraseology, as "objectively counter-revolutionary." If Bukharin, or an equivalent figure, had indeed come to power in the post-Lenin years, and rejected the Stalinist project, the USSR might truly have gone in what Carr and Stalin saw as a "counter-revolutionary" direction (as it did when the comparable figure of Gorbachev came to power).

Carr would accept any suitably sponsored "fact." For example, he wrote in 1966 that in India, where "liberalism is professed and to some extent practiced, millions of people would starve without American charity. In China, where liberalism is rejected, people somehow get fed. Which is the more cruel and oppressive regime?" Of course, the facts of the devastating and state-produced famine a few years earlier under Mao's Great Leap Forward were not then available to Western academics. In the past decades, Chinese Communist publications, including long-suppressed census figures, have made everything clear—the only question now at issue being how many tens of millions suffered. Carr's assumptions were, in fact, the result of accepting official Communist accounts—this being no more than a particularly egregious example of that intellectual, or rather unintellectual, prejudice.

## 6.

Carr several times maintained, and this is central to his thought, that the past cannot be understood except from the point of view of the future—the future, that is, as conceived by historians. His constant conviction, even late in his career, was that the Soviet Union, with all its rather belatedly noted excesses and blemishes, was on the right track.

This was in part because he still saw the planned economy, even in the most Stalinist sense, as the "future," and "industrialization" as the expansion of coal-and-steel modernization (another lost cause). And he still had hostile points to make about "bourgeois democracy" as against the proletarian kind. All gone down the plug-hole.

Carr did, for the most part belatedly and inadequately, criticize the inhumanities of Stalin's regime. But he continued to object to "moralizing," in the sense of attributing wickedness to Stalin—or even Hitler. This perspective, still found these days in certain sections of academe (in people who, however, seem to have come to it independently of Carr), is now called being "nonjudgmental." But neutrality on such issues is itself a moral stance, and this human failing goes with a smug affectation of being above the battle. Carr's view that history is not, or not much, interested in the losers has long been criticized as both insensitive and uncomprehensive. But the past decade has relegated his favorites, the proletarian revolution and the planned economy, to the status of . . . losers.

In terms of both ethics and realism, we must prefer the great British historian Norman Cohn's remark that "Communism and Nazism have been inspired by fantasies which are downright archaic." And, above all, a crucial point largely missed by Carr, and one that greatly contributed to the decline and fall of Soviet Communism, was the absence of even residual intellectual and political liberty. As even the great German revolutionary Rosa Luxemburg foresaw, this led not only to brutalization but also, even more destructive, to stultification.

Carr will, I imagine, be seen as a representative of that elitist and condescending section of British establishmentarianism which was, to one degree or another, seduced by the idea of a planned society, regulated, to the benefit of all, by the equivalent of their nominees.

Unlike the true Stalinists and their dupes, who denied the excesses of the period, Carr, as we have said, in a general way at least, admitted them—and *still* took a positive view of the Soviet phenomenon. He accumulated a vast amount of material and with it a mountainous prestige. But, of course, knowledge is not the same as judgment—a point relevant in many other fields as well.

Carr's enterprise was carried on after his death in 1982, but his successors, though to some extent skewed by the direction of his aims, were serious scholars, and not into the semidenial of the ills of Stalinism that persisted in a section of academe.

7.

How are we to sum up the realities of the Stalinist planned economy?

First, there were some successful products, such as the Moscow Metro.

Second, these were nothing like the claims made then—and later—and could and would have been achieved, with far fewer negative effects, under a Bukharinist (or indeed any other) regime.

Third, and especially with the gigantic—and often merely exhibitionist—projects, there was far too little in the way of serious study of the objective factors, in spite of serious comment from such as Peter Palchinsky, the Soviet civil engineer later shot by the secret police, and others who warned, for example, that building the "world's greatest steel mill" at the site of the Magnitogorsk iron deposits was unwise, because fuel had to be brought in by land, and when the deposits had been exhausted, not only fuel but iron itself needed transport to the site (see Loren R. Graham, *The Ghost of the Executed Engineer*). And this was one of the more successful, and not totally misconceived, efforts, unlike for example, the much-publicized Baltic–White Sea Canal, opened officially on August 2, 1933, which was never of much use. Others, such as the "world's greatest" dam, at Dniprostroy-Dniprohes, worked, but irregularly, and, as often with these dams, ignored the cost of economic losses in the flooded area—worse in this case than in most.

Fourth, the human cost was only payable at the price of extreme repression. In the original conception, it was planned that Magnitogorsk would contain, in addition to the steel mills, a model "workers' city" for its employees. But there was never any funding to spare. Right up to the 1980s, the area was characterized by filthy barracks low on heat and hygiene and a bitterly sullen, suffering population.

The poverty and exploitation were handled simply: they were simply denied. And this is to say nothing about the forced labor that provided part of the Magnitogorsk workforce, as it did the whole workforce of Dalstroy, the organization set up to oversee Kolyma, and of other projects. We shall be saying little here of the Gulag, which has been well covered by Anne Applebaum and in forthcoming work by Oleg V. Khlevniuk and others, but it should very much be borne in mind, both in its economic and human perspective.

Another important qualification sometimes omitted by observers of what they take to be a planned economy is, apart from the misthinking of the authorities, a further set of obstacles at a lower level. In the first place, the engineers and managers were largely underqualified. As we have said, the "cultural revolution" of the late 1920s was intended to produce, in the economic as well as other fields, a generation of specialists from the party-selected nonbourgeois classes. But the training of these had been irrationally hurried. And as the old industrial elites were removed and often, like Palchinsky, shot, the new men were highly inadequate.

Worse, throughout the 1930s, any industrial or transport disaster (of which there were many) was blamed on the engineers. From the 1928 Shakhty trial on, we find these exercises in admitting failures and blaming them on these unfortunates. A reading of some of the accused's testimony at the Pyatakov trial in 1937—the tip of the iceberg—gives some idea of what was a nationwide destruction of the key personnel. This, of course, made a bad situation worse.

If we look—a random check—at the published lists of those shot and buried in the Donskoi Cemetery (complete with prison photographs), we come across sequences such as engineers and others from the capital's power grid, Mosenergo, accompanied by four minor railway officers, shot on

October 21, 1937; eight Moscow tramway engineers and other tramway officials shot on January 11, 1937, as terrorists; and so on.

Even now, some Western fans of the planned economy rely (as one can understand) no longer on figures of the official Soviet type, which almost everybody now knows to be faked to a high degree, but on ones extracted from more confidential documents. These deductions are more credible, but it is hard to think of them as providing serious results.

We are not concerned with this point. But it is strikingly evidential to note some of the giant projects that were still under way when Stalin died, and were abandoned at once by his successors. These include—and specifically as of no use to "the national economy":

the Main Turkmen Canal,
the Volga-Ural Canal,
the Volga-Baltic Waterway,
the Lower-Don Dam (and the port at Donetsk),
the Salekhard-Igarka "railroad of death,"
the tunnel to Sakhalin under the Strait of Tartary.

All were, even by Soviet standards, worthless—a good argument against the planning system.

*Chapter XI*

# Inside the New Society

⎯⎯⎯ ∞∞∞ ⎯⎯⎯

### 1.

The horrific events of the period after the rural terror of 1930–33 were clearly understood a generation ago. The facts were undeniably available even before the collapse of the regime.

Since then, there has been a flow of further evidence, some of it striking, but none of it affecting the substance of our knowledge. The account of the period given in my *The Great Terror,* originally published in 1968, remains generally valid, both as a political history and as a presentation of the experiences of the unfortunate populations. Brought up to date in 1990 with the evidence that had meanwhile emerged, it retains its general soundness and scope. There are, nevertheless, substantive points based on later information that call for comment.

It would be contrary to our purposes to avoid mention of the point that it was precisely in the late 1930s that Western admiration of the USSR and of its leader reached its highest point. And, above all, this included acceptance by many of a vast output of total falsehood. Western addicts were required to believe that most of Lenin's leadership had become Nazi spies . . . and much else. The public "trials" in which these and many others were so presented were not minor or peripheral. They were the main public, and heavily publicized, events of 1936–38, though they do not represent anything like all that the terror meant to the population.

### 2.

Much evidence was rejected in the West as indirect or secondhand. In the then circumstances this was inevitable—as it still is on various events of, for example, ancient history. (We only have two "documents" on the Second Punic War, about which we nevertheless know a great deal.)

More generally, Edward Gibbon writes that historical evidence is often "imperfect and partial" but that even such can contribute to "the whole" if properly allowed for and used in conjunction with other material. He adds, "a historian may use such material without making himself responsible for all the circumjacent errors or inconsistencies of the author whom he has quoted."

Most of the older, indirect evidence for the Stalin period is now confirmed by documentary or firsthand sources. There are, it is true, events for which no proofs exist and for which the secondary evidence is not quite conclusive. It is largely on such matters that academic skepticism still exercises itself. One of these events is the assassination of Sergey Kirov on December 1, 1934.

We do not have final "proof" or "certainty" of Stalin's responsibility. Let me quote another competent historian: Macaulay writes, in his essay on Warren Hastings, "The rules of evidence in law save scores of culprits whom judges, jury and spectators firmly believe to be guilty. . . . But it is clear that an acquittal so obtained cannot be pleaded in bar of the judgement of history." Instead of proof, we have an accumulation of suspicious facts. And we have a highly suspicious suspect. The Russian historian Oleg V. Khlevniuk, when it comes to the Kirov murder, does not exculpate or accuse Stalin, saying merely, in his 1996 book *Politburo*, "there are not enough facts available to settle the question." "Political murders," he adds, "are prepared in strict secrecy, and orders for them are not registered in documents."

As to the absence of direct written evidence, let us look at the murder of the Soviet Yiddish actor and director Solomon Mikhoels in 1948. If Stalin had survived Beria, or the latter had not repudiated the anti-Semitic line, no evidence of this supposed car accident would have emerged. As it is, we now have transcripts of the interrogations of the MGB officers concerned (in *Ubiystvo Mikhoels,* by Victor Levashov), two of them saying specifically that they were instructed to put nothing on paper! The order came directly from Stalin to MGB chief Viktor Abakumov, and from him to the actual murderers.

Relevant secondary sources on Kirov have been available for many decades. They represent, in the main, secondhand rumor within the NKVD, sometimes with detail that can be shown to be erroneous (the sort of material Gibbon had to handle as best he could). We have long known, for example, a report that Kirov opposed and prevented an attempt to impose as head of the Leningrad NKVD the appalling Yezhovite E. G. Evdokimov. This was confirmed a few years ago in a Ukrainian document. We now have the fact that Evdokimov lasted three days. Kirov would not accept him, so he clearly got the post behind Kirov's back. Our unofficial source gave the date wrong (it was 1931), but, as so often is the case with these indirect reports, the facts were right.

This is only one of the points establishing divergence between Kirov and Stalin's regime—of course, not that the absence of such conflict would have saved a figure from Stalinist liquidation. That Stalin did not object to killing even his supporters is clear enough from the record. Of the six members and candidate members of the Politburo who died between 1937 and 1940, Valerian Kuibyshev is the lone probable natural death (though his son, then in his teens, believes it to have been murder by a newly intruded NKVD guard). There is no evidence that Stalin was on bad terms with Stanislav Kosior or Robert Eikhe or many other high-level victims. But the real question is, was the Kirov murder crucial in Stalin's drive to total power? Yes, it was. He would not have gone in for murder in such circumstances? Why not? And, of course, all those who held even highish posts in Leningrad under Kirov were shot.

But the case for Stalin's supposed innocence seriously distorts a more important question: Did Stalin meet any opposition, or reluctance, from the by 1930 wholly pro-Stalin, anti-opposition Politburo? The argument put forward was that there was no "record" of such. But this was based not on records of discussion, which indeed hardly existed, but on the documents finally agreed on in the Politburo. We have always had reports, from several good sources, of disagreement on such matters as Stalin's proposed shooting of rebellious party members in the early 1930s.

Evidence of disagreement was indeed kept quiet. When Stalin was on holiday, Lazar Kaganovich reported to him. We have for some time had a letter from him to Stalin of August 2, 1932, saying that two (unnamed) members of the Politburo had objected to or criticized the draft of the August 7, 1932, terror decree's vital second and third paragraphs (see *The Stalin-Kaganovich Correspondence, 1931–36*, edited by R. W. Davies and others). Even lesser documents long available give evidence of such clashes, on grounds of insufficient subordination, including a sharp dispute between Kirov's number two, I. F. Kodatsky, and Molotov (which Khlevniuk covers at length).

With much unofficial and such slender official evidence, we had enough to cover this historically important issue. That is now overwhelmingly confirmed by the documents quoted in Simon Sebag-Montefiore's *Stalin: The*

*Court of the Red Tsar.* In his absences, Stalin had, as always, relied on Kaganovich and Molotov, but they had allowed the Politburo to take a "incorrect and dangerous" position, sponsored by Grigory Ordzhonikidze, with even Kaganovich "in the camp of reactionary elements." Their resolution was annulled. The question of opposition is important to our understanding of the extent to which Stalinism was Stalin's own creation. He was later to obtain a more acceptable Politburo.

### 3.

We now have more detail on other matters. For example, on the 1936 Zinoviev trial: when Nikolay Yezhov himself was later arrested, the police record listing his property included one bullet labeled "Zinoviev," one "Kamenev," and two "Smirnov" (who had presumably needed a second shot). We now have better confirmation of the role of the staff and students of the Gorky Pedagogical Institute in the affair, and also of Stalin having only Kliment Voroshilov and Yezhov at his meeting with the two chief accused.

On to 1937. We know more now than was earlier available about the progress of the extreme terror, and of a key, or at any rate striking, event: the suicide ("or murder," as Khlevniuk has it) of Ordzhonikidze in February 1937, presented at the time as a heart attack, testified to by four doctors, including the People's Commissar of Health. The full text of Stalin's speech at the crucial "February-March" plenum that followed has him several times praising Ordzhonikidze, then deploring his having, behind the party's back, kept up a relationship with the deviationist V. V. Lominadze (himself a suicide in 1935). Such an accusation leveled at a living Communist at the time would have been followed by arrest and purge. So we now have even better reason than before to see a hostile relationship, already deducible from the later arrest of his family, the change of place-names previously given in his honor, and so on. And we now have, too, in the decensored version of Anastas Mikoyan's memoirs, the point that for several years Stalin suggested to his circle that Ordzhonikidze had been a British spy.

### 4.

The most sensational event of 1937 was the arrest and execution in June, after severe torture, of leading Red Army generals and the suicide of the chief army commissar, Jan Gamarnik. Much more is now known about the massive army purge that followed, in which a great majority of the trained military leadership perished. Everything substantial was described some years ago. Here I will add only one small but telling postscript. "Wives of Enemies of the People" was a penal category. Fifteen such wives were shot on August 28, 1938. But Tukhachevsky's, Uborevich's, Kork's, and Gamarnik's widows were only given eight years imprisonment. We now know that Nina Tukhachevsky and the others were retried and shot in 1941, after the outbreak of the war, whose disasters their husbands might have helped the country avoid.

On a related point, the decree of April 7, 1935, extending all penalties, including death, down to twelve-year-olds, had been published in the Soviet press, attracting a fair amount of hostile comment abroad. (The French Communist *L'Humanité* was reduced to arguing that children matured faster under socialism.) One unstated reason for the public stance seems to have been to put pressure on arrested victims: a copy of the decree is reported as displayed on interrogators' desks.

Later in 1935, the Stalin devotee Romain Rolland, the French writer, saw Stalin in Moscow. Their conversation was recorded but noted as not to be published without Stalin's permission, and in fact it is only now available, as Roy Medvedev tells us in *Moscow News* (August 13, 2002). Rolland asked about the decree which had made this bad impression in France. Stalin defended it as follows, though his reluctance to publish this defense is understandable.

> *This enactment has a purely educational importance. We have thus sought to deter not so much juvenile delinquents as those who involved children in crime. Groups of 10 to 15 boys and girls were identified in our schools that set out to kill or corrupt the foremost students of both sexes. Foremost students were drowned in wells, assaulted, battered, and terrorised. It was established that such children's gangs were organized by adult criminals. The enactment was promulgated to intimidate and disorganise adult gangsters.*

We have a later (unpublished) decree, of August 15, 1937, on the treatment of children of enemies of the people. Those over fifteen were to be tried like their mothers. "Socially dangerous children" were to be sent to labor camps or colonies or "children's homes of special regime." Nursing babies up to one or one and a half years old were to remain with their sentenced mothers in camps. Orphans aged one or one and a half to three years old were to be sent to "homes" near their family residence; orphans from three to fifteen years old, to these homes away from their relatives, and not in or near the main cities or the state frontier.

As to conditions faced by mothers and infants in the camps, we have a report by the head of the First State Section of the Sanitary Department of the Gulag on infant mortality in the first half of 1943. Among children of *volnonaemni*, that is, of nonprisoner mothers, the rate was 0.47 percent. Among the children of mother-prisoners, it was 41.7 percent. As the official points out (in *Voprosy istorii,* 2001, no. 6), this truly extraordinary difference was due to the latter's having sunk below sustenance level.

5.

On the 1938 Bukharin trial, we now also have interesting new material. This includes the list of possessions confiscated from the NKVD chief Genrikh Yagoda (as with Yezhov later) by the official search team. Among the items divided on the list into 130 categories were 1,229 bottles of wine, 11 "pornographic" films, many items of men's and women's clothing (often from abroad, as with 91 berets), a fair amount of money, "an artificial rubber sexual member."

On the trial itself (a vast public falsification that took in such people as American ambassador Joseph Davies), we now find that the public record, published in many languages, including English, was even to some extent *re*falsified after the trial. We now have the stenographic report of Bukharin's final words, which contains several dozen cuts and changes, often substantial—and often in Stalin's own handwriting.

6.

More centrally, we did not originally differentiate enough between the party, state, and army purges and the mass terror, assuming that the latter was an extension and by-product of the former. Stalin personally signed orders for some forty-four thousand executions, but these were mainly of party, army, and police officials.

There was an overlap, but "mass operations" against the population were differently conceived. We now have a set of decrees, starting in July

1937, ordering specific execution and imprisonment targets for "troikas" in each province and republic. The largest single category was "anti-Soviet elements." This included former kulaks, former officials of the tsarist state and army, former members of non-Bolshevik parties, religious activists, "speculators" . . . a significant proportion of the population.

Thus we see, quite apart from the purges of the party, the army, the engineers, and the intellectuals, an operation consciously designed to rid the country of those socially unassimilable to the Stalinist order. It has been plausibly argued that the main motivation for the terror was what it would be polite to call paranoia. We can now add that one of its components was a version of Marxism.

The next-largest category was "national." There were instructions on Poles, on Germans, Latvians—even on Harbintsy (former workers on the Chinese Eastern Railway).

The prescribed figures were increased from time to time. And whole new targets were set early in 1938. In any case, the apparent strict formalities implied were not strictly observed. We have an instruction from Vasili Mironov, head of the Novosibirsk NKVD, telling his operatives that they may double the figures if they want to. At the same time, local party secretaries themselves would request increases in the numbers. And a new set of lists soon appeared in early 1938.

These lists were presented in the form of "albums," each containing the names of those accused and sentenced by provincial and republican troikas in fulfillment, or overfulfillment, of the numerical targets set by Stalin and Yezhov, and these albums were sent to Moscow for approval. Against each name for sentencing, the central NKVD or its employees only had time to put in either a number for the years of imprisonment or the single letter "R," for *rasstrel* (shoot). From July 1937 to November 1938, 767,387 were sentenced (386,798 to death) in the general anti-Soviet category, 350,000 sentenced (247,157 shot) in the "national" category (though in Sverdlovsk, for example, a great majority of those so listed were not really of the specified nationality).

An illustration of the attitude towards those considered unassimilable into the Stalinist state is the fate of 170 blind, legless, and otherwise disabled men sentenced in Moscow to short terms of imprisonment in late 1937 for such offenses as begging at railway stations: they were resentenced and shot in February–March 1938. (The rationale seems to have been that they would be no use in labor camps.)

7.

Another important advance made since the publication of the last edition of *The Great Terror* is that we now have a complete record of the organization and staff of the NKVD, including the fate of the latter.

Yagoda's department heads were purged in 1937, among them Molchanov, who had organized the Zinoviev trial, while Kurski, who had worked on the Pyatakov case, committed suicide. Almost all had been purged by early 1938. We now have the true story of the fate of Avram Slutsky, chief of foreign intelligence, whose death on February 17, 1938, was announced as a heart attack (and he was given an honorable burial for having "died at his battle post"). We had long had a less official version—that he had been poisoned in the office of Mikhail Frinovsky, Yezhov's deputy people's commissar. We have now learned that the other deputy people's commissar, Zakovsky, seized him, and Alekhin (head of poisoning) ran in and gave him the injection. He was later (posthumously) purged. Zakovsky too (shot in August 1938), and Frinovsky (shot February 1940).

The personnel taken over by Yezhov and not purged in 1937–38 were largely shot in February–March 1939; and the new Yezhov cadre with Frinovsky, in January–February 1940. It is a curious point that we have Frinovsky's confession, as extorted by his Beria-style successors. Among much else, he is made to admit that in his time he had extorted false confessions by methods contrary to "socialist legality."

Quite recently, some Western commentators claimed that Stalin gave up torture after Yezhov's reign. However, as has been known since Khrushchev's time, Stalin issued a directive early in 1939 to the effect that "physical" methods were correct. And we know, in fact, that they were used on prisoners, from Politburo members down, at the very time Frinovsky and company were facing those accusations (and of course, that torture was massively employed throughout the Stalin period, as with the victims of the secret 1952 Jewish Anti-Fascist Committee trial, at which some of the accused exposed it).

How, in 1939, did Stalin reconcile these positions? Not, of course, by releasing or posthumously rehabilitating those from whom Frinovsky and the others had "illegally" extracted confessions. Stalin's own words explain his method of having it both ways: "the practice of the method of physical methods was befouled by the villains Zakovsky, Litvin, Uspenski and others. But that in no way discredited the method, if it is correctly practiced" (see S. A. Papkov, *Stalinski terror v Sibiri*).

8.

A central characteristic, seldom actually omitted from nonjudgmental accounts of Stalinism, was indeed torture. It was applied on a huge scale to produce a totally false picture of terrorism, sabotage, and espionage.

Even the ostensibly nonphysical methods used in 1936 are described by victims as both mentally and physically devastating. One man arrested briefly told me that the comparatively mild-sounding *stoika*, when a prisoner was kept standing against a wall for days, was hardly bearable. Torture is, one might say, a worse crime against humanity than killing. At any rate, the list of Soviet high-rankers who chose suicide rather than submit to arrest is remarkable, from the former Politburo member Mikhail Tomskii to the chief political commissar of the army, to the head of the Byelorussian government, the head of the Ukrainian Communist Party, and the heads of the Leningrad and the Moscow NKVDs.

What has now emerged most strongly is the effort, the sheer mass of the documentation, that went into the structure of lies. The interrogations and confrontations often produced tomes of paperwork, employing a large staff of interrogators and secretaries, with page after page of ever more complicated falsehood. The whole regime was, indeed, based on what Pasternak called "the inhuman power of the lie," but the sheer mass of false detail is astounding. And in some important cases, we know that Stalin himself read the "protocols" (the *Pravda* journalist Mikhail Koltsov's two volumes, for example).

Another oddity, which one might have thought detracted from the credibility of the accusations, was that the victims were often accused of engaging in espionage for four—or more—different countries. These large-scale attributions of terrorism and treason were, of course, reflected in the great public trials, and in the immense propaganda barrage put out not only in Russia but on a world scale.

And accompanying the assault on imaginary enemies was the parallel uproar about imaginary triumphs.

9.

Just as terror against your engineers is clearly bad for industry, and terror against your trained senior officers has a deleterious effect on your military efficiency, it can be argued—if less irrefutably—that terror against your writers and poets, historians and scientists is harmful to society.

As to the last named, even before the release of new material we knew of the fate of the leading astronomers accused of terrorism. But we have only recently been given the document on the purge of the USSR's leading physicists: the case of the Kharkov Physics Institute (a survivor of which, Alexander Weissberg, was one of the best pre-Khrushchev sources on the terror). Some were shot, some like the great Lev Landau merely imprisoned, and the institute was liquidated.

Still, the physical sciences—except, of course, for biology—recovered. The terror against the humanities, however, was a matter of destroying not only its more individual representatives but also truth and thought. A vast cultural apparat took over the control of the mind itself.

This involved the massive inculcation of falsehood from which the Soviet citizen had no protection, and which was also imposed on Soviet sympathizers in the West and elsewhere. The Austrian Communist leader Ernst Fischer, in his autobiography, tells how his wife later asked him how he could have believed that Trotsky and most of the old Bolsheviks were Nazi agents and not the obvious alternative that the story was a fake. He found it hard to answer.

## 10.

This is all now well established, though there are still some Westerners that take some Stalinist "documentation" at its face value.

Dead bodies were a common product of the Stalinist system. But minds did not do well either. They had to endure a continuous barrage of untruth. It can be argued that the Soviet Union's main negative characteristic—with plenty to choose from—was falsification. One finds it right from the start. But in the 1930s, after the disastrous failure of collectivization, the disjunction was complete. Henceforth, two different Soviet Unions existed—the official one, a flourishing and happy country (beset, though, by traitors), and the real one, overrun by poverty, squalor, and terror, and with a crushed population.

The prettier of these pictures was not only compulsory in all Soviet media and deniable by citizens at the cost of their liberty or lives. It was also, as far as possible, conveyed to the outer world and especially (as we have said) to a stratum of the Western intelligentsia, many of whom were even taken in by, for example, the official denials issued by Soviet representatives in the West of the very existence of the 1933 famine, let alone its causes.

The most falsified area of all was history, and especially the history of the revolution itself. And to the connoisseur of falsification there is something especially striking about the way in which the Soviet *visual* images were massively and pervasively amended. (More recent and particularly striking work has been done on this by the British photographer David King; see his 1997 book *The Commissar Vanishes*. New versions of old photographs, designated to remove unpersons from the record, are the main theme.)

With modern technology, such visual revisionism would no doubt be simple. We have to admire the skill of the artists working with more primitive technology who created what must be seen, considering their context, as minor masterpieces. We find two different types of visual unpersoning: first, the crude and simple blacking out of faces in books; and second, and far more striking, the actual faking of photographs to remove unwanted figures.

From even the earliest Soviet phase, under Lenin, we find a splendid photograph of a demonstration in which a sign over a shop reading "Watches: gold and silver" in the original is transformed to read "Struggle for your rights" in the faked photo. But this was small stuff compared with what came to be normal from the 1930s on.

Favorites have always included the picture of Stalin in exile in Siberia, where Kamenev, in the later versions, has been turned into a bush; the one of Lenin in 1917 addressing a crowd in which Trotsky and Kamenev have disappeared in the corrected version; and the one of Stalin and Yezhov at a great slave-labor project, the Moscow-Volga Canal, in which Yezhov becomes a stretch of water. We may note that this was also the practice in Mao's China, though done less creatively, where we see succeeding versions of a Politburo photograph with unfilled gaps appearing. In the Soviet case, unpersons were not simply blacked out or merged into other objects but shifted around to fill up such gaps.

To change an existing painting in suitable fashion was more difficult than the photographic equivalent, a fine example being a painting of Stalin and others looking over the White Sea–Baltic Canal, in which "others" originally included Yagoda, who is now painted as a jacket hanging on a railing.

There were, indeed, two categories of people removed from the visual record. The first group, people like Kamenev and Trotsky, had their revolutionary pasts destroyed (and were, of course, murdered) but continued to exist in Soviet history in their new roles as terrorist agents of Hilter–they were thus "ungoodpersons" rather than "unpersons" proper and they reemerged in the pictorial record only in political cartoons, where Bukharin, Trotsky, and the others figure as mad dogs on Nazi leashes.

Of course, falsification abounds in history, from ancient Egyptian stelae registering defeats as victories through Napoleon's *Moniteur* reporting Trafalgar as some ships lost in a storm. We can even find odd cases of unpersoning. After posthumous *damnatio*, Roman emperors' names were hacked out of inscriptions (and in one case, at least, the third "G" of AVGGG, signifying the three Augusti, now reduced to two, has been chipped away for good measure). Still, this was a rarity. Nor is it exactly a parallel, though worth our attention, when we find a print by Peter Street from the 1660s in two otherwise identical versions: the head of Lord Protector Richard Cromwell has been replaced in the later one by that of Charles II (see Francis Haskell's splendid *History and Its Images*). But this was no more than a labor-saving device by a busy producer, and Richard Cromwell, far from being removed from history or from life, died over fifty years later in retirement in Hertfordshire. More generally, as Orwell noted in *1984*, while the newspapers and history books of "Oceania's" past were "colored and biased," "falsification of the kind that is practiced today would have been impossible."

As we have said, one baffling notion, still to be found among academic students of the Soviet period, is that "documents" are, per se, a reliable source of information. These photographs are, of course, documents, and much Soviet typed or printed material is of the same level of credibility. (If one of the Stalinist photo-revisions was all that had survived, it would doubtless be accepted by researchers.) It is true that there is more leeway in the falsification of nonvisual documents, since they are usually invented out of the whole cloth rather than being revisions of earlier material.

The rehabilitation of Stalin's victims (others had to wait a generation) began in the late 1950s under Khrushchev. Even then, some of those deleted from the photographs were still given fake death dates—since even the secret NKVD records had also been falsified, so as to transfer some deaths to a later period.

The present writer can add a coda to the whole phenomenon. In the mid-1960s, some of those shot after the Bukharin trial in 1938 were rehabilitated—though a number were not (which in itself is absurd, since the confessions of all linked them in a single close-knit conspiracy). The question now arose of rehabilitating Faizulla Khodzhayev, the Uzbek Communist leader who had been one of the victims. Meanwhile, a local party history reprinted (well, not quite) a photograph taken in the 1920s. As originally published, in those early days, it showed Khodzhayev sitting in the front row. In 1964, he had not yet been formally rehabilitated, but those in the party machinery were plainly aware that the procedures for rehabilitation were afoot. Thus, to black him out altogether would be politically short-sighted, while to put him in would be to anticipate official action. The decision was made to print the photograph with one small change: the greater part of Khodzhayev's face was concealed behind a large beard that had not appeared in the original photo. In case readers wish to check, the two versions are to be found in *K istorii revoliutsii v Bukhare i natsional'nogo razmezhevaniia Srednei Azii,* by F. Khodzhayev (Tashkent, 1932) and *Partiinaia organizatsiia Tadzhikistana v 1924–1926 godakh,* by A. V. Makashov (Dushanbe, 1964). We chance to know from the literature that Khodzhayev never had a beard (see Dr. Donald Carlisle's article in *Kritika,* fall 1971). All this serves to provide a further insight into these (to us) alien mental processes.

We have suggested that the 1932–33 slaughter of a wide swathe of the Soviet Union's population might have had a rather negative effect on the Soviet economy. When it comes to the differently targeted terror of 1937–39, we find further negative effects. When your industrial incentives involve a continual mass purge of your engineers, managers, and railway-men, it implies a certain departure from what anyone would normally look on as a planned economy, or a sane society.

## 11.

A s for Western assessments, a whole range of Stalinophilic writing by journalists and scholars has been devastatingly exposed over the past half century. But there are examples of compulsive blindness affecting even governmental circles, from the 1930s on. The U.S. State Department had an excellent Russian Department. In 1937, it was disbanded and its experts dispersed. George Kennan writes of "this curious purge" that there was strong evidence that it was ordered by the White House, and Eleanor Roosevelt has been given as the probable initiator. In any case, a well-informed, highly professional body was destroyed, and much real thinking and information about the USSR was thus wantonly denied to the U.S. government. Harry Hopkins, who became a chief American negotiator with Moscow, is quoted as asking a State Department expert if he belonged to the "anti-Soviet clique."

## 12.

Study of the realities of the Soviet experience, after the debacle of the Webbs and others, began to be reasonably well conducted in the post–World War II period—partly because those concerned often had had direct experience of international or Communist affairs. This quality of analysis was partly lost, as far as one level of academe was concerned, in the 1970s. "Revisionism" became common in such circles. And though it was no longer possible to present a fully Potemkinized or Webbized account, various ways of toning down the realities remained the alternative.

The main trouble was, and is, that since attention to the factual was no longer compatible with these views, a degradation in the mental level served instead. And by the late 1970s, those who had adopted fashionable counterfactual agendas were rising in academe and deploying power and contacts.

What is truly deplorable is a different, and mind-boggling, phenomenon. An American academic element, with a poor record of work, in some cases, has today become parasitically dependent on genuine (Russian) Moscow researchers. The trouble here is not one of opinion but of minimal qualifications, so that some sets of documents, very useful in the original Russian, are published in the West with truly debased editorializing and analysis (so much so that, as I write, the leading Moscow historical journal has, coolly but devastatingly, noted the fact). It is a question of the merest incapacity. This is not the only example of academic dumbing down, though it is one that, as many in the field have observed, is so openly silly as not to present any challenge in the long run. But meanwhile, it is an appalling distraction.

## Chapter XII

# With and Against Hitler

⊰⊱

### 1.

As we have said, this book is not a work of history. It merely records events that affect our understanding of the totalitarian, and our own, development. And even on these, we do not rehearse what is already generally known but examine, in those contexts, vital and often unknown or neglected evidence—and thus of course undermine established misevaluations.

The story of the Nazi-Soviet Pact is well known, though it still often tends to be brushed aside when it does not fit certain ideas or agendas. People should, indeed, be reminded of at least some of the actions of the time. The joint invasion of Poland in 1939. The Katyn massacre in 1940. The Soviet-German naval cooperation. The handing over to the Gestapo of German Communist refugees in Soviet exile. The publication of Communist papers in Western Europe for some time after the Nazi invasions. But perhaps above all the peace movements (including peace with Hitler) pursued by the parties in a campaign that compromised (one would have thought irretrievably) the record of many on the far left in the United States as well as Britain. This was not the last peace activity to be run from Moscow. (And, in connection with some of our earlier comments on general words, let us note the Soviet ban, on Stalin's direct orders, on the hostile use of the word "Fascism.")

The whole experience is one to be remembered and very much taken into account by all serious minds today. But we shall say no more here, but turn to the often equally misevaluated events of the war which for the USSR started in June 1941.

### 2.

The clash that followed between the quondam allies has also been researched in detail, both militarily and politically, in both Russia and the West.

Russian losses were, as we know, enormous, far greater than those of the Western powers, or of Germany. These are even now, sometimes, put to the credit of the regime. The soldiers fought bravely and tenaciously. The civilians died in huge numbers. But far from this giving justification to the regime, the opposite is largely true.

One still sometimes reads, even in books and periodicals not (or no longer) subject to old prejudices in favor of the Soviet Union, that Stalin's industrialization was the saving of Russia in World War II. This residual error is untenable for several reasons.

First, as we have seen, the crash industrialization after 1929 was irrationally pursued and falsely celebrated. Much effort and investment went into wholly or partially worthless grandiosities.

Second, within military-industrial planning proper, there was a great deal of irrational subjectivity, as when Stalin insisted on heavy cruisers. (The naval commanders who opposed this being among the few purge victims to be publicly, and of course posthumously, denounced for such errors at the 1939 Party Congress.)

Third, of course, much of the industrialization effort was effective–as with the T-34 tank, which was better than any the Germans deployed. But a great deal of military equipment was lost in the opening battles. The only real positive achievement during those disastrous days was the successful transfer of part of the industrial equipment to locations further east, beyond the reach of the German penetration.

Fourth, but, as Stalin himself put it, much industry was nonetheless lost to the enemy, together with much of the vital food-producing areas.

Still, it is maintained that the USSR defeated the Germans and that *therefore* the Stalinist 1930s were retrospectively justified. This is the judgment expressed typically, and which probably has the largest readership, in Eric Hobsbawm's *The Age of Extremes*, in these terms: "It turned the USSR into a major industrial economy in a few years and one capable, as Tsarist Russia had not been, of surviving and winning the war against Germany. One must add that in few other regimes could or would the people have borne the unparalleled sacrifices of this war effort."

This is thoroughly misleading. The Russian army in World War I suffered defeats, but none as devastating as the deep penetrations of 1941–42. The collapse of 1914–17 was from the top down (and as against the 1940s, the Russians had given up internal security in the army!).

Unlike 1914, this time the German threat was total and openly devoted to the destruction of Slavdom. As Stalin himself is reported saying, if the Germans had behaved as well as they had in World War I, they would have won. On paper, the Germans' chances of victory were slim. The astonishing thing is how near they came to success.

The disasters of 1941 were due in large part to Stalin's mishandling of the situation, as has long been made clear by Russian and other writers on the period. And, still more important, his decapitation of the army in the purges had left a half-trained military leadership, as again all sources agree. Then, also, Stalin was wholly responsible for ignoring warnings that the Nazis were preparing to attack—one result of which was the destruction, on its airfields, of much of the Soviet air force.

Russian scholars are now emphasizing Stalin's other huge military error: the wholly defective deployment of the Soviet forces. Against the advice of some of the generals, when annexing the gains of 1939, Stalin ordered the abandonment of the fortified line along the old Soviet frontier and had the armies go forward to a new one. The old forts and other resources were abandoned. But the new ones had not been completed, and were in any case exposed and easily overrun. Meanwhile, in the retreat, the old ones had become unusable. (It seems that one of Stalin's motives for the forward move was to bring his forces into a position from which they could advance, when feasible, into the West.) All this resulted in huge losses, mainly of the best-trained soldiery. Stalin was personally responsible for, among other such things, the disastrous attempt to hold Kiev, against which his advisers had all warned—the biggest defeat of the war.

Stalin relied, in some cases well into 1942, on the survivors and accomplices of the purge, now in high command positions. Kliment Voroshilov, Semyon Budenny, and Grigory Kulik were disastrous as army leaders, while the purely political Lev Mekhlis contrived a catastrophe of his own in the Crimean Peninsula. Meanwhile, generals commanding at the front were shot in July 1941. In October 1941, a group of experienced officers, including three successive heads of the air force, were shot. One of their co-accused, General Kirill Meretskov, was indeed released (though he said he found it troublesome to be at meetings that included Deputy Police Minister Vsevolod Merkulov, who had personally tortured him). A further group perished in February 1942. A number of loyal Soviet generals over and above those executed in 1941–42 were shot, more still when the war was over.

Then this was Russia's only war in which large numbers went over to the enemy, including five generals and numerous colonels (nothing comparable happened in tsarist times). And all this *in spite of* the obvious horrors—and anti-Slav racism—of the Nazis. Apart from these, there were scores of thousands of anti-German, but also anti-Soviet, partisans in the Ukraine.

3.

The Stalinist grip nevertheless had one major positive effect on the war effort. After the initial chaos, there were many broken units and much desertion. Apart from those taken prisoner, the NKVD reported to Beria, who reported to Stalin, that by October 10, 1941, 667,364 soldiers who had left their units and "escaped from the front" had been rounded up: 632,486 had been formed into new units, 25,878 had been kept under arrest, 10,201 of them shot. (And this of course continued. Anthony Beevor's classic *Stalingrad* notes over ten thousand military executions during the Stalingrad campaign.) It may indeed be argued, and this is not to rebut the ruthlessness, that it was one of the conditions for the narrow margin of victory over Hitler. (And more than nine hundred thousand Gulag prisoners were released into the army, mostly into penal battalions, used for such tasks as charging across minefields.)

This presents us with certain ethical, or moral, problems. Was this extreme ruthlessness justified by the continuing Soviet struggle against Nazism?

Which, of course, raises the question of how much ruthlessness is justified in what circumstances. One has the feeling that the matter has not been adequately thought through by most of those prepared to moralize in this and other similar contexts.

A Russian–Jewish, too—once said to me that the best outcome of the war would have been a German victory over the Soviet regime, followed by a Western nuclear destruction of Nazism. "But you would have been dead." "Yes, there *is* that."

4.

It is now clear that the Western allies failed to engage Stalin, even on matters where dispute could not have been in any way harmful to the Soviet war effort. Even, what is more, on issues in which their concepts of human rights and laws were grossly and indefensibly crushed.

An early example was the case of Henrik Ehrlich and Victor Alter, both leaders of the Jewish Social Democratic Bund in Poland. Ehrlich had been a member of the Petrograd Soviet in 1917. Both had since been prominent in Polish and European politics. They were both arrested in 1939, chancing to be in the part of prewar Poland occupied by the Soviets. Condemned to death, they were pardoned and, in the summer of 1941, released. They were then approached to head an international Jewish Anti-Fascist Committee. They were rearrested in December 1941 and never seen again.

The Bund had veterans in the United States, in particular the labor leader David Dubinsky. He organized protests. But these were not pressed; indeed, he was openly discouraged. In the event, Ehrlich committed suicide in jail in 1942, while Alter was shot in 1943. To a query from Americans, the Soviet embassy in Washington eventually said they had been shot for calling on Soviet troops to surrender to the Nazis.

Here was an occasion where a Western stand for international justice might have found a crucial issue—and perhaps, if successful, have induced Stalin to meet, at least to some extent, the standards to which he should have been held. (Nor will it do to argue that we should not have interfered in Soviet affairs. They were mounting huge political campaigns in the West at this very time.)

5.

The Western allies were later faced with a direct moral-political challenge of another kind, when the Nazis announced the discovery of mass graves in Katyn. There was even then little doubt that the Polish officers and others had been killed when in Soviet hands in 1940. In the first months of the German invasion, Stalin had made some approaches and some concessions to the Polish government and parried inquiries into the missing Poles. When the Katyn graves were discovered in 1943, Moscow attributed them to Germany (indeed, the Soviets only admitted the truth some fifty years after the event).

The West was faced with an irreconcilable mix of motives.

1. Britain had gone to war in 1939 because of the German attack on Poland. Over the entire war, Polish army and air force units had fought the Germans on Allied fronts.

2. In this context, Stalin had (as is now fully documented) ordered the killing of the Poles—to the number of about twenty-one thousand—after they had fallen into Soviet hands when the USSR invaded eastern Poland in 1939.

3. This was no minor ethical outrage that could be minimized or finessed. Stalin denied it and attacked the Poles for suggesting an inquiry, eventually imposing a small Stalinist clique as the Polish government (while arresting and repressing the representatives of the genuine underground Polish government).

*But*, at the time of the discovery of the graves, the Russians were bearing a very high proportion of the effort to defeat Hitler. That is to say, the Russian soldiery were doing so. At any rate, unless Stalin had confessed (and, say, blamed the NKVD), any hint of Western disbelief in his story and belief that he and his regime had committed so vile a crime would have been seen as a stab in the Russian back. The result was the effective suppression of the truth, and of other Polish objections to Soviet conduct, in the interest of anti-Nazi unity.

Without pursuing the matter further or inquiring whether giving in to Stalin on this, or even more on other issues, was the best policy, we find that this is an example—an extreme example, in fact—of the same type of moral and intellectual problem faced today, for in the West, political argument is continual about whether and to what extent we should ignore various deeds by states that are, for the immediate crises, our allies.

## 6.

The Red Army's revived resistance to the German invasion was indeed splendid, but, as Stalin himself put it to then U.S. ambassador to the Soviet Union, Averell Harriman, the Russians were fighting "for their homeland, not for us." Vasily Grossman, himself present at Stalingrad, writes in his *Life and Fate* of a brave officer certain that he was not only fighting the Germans but fighting for a new Russia, that the victory over Hitler would be a victory over the death camps in which his father, his mother, and his sisters had perished. And Russian writers from Pasternak to Sakharov note something like this as dominant in the expectations of the returning soldiery, when the war ended.

The present writer was attached in 1944–45 to the Third Ukrainian Front, and found the Soviet soldiers friendly, above all high-spirited—and unsubmissive to their political officers (though our main concern was the Bulgarians, whose armies now served on the flank, and in any case we saw none of the excesses the Yugoslavs were to complain of).

Once, another British officer and I were held up by a squad of

Communist partisans, now made policemen. We had forgotten the password. But some Soviet soldiers came up. We explained that we were Allied officers being harassed by these troopers. The soldiers at once seized them and hustled them off. On another occasion, a subaltern in my regiment and I were with a group of Soviet lieutenants in a bar-restaurant. The other Briton present and a Soviet woman officer had taken to each other. We all, the rest of us (six or seven), more or less smuggled them out past the surly looking Soviet town commandant.

But more striking was when I had to go with an RAF Group Captain to the funeral of a Soviet general who had been killed in a mislocated RAF attack on his column. After the rites, the Group Captain brought out his maps to show the Soviet general in charge of the funeral how the British squadron had misread a similar junction of rail, road, and river. The Soviet general waved it aside as the sort of thing that happened in war. This was so much contrary to the Stalinist practice of seizing on every conceivable Western act of the sort as an unappeasable crime, that I wonder how the general survived. Perhaps he didn't. The writer Konstantin Simonov wrote later that the qualities Soviet soldiers brought home after the war were unsuited to the Stalin regime and were part of the tide of feeling that made the postwar repression crucial to continued Stalinism.

Stalin was concerned then, and later, to crush anything resembling disaffection. And, to go forward briefly, after victory, things were to grow worse. The independent spirit Simonov had noted among the soldiery did not prevail. One example we have is of a conversation bugged by the secret police between two generals—Gordov and Rybalchenko. They speak of "only the government living, the broad masses beggared"; that "It was necessary for us to have genuine democracy"; that "the people is silent, it is afraid." Both generals were arrested at once, in January 1947, and soon shot.

A different incident in the postwar terror was the "disappearance" of the wife of Stalin's old army protégé Marshal Kulik. He and anyone else concerned were told she simply could not be found. It is only in the last few years that we have discovered she had been "sentenced" by a MGB tribunal and shot by the top executioner, Blokhin (about whom, on a different occasion, David Remnick found the interesting detail that when shooting several hundred at night, he wore waterproof and bloodproof clothes, cap, and gloves; see Remnick's *Lenin's Tomb*). The reason for Stalin's odd decision on Mrs. Kulik is unknown. But Kulik himself was later caught speaking subversively and was shot in 1950.

7.

T he regime, then, barely survived, through the sacrifice of its people and the help of its allies, a disaster for which it was itself largely responsible.

After the first six months, American supplies came in on a vast scale (19.6 million tons). There has been little written about American and British aid to the Soviet war effort. Or rather, though full accounts, with figures and tonnages, have been produced, they remain unknown to the mass of the relevant public—rather as there is so much neglect of the huge and vital American effort against the 1921 famine. Marshal Georgy Zhukov said later (in remarks bugged by the secret police and reported by its then head to the Politburo):

> *Now they write that the Allies never gave us any aid. But how can one deny that the Americans sent us so much material, without which we could not have formed reserves and continued the war. . . . We received 350 thousand motor vehicles, and what vehicles they were! . . . We had no explosives, no powder nothing to fill rifle cartridges with. The Americans really helped us with powder and explosives. And how much rolled steel they sent: we could never have organised the production of tanks so quickly if it were not for American help with steel. And now the entire affair is presented as if we already had everything in abundance. ("G. K. Zhukov: neizvestnye stranitsy biografi,"* Voennye arkhivy Rossii, *vol. 1 [1993])*

The shortage in 1941 of even such basic military supplies as ammunition was, of course, noted earlier by Khrushchev.

There was a fair amount of British aid too, surprisingly so for a country that had little to spare. The main British contribution was in the convoys sent to Murmansk, subject to constant attack from the German battleships in occupied Norway. One major convoy was almost totally destroyed. Finally, the Barents Sea battle, in 1942, where a small British squadron defeated a larger and more powerful German one, virtually ended the struggle. My friend the writer Alan Ross, who died in 2001, tells of being caught in a waterlogged hold floating with sailors' bodies, before his cruiser could be righted and the battle resumed. Another friend, the poet Donald Davie, was a Royal Navy radio operator in Murmansk and heard the Commodore reporting the numbers and size of the German squadron, ending "I am attacking," which Donald said was the greatest thing he ever heard. (A few days later, the Commodore arrived in Murmansk. He had lost an eye.)

Of course, Russian losses were by far the greatest, in part because (particularly in the last phase) Stalin ordered attacks regardless of casualties. They were, at lowest, twenty or thirty times as great as Britain's. But when we turn to the ruling bodies, the proportions are strikingly reversed. The Soviet Central Committee suffered the loss of one of its members, surrounded at Kiev (plus another who seems to have gone over to the Germans). The British House of Commons, four times as large, has twenty MPs on its war memorial.

The immense scale of Allied supplies produced almost nothing in the way of recognition, let alone cooperation. In this context, it is instructive to quote Stalin in a secret message to his ambassador in London Ivan Maisky, since this—on October 19, 1942!—well illustrates the mind-set that fueled the Cold War (which we shall treat later): "all of us in Moscow are getting the impression that Churchill is sustaining a course towards the defeat of the USSR, in order to come to terms with the Germany of Hitler or Brüning at the expense of our country"—a remarkable example of Stalin's deeply established attitude towards the non-Soviet world. And the coming of peace simply meant its now largely untrammeled development. The peoples of Russia and Sovietized Eastern Europe, exhausted by the war, faced ever-worsening oppression. And even in the freer world, with lesser stresses, those concerned to face the perspectives of reality did so under constant anxiety and apprehension, which expressed themselves at the time as proceeding

*While the days like rotten stone*
*Crumble from the future's cliff.*

## Chapter XIII

# Cold War: Heated Imaginations

—————⊗⊗⊗—————

### 1.

In this chapter we shall not be dealing with the whole reality of the Cold War. This has been done before. (My own last analysis was in *Reflections on a Ravaged Century*.) But demonstrations have little effect on an evidently unteachable corner of academe—not only academe, of course, and we shall be coping with the awful example of Ted Turner and the CNN later.

So, down to essentials.

The Soviet Union, right up to the eve of its collapse, was committed to the concept of an unappeasable conflict with the Western world and to the doctrine that this could only be resolved by what Foreign Minister Andrey Gromyko described, as officially as one can imagine (in his 1975 book *The Foreign Policy of the Soviet Union*) as world revolution: "The Communist Party of the Soviet Union subordinates all its theoretical and practical activity in the sphere of foreign relations to the task of strengthening the positions of socialism, and the interests of further developing and deepening the world revolutionary process." (One could hardly be franker.)

The concepts and motivations had, of course, been central from the start of the regime. When, after World War II, Stalin turned to the new international problems, this was clearly the perspective in which he saw them, and the basis on which he operated, as indeed was obvious enough and soon understood by most observers. However, one still finds academic comments like, "Early views that the Soviet Union had a clear blueprint for world domination have been discredited." Since no such view has ever been advanced, the intention seems to be to cast doubt on the view that the general Soviet intention was to advance its borders when and if possible and that, until abandoned and denounced by then Soviet foreign minister Eduard Shevardnadze, the USSR's foreign policy was based on permanent irreconcilability with the non-Soviet world, and, in fact, with the long-term intention of destroying it.

Without again rehearsing the whole story, can we briefly develop the main elements of a foolproof case? I think so, especially as we now have even more striking material from the Soviet archives than we did two or three years ago.

Foolproof? Well, first, it seems, we should make one or two obvious points, or points one might think obvious.

First, to present the actions and admitted motives of the Stalinist and post-Stalinist Soviet Union is not to say that America, or the West, or its allies were angels facing demons. They were more like humans facing monsters, with the human capacity for error and sin. It seems best to get that out of the way. And to note that to describe Hitler's war on Poland in 1939 by selecting a few successful Polish counterattacks, ignoring all other data, and thus proving Polish aggression, is more or less what is done vis-à-vis the West and Moscow on the Cold War.

Still, further confirmation of the adult view has been continually emerging from the Soviet and other records, and it is worth deploying some of this. A group of diplomatic advisers (who had been members of the Soviet Foreign Ministry commission on the preparation of peace treaties), including Maxim Litvinov and Ivan Maisky, recommended at least a temporary détente with the West. All the objective factors favored this. But even though this plan accepted that in the longer term the West and the USSR were still irreconcilable, Stalin rejected it completely.

It is only recently that we have had the letters written by Stalin to Molotov in 1945–46, when the latter was outside the USSR in negotiations with the Western powers (so that the highest level of secrecy, "word of mouth only," was not available).

We had always thought of Molotov's stance in these negotiations as the most uncooperative and hard-line conceivable, earning him the nickname of Stone-bottom. But we now find Stalin continually upbraiding him for inadequate hostility to the West. Molotov was blamed for having relaxed censorship on foreign journalists in Moscow. And in November 1945, in Stalin's absence, *Pravda* had been allowed to print a speech of Churchill's praising the Soviet war effort and Stalin personally—this was "servility towards foreigners." And when Molotov returned to Moscow, he was, on Stalin's orders, formally reprimanded by a commission of the Politburo. A recent collection of Russian Foreign Ministry papers dating from September 1945 to December 1946 (edited by Vladimir Pechatnov) shows that not only in connection with Molotov, Stalin demonstrated unremitting hostility to the United States and Britain. (The softer ideological, or at least tactical, line was of course also to be found in Browderism. The CPUSA fully accepted its general secretary Earl Browder's move to a more liberal Communism in 1943. A public rebuke, drafted in Moscow but signed by the French Communist leader Jacques Duclos, resulted in an equally full acceptance of the opposite view in 1944, the third of the CPUSA's disciplined about-faces [1939, 1941, 1944].)

So even Molotov was too mild for Stalin. Litvinov much more so, even going to the length that when asked by the American envoy Averell Harriman in November 1945 what the West could do to satisfy Stalin, he answered, "Nothing." In June 1946, still in that post, he warned a Western journalist that the "root cause" of the confrontation then reached was "the ideological conception prevailing here that conflict between the Communist and capitalist worlds is inevitable"—that is, no more than the doctrine long since announced by Lenin that "a series of frightful clashes" were bound to occur between the two systems, leading finally to the world victory of Communism. When the correspondent asked Litvinov, "Suppose the West would suddenly give in and grant all Moscow's demands? . . . Would that lead to goodwill and the easing of the present tension?" Litvinov answered, "It would lead to the West being faced, after a more or less short time, with the next series of demands."

What this demonstrates above all is that the power to create an unappeasably hostile world power and a complete confrontation was in the hands of one man, and that Stalin had the determination, if necessary against anything like peaceableness in his own party, to disrupt all chances of a tolerable postwar world. This untrammeled autocracy is often seen, by those who have never encountered anything like it, as an offense to political theory. We have, of course, come across it before, over domestic issues. It now became a global threat.

Thus, it seems clear from this, as from much else, that had Stalin not recovered from his illness in late 1945, the USSR would not have been launched on the calamitous course that followed. This is, of course, not to say that Stalin was against making small, and temporary, concessions that did not affect the realities of power. This was seen in the legalization of the antifascist opposition parties in Bulgaria in 1945, in the broadening of Moscow's Polish regime to include Stanislaw Mikolajczyk from 1945 to 1947: all temporary. Stalin, in fact, gave the direct recommendation to the East German Communist leaders to "zigzag"—a word he used several times.

2.

As Orwell pointed out, even mild Western expressions of distaste for Communist actions were almost always called "rabid"—in fact, a useful marker word.

Anyone who looked at the journals and propaganda of the Soviet side, including the output of, for example, the French Communist Party, would have found that "Anglo-American imperialism" was constantly described as intent on a new world war, Westerners as "frenzied" enemies of peace and popular liberties.

Those interested in the period should read the minutes of the three meetings of the Cominform in 1947–49. The tone, which was of course to be found in Soviet and other East European newspapers in every city and province, is far and away more virulent than that of any but the most extreme "anti-Communism" in the West. The content, too. So this, from the most high-level Communist assembly, managed by Stalin's immediate subordinates Andrey Zhdanov and Georgy Malenkov: "Like the Fascist aggressors the Anglo-American bloc is preparing for a new war." "The bosses of American imperialism draw up their plans for world war." One often finds such things as the West's "kindling of war psychosis and hysteria." The American press is "a torrent of preaching in favour of a new war." Western socialists are often attacked, sometimes by name: "Bevin, Attlee, Blum," and others are "accomplices of the warmongers." And so on. Indeed, "the right-wing socialists" are branded the worst enemies of peace.

To return to the Cominform document, the Tito regime, which typically "marches in the front ranks of the instigators of war," is a "fascist gang," committing "an act of treachery and betrayal unexampled in history." Apart from endless abuse, the Titoites were the subject of a formal resolution titled "The Communist Party of Yugoslavia in the Power of Murderers and Spies."

The trial in Budapest of the Communist minister Laszlo Rajk and others (which has long been exposed as a Stalinist fake) is taken as proof of the Titoite treachery (and was publicized in Poland, for instance, "with an initial print of 100,000"). On Titoism in general an interesting quotation from the Western point of view is in a Cominform speech by Jacques Duclos of the French Communist Party. The Yugoslavs are accused of "frenzied propaganda activity" in France, where "some intellectuals, on the pretext of objectivity, listen to what they say" (but huge demonstrations have been organized against them).

As for this type of Soviet interference in Western domestic affairs, we now have an astonishing later example, and one that should silence those who still maintain that the Western Communist parties were granted any autonomy by Moscow. In 1951, years after the dissolution of the Comintern, Harry Pollitt, leader of the British Communist Party, was instructed personally by Stalin in the preparation of a new party program. Pollitt then gave his draft to Stalin, who extensively rewrote it, even bothering to rework such sections as that on agriculture, and finally changing the title from "For a People's Parliament and a People's Britain" to "For a Progressive Worker's Government and People's Democratic England."

In this connection, one should mention another case of just this period—in *Report on my Husband,* by Josefa Slánská. Rudolf Slánský, whose death certificate his widow got some two years after his death in 1952 ("cause of death: strangulation from hanging"), was a leading Czech Communist. His widow's description of his interrogation and trial for offenses of which he was totally innocent is revelatory, as is her own arrest, maltreatment, and exile. Slánský had himself been prominent in the Stalinist takeover in Prague in 1948. But the charges of espionage and terrorism in favor of American imperialism were, of course, vicious fantasy. It is less the mere inhumanity than the moral squalor of Stalin that emerges with exceptional vividness from such a case. (The execution was greeted thus by the Communist press: "The imperialists and their agents have suffered a new and heavy defeat in their war plans for world domination.")

Among the accusations leveled at Slánský was his recruitment into his conspiracy of Spanish War veterans of the International Brigade (always a suspect category in the Soviet bloc; Yugoslav veterans of the brigade headed by Vladmir Čopić himself had been shot in Moscow in 1939).

As to the idea of moral equivalence between the West and the Soviet bloc, this was also, of course, applied to their domestic affairs. The Rosenberg case was, and is, cited as comparable to the Soviet liquidation of the Jewish Anti-Fascist Committee in 1952. Yet there are profound differences: The Rosenbergs were, though she only peripherally, indeed espionage agents of Stalinism, while the Jews in the Moscow 1952 Anti-Fascist Committee case were totally innocent. The Rosenbergs were not tortured. The Rosenbergs had a genuine trial, and their false, though ideologically loyal, pleas of innocence were widely publicized; and if they had chosen truth rather than Stalinism, they could have been spared (there are arguments for lenity, but they must not obscure the realities).

## 3.

How to explain the persistence of the opposite view, on this and related matters?

In and after the 1960s, a radicalized new intake into academe took place. As these academics aged, and rose in their profession, they increasingly deployed an anti-American or anti-Western attitude. The trouble was not their opinions as such, but the repetition of largely, sometimes entirely, false accounts of the international events of the period.

One American professor of the vintage even managed—quite recently—to intrude a piece into the normally harder *Times Literary Supplement,* arguing that the immediate end of the war in Europe saw a vast military and general effort by the United States to impose its control over the Continent. This view (about a time when there was a massive withdrawal of American troops!) saw the imposition of puppet regimes in the non-Communist section of the Continent. Yes, how we remember the U.S. tanks carrying their quislings to power in Oslo and London, Brussels and Copenhagen, while elected governments were nowhere to be seen, having doubtless been given political asylum and freedom in the East of the Continent.

The view much promulgated today in these circles is less that the Soviets were always in the right (though that too is found) than that the United States was at least equally to blame for the Cold War.

Perhaps we should further reconstruct the historical scenario some seem to accept. In the late 1940s, according to this, we see a Russia with a free press, the open advancing of pro-American views, a multiparty system; in America, a rigid dictatorship. The governments of Western Europe are run by members of the American Fascist-Capitalist Party, though after a few years many of its British, French, and Italian leaders are accused of being agents of Russia and executed after torture. In 1952, America's leading Jews are tortured, then executed without publicity. In 1953, demonstrations in favor of Russia are put down by American troops in Paris. In 1956, a socialist rebellion in Belgium is similarly suppressed. In 1968, the Capitalist Party in Italy, hitherto loyal to Washington, moves to a more humane capitalism; troops from the United States and its European satellites intervene. In Germany, the American foothold in Berlin is surrounded by a wall, to prevent people escaping to the liberal East German Republic. . . and so on and so on.

You see what one means by moral equivalency?

A more nuanced, moderate reckoning accepted the Soviet realities but balanced them with equal American or Western offenses, leaving that side of the story much as given above. (On the Berlin Wall, the fact of its construction by the Communists would be admitted, but its necessity blamed wholly or partly on the West.)

"The Cold War mentality" is a term employed in a more or less derogatory sense to describe those who were right and were later proved right beyond rational dispute about the nature and origins of the Cold War. It is commonly used to suggest that those who wrote of the Soviet Union and of Soviet intentions and actions in a hostile spirit were biased, or even that they demonized the USSR from political prejudice, while more recent and less hostile presentations of the facts are thereby more "objective" and "nonjudgmental."

In reality, as we have noted earlier, from the newer knowledge of Soviet and East European internal affairs that has emerged in the 1990s, the substance of Soviet foreign policy now appears to have been even worse than we had thought.

Our view was, briefly, that until Gorbachev and Shevardnadze, the Soviet Union's foreign policy was based, as the latter put it, on irreconcilable hostility in principle to the West and to other non-Soviet states, so that the policy pursued by the United States and its allies—denying the Soviet Union military and other superiority—though sometimes pursued rather shakily, was right in principle and successful in practice. As I put it in my *Present Danger* in 1976, the aim of the West was to make the expansionism inherent in Soviet policy impossible, thus making possible the evolution or collapse of the system based on it.

These propositions were denied at the time by some circles in the West and are still, if not exactly denied, regarded as prematurely deduced on irrational grounds. It was believed that a "Cold Warrior" became opposed to the Soviet system because of some irrational predisposition, and—if a historian—his motives were, at the least, to deliver a distorted anti-Soviet brief. The idea seems to be that if one can show that opposition to the Soviet threat was in part based on a dislike of Soviet actualities and intentions—that is, "emotions"—then the opposition cannot have been objective. But, of course, the

Soviet system was indeed disliked, even detested, *because* of its record and intentions, as seen by those historians who were not prejudiced in its favor.

As just such a historian, let me provide an example. I was in the Balkans from 1944 to 1948 and saw the whole process of Stalinist takeover in Bulgaria, with the antifascist democratic parties suppressed and their leader, the excellent Nikolai Petkov, hanged (where he was followed after I left by the Bulgarian Communist leader Traicho Kostov). Even those of us who had originally thought better of the Soviet occupiers, or at least had expected them to improve, were wholly disenchanted. And, of course, every Westerner who had in one way or another been involved in the realities felt the same way. However, for years I did not write anything on this theme. It was only when it became clear that there was much that had been kept secret, or inadequately reported, that this changed. Even so, my first research (as Webb Fellow at the London School of Economics) was an analysis, from various sources, of the realities of political struggle at the highest Soviet level from 1945 to 1960. The regime and its leaders do not come out of this particularly well, but without emphasis on the regime's truly negative side. My motive in writing it was above all curiosity.

Of course, when it became equally apparent that there was no full registration (or as full as was then possible) of the much more horrifying facts of the terror of the late 1930s, curiosity remained one motive, leading to my *The Great Terror* in 1968. Of course, no one could deal with this, or other themes I wrote of later, unless judgmental as well as inquisitive; and those who denied the negative characteristics of Soviet Communism were deficient in judgment *and* in curiosity—gaps in the teeth and blinkers on the eyes.

One of the oddest of the verbal expressions is the condemnation often to be found in the West of "triumphalism." This strange term is used to deplore any sign of being glad that the Soviet Union failed and that the Western world "triumphed" (nowadays, of course, there is an "ism" for everything). It seems to imply, above all, that such an attitude is in bad taste. The poor, unfortunate totalitarian anti-Western regimes collapsed, but one shouldn't crow.

What one suspects here is the feeling not so much that the West should not be openly pleased with what happened as that those in the West who were, or were in general, right about the Soviet regime should not be "triumphalist" over those who were wrong. One may agree that it is more important to help them reform their methods than to rebuke them. But how can it be done without some public analysis of their errors, which, after all, had a very deleterious effect on part of the Western mind? Let's not be smug; but let's be rigorous.

# Chapter XIV

# A Gaggle of Misleaders

## 1.

The following examples of well-received misperception and misrepresentation of the key events of the period are selected, not quite at random, but so as to provide a wide view of the phenomenon and specifically of one variety of its manifestations. We have avoided, as we have earlier in this book, the products of a total ignorance, however pretentiously presented—as with the Webbs. And we have stuck to examples with, in each case, heavy intellectual claims to acceptance. It is a vivid haul of misunderstanding and misdirection, at various levels of IQ and influence.

## 2.

### C. P. Snow

The English writer C. P. Snow, later Sir Charles, later Lord Snow, is a stunning example of a deep emotional attachment to bureaucracy, to state supremacy, to quasi-Marxist—and to pro-Soviet—delusions.

His novels, characterized by the critic D. J. Enright as suffocatingly smug, but praised as "naturalism" because in reality "people talk in cliché . . . and life consists largely of banal situations." But his work nonetheless comes to life when a thirst for power emerges. As one of his prime characters (clearly the author's alter ego) naively confesses, "He longed for all the trappings, titles, ornaments and show of power. . . . He wanted the grandeur of the Lodge, he wanted to be styled among the Heads of Houses." And that is merely in academic intrigue, which was the theme of his *The Masters*. Canon Raven, the mild pacifist head of Christ's College, later sent a short letter to the *Spectator*: there had been no real operation like it except one, mounted by Snow, which had failed.

When Snow went into politics, while producing an even duller novel, he spoke of "A kind of pleasure, the pleasure, secretive but shining, they got from being at the centre of things." His own political career produced one hilarious, undull moment. As a junior minister in one of Harold Wilson's Labour governments, while defending its Comprehensive School policy, he was asked—in a debate in the House of Lords—why his own son was sent to Eton, and answered so that he could meet those he would know in later life. Wilson was understandably aghast at this super-silliness.

So far, a type: a subject for negative diagnosis. But, in our more general context, it gets much worse.

Snow is best known today for his "two cultures" controversy with the literary critic F. R. Leavis (of which Philip Larkin wrote me that while Leavis was a bit crazy, of course he was right as against Snow). In our context, it was an example of Snow's claim to a reliance on Science. He noted that many of the earlier generation of scientists had been, and in the Cold War were often still, "leftwing" or "radical," and that their view of the world scene was therefore so much the better for it. These included the British bio-chemist and authority on Chinese science Joseph Needham, who supported the Chinese Communist allegation of American germ warfare, on the grounds that reputable mainland Chinese scientists had confirmed it to him! But above all, Snow cited the British physicist J. D. Bernal, a "militant Marxist." And later, in his high-establishment Rede Lecture, in which he first put forth his "two cultures" argument, he said that "scientists have the future in their bones," citing Bernal's *World without War*, against George Orwell's *1984.*

Bernal, whose politics and political writing were totally Stalinist, was, as it happens, a target of Orwell's. Bernal had urged an "ever-closer understanding between Britain and the USSR." In an editorial in *Polemic*, Orwell asked if he meant that Britons could move freely in the Soviet Union and that Soviets were to be encouraged to read British newspapers, listen to the BBC, and "view the institutions of this country with a friendly eye." And he answered himself, "Of course he didn't," all he meant was that "Russian propaganda in our country should be intensified and that critics of the Soviet regime (darkly referred to as 'subtle disseminators of mutual suspicion') should be silenced."

Snow himself was a sort of democrat sort of socialist. But it is his record on the USSR that stands out. He often visited, and was put up by, for instance, Yuri Zhdanov, earlier head of the party's Culture Department, but now demoted to be head of a university. He also frequented the conformist writers—eventually publishing in 1966 a collection of Soviet short stories, in the preface of which he argued that we should not look at Soviet literature with any political considerations in mind, accepting as fact such things as that "frontline soldiers in dugouts sang the war poems of Surkov [Stalinist hack]."

The phrase "cold war" occurred frequently in this preface. It meant drawing attention to any facts or expressing any opinions unpalatable to the Soviet leadership. Snow assured us that it was wicked to look at Soviet literature with any political considerations in mind, since we would not do so with the literature of other cultures. This really is fantastic! Soviet literature, as we were told day in and day out by Soviet politicians, cultural bureaucrats, and orthodox writers themselves, was (or should be) "a weapon for Communism."

In a country where a good deal remained unpublished for political reasons, it was impossible to look at what was published without some consideration of what made it acceptable. And the fact that when the cultural bureaucrats relaxed a little, a literature of moderately outspoken revolt immediately started getting published was something to which one could not simply blind oneself. But of course the Snows (his wife was cosignatory) did not mean what they said. They would have had us accept Soviet literature as indicating the hearty adherence of Soviet writers to the Soviet establishment—a political message was all right, you see, as long as it was on their side. But Snow found it possible at the same time to maintain that Soviet writers could reproach English ones with "being too willing to distort the truth for the sake of the drama."

For Snow, Soviet literature was produced by writers "devoted to" their country's political system and, in spite of disputes among themselves, in general accord with the party and with each other. Though the older ones had lived through difficult history and had had bad times, "they were always respected by their colleagues, even in the middle of bitter disagreement." And that is all Snow had to say about the troubles of literary men in a country where large numbers perished in labor camps or before firing squads or committed suicide; where, as Snow's book came out, Olga Ivinskaya, the literary executor of the country's greatest writer, Boris Pasternak, himself lately dead in disgrace, was in jail for attempting to secure the publication abroad of his surviving works.

Snow thus consciously aligned himself not only with the British establishment, which is bad enough, but with the worst foreign one he could turn up. One is reminded of the controversy between Lord Acton and Bishop Creighton, when the Anglican Creighton was inclined to excuse Pope Innocent III's persecutions on administrative grounds, while the Catholic Acton condemned them absolutely for reasons of inhumanity. Each of these solidarities—the bureaucratic and the humanist—in fact transcend mere political and religious allegiance.

Many Communists kowtowed less deeply than Snow. He remains an exhibit of a certain habit of mind.


3.

Simone de Beauvoir


It is only reasonable that we should include a French representative among our misleaders—it was, after all, France where the attitude flourished most greatly before it imploded a few decades ago. But who? Sartre and others have been winnowed (one hopes) to dust. But de Beauvoir is someone known (and published) in the English-speaking world; and, as a bonus, an example of the attitude as applied to China.

The main interest of Simone de Beauvoir's China book *The Long March* is that it gives the reader a postmortem chance to see for himself the qualities that once dazzled a lot of people. Yet it also presents, in an extreme form, the abstract bitterness that is to be noted in some degree even among the intellectuals of the English-speaking countries, and this reductio ad absurdius can illuminate the absurdum we had here already. Then, too, it might be thought to gain a sort of Draculan vitality by attaching to what was more or less a live issue—the lasting tenderness of some of our own little Bourbons towards Asian totalitarianism.

Throughout five hundred tedious pages, de Beauvoir sneeringly refutes the arguments of anonymous or unrecognizable Aunt Sallies. She denounces others for not giving firsthand information but herself quotes party novels as true descriptions of how things happened! (This was, of course, before the intellectuals took advantage of a brief "thaw' to tell quite a different story. Her own leading informant, the veteran Chinese woman writer Ting Ling, was among those purged for such liberties.) But in any case, de Beauvoir denounces hostile firsthand information as suspect too. She takes the line that the existence of *any* false charges against the Maoist leaders clears them completely (just as, no doubt, the Nazis are to be acquitted because one accusation against them, of responsibility for the Katyn massacre, was a viciously motivated invention). But if all unofficial information was to be dismissed as manufactured by evil propagandists in Hong Kong, official admissions were no good either, for they were quoted "out of context." It would be interesting to know how one can quote out of context, to take one example, the admission by the Kwantung executive that as soon as it was (temporarily) permitted, there was a mass exodus of peasants from the collective farms, which the author saw as both voluntary and popular.

De Beauvoir's other main lines of argument involve justifying things on the grounds that there were abuses in the West too (on the principles Orwell defined, in *The Lion and the Unicorn*, as "two blacks make a white, half a loaf is the same as no bread") and pointing to the undoubted faults of the old regime. The sort of intellectual chicanery she was capable of may be seen in her attitude to the official admission that the peasantry showed no enthusiasm for expropriating and executing the "landlords," so that party militants had to be sent in to take charge of the matter. The peasants really *did* want to do as the party ordered, she argues, but needed these intruders to help them to shake off the "hypnosis" the landlords had them under. A real Jacquerie!

She justifies the controlled press on the grounds that only thus could the regime "explain" things to a hitherto uninformed population—as, of course, in the case of the "germ warfare" hoax. More often in her arguments there is not even this residual intellectualism, but just inept propagandist inaccuracy. For example, she asserts that Soviet economic assistance was "disinterested" and not a "deal," on the grounds that the Soviet Union did not want and could not transport Chinese wheat. The terms of the three relevant agreements (1950, 1954, and 1956), even as published, provided for full Chinese repayment: wheat was not mentioned, but various other types of goods were—and, failing them, gold or U.S. dollars. And she attributes the destruction of Manchurian industry solely to the Japanese and the nationalists. Most of it was actually due to the Soviet looting of machinery (estimated in the Paulley Report as the value of two billion dollars), admitted to by the Soviets themselves in a note of January 1946 to the then Chinese government, justifying it as "war booty."

But maltreatment of facts is, after all, only a minor component in that unique Sartrean blend of intellectual and moral disintegration which most Frenchmen would have been ashamed to learn was presented to an Anglo-

American audience as the fine flower of *la logique*. There is something a little un-Voltairean, is there not, in Catholics being accused of preferring a "flashy martyrdom," which they could have avoided by submitting to government control? But let us take a point on which everything I have said about the author's methods of argument and standards of moral judgment is demonstrated with clinical purity. She deals with "family and country allegiances." In China, if these conflict, she argues, "country must be chosen; but the same applies in the West when similar conflicts arise." She gives an example: a French racing driver who finished the course after hearing of his brother's death. In war, too, French parents were prepared to see their sons risk their lives "in Indo-China, in Algeria." Owing to considerations of cash, "bourgeois" blood ties were less firm than those encouraged in China, and hence the bourgeoisie was hypocritical in damning the Maoists on this issue. In addition, in a revealing footnote, de Beauvoir argues that "the entire Right praised the conduct of the Francoist general who let his son be shot rather than surrender the Alcazar," while if a son had done the same by his father in the Chinese Civil War, horror would have been expressed.

You see at once the barren dichotomy—if you are not pro-Mao, you are bourgeois, "Right," or pro-Franco. You note the crude "you're another" method of defending an alleged abuse. What is not immediately evident is what exactly it was about the state's attitude to the family that was deplored by some observers of the Chinese scene. To take a single example, an article appeared in the official *China Youth* at about the time de Beauvoir was in the country. The author, Chen Yi, was dealing with letters from young people who felt loath to denounce their relatives. First a girl was told why it was her duty to put the finger on her husband. Then advice was given to a youth whose father, though no longer a practicing counterrevolutionary, had once been a despotic landlord. This is how one of the young comrade's qualms was dealt with:

> *You wonder how you are going to face your father if, instead of being sentenced to death, he is afterwards set free. If your father is not sentenced to death, but released by the government authorities after they have educated and reformed him, why should he retain enmity against you or seek to harm you on the sly if he has really reformed and intends to start life as a new person? He will even be grateful to the government and to you for his salvation. However, if he has not yet truly reformed and retains enmity against you, you can still denounce him again.*

And in fact there were literally hundreds of cases of such familial denunciation reported in the Maoist press, often followed by ceremonies of congratulation for the young denouncers, as with the public award of the title of "model security worker" to a Shanghai student for reporting his father. A Chengchow high school boy was specially commended: he had actually assisted in carrying out his father's arrest. Are these acts strictly comparable with those of the racing driver, the soldier's parents, the Franco general? Might not de Beauvoir's old mentors in the philosophy department at the Sorbonne have muttered "*distinguo*"?

To turn from this to the true voice of French left-wing humanism, we may choose Camus' analysis. The motive, he said, of these pseudo-leftists with a "passion for slavery" was not that they loved the totalitarians, but that "they heartily detest part of the French." For all their double-talk, "none of the evils which totalitarianism claims to remedy is worse than totalitarianism itself." He added, and the words applied elsewhere in the West too, "the Left is in full decadence, a prisoner of words," needing as treatment "pitiless criticism, the use of the heart, sound reasoning and a little modesty." Hitherto, the essential Frenchwoman—Héloïse or Mlle de Lespinasse or whoever—has always and everywhere been admired for sensitivity and intelligence. Even the *tricoteuses* have probably been maligned; at least it is not alleged that they let their knitting get into such a fearful tangle.

4.

John Kenneth Galbraith

Another, like Snow, from highish-level establishment circles. And also one accepted, or listened to, largely because he presents his themes in a way persuasive to such a public, which is not so common among (let alone respected among) the professional economists. To take a pundit seriously on these grounds is (as in a different way in Hobsbawm's and Snow's cases) like saying, "This is a beautifully printed and finely bound railway timetable." Yes, but its train times are wrong.

Galbraith's comments on the Soviet Union in 1985, when the system was on the point of collapse, are worth citing, if only to illustrate a lasting defect in his point of view: "The Soviet system has made great economic progress in recent years. One can see it in the appearance of solid well-being of the people in the streets." And he felt able to say that, unlike the West, the Soviet Union "makes full use of its manpower." This last is about as far from the reality as it would be possible to imagine. But Galbraith's longer-term takes on the regime were more theoretical—in particular, his view that the Communist and Western systems were "converging."

My first direct encounter with this argument was when, giving evidence to a U.S. Senate committee, I described Galbraith's position as a belief that since "we have factories, they have factories," convergence would follow. Galbraith wrote me, calling on me to apologize to the senators. I replied that my phrase was, and was obviously intended as, a simplification, but that not much simplification was needed—and supported this by a number of quotations from him. He replied that if I wouldn't apologize, he'd rebut me to the senators himself.

As it happened, I had to testify to the same committee some months later, and this time I went to the trouble of relying on actual quotations. The supposed economic convergence seen in Western and Soviet-style operations appeared in reality to amount to little more than the fact that certain organizational forms were, or were believed to be, particularly suitable for modern industrial production. Galbraith told us (in the *Times*, October 8, 1969) that "the cultural shock in passing from Magnitogorsk to Pittsburgh is infinitely less than in going from either of these cities to a typical farming village (the archetypal economic form) in China or India." The relationship between the individual and the "industrial and public bureaucracy" was, he felt, the same. Even in the broadest sense, it is difficult to see that such resemblances should automatically be regarded as having any deeper significance than, say, the fact that the old Ford mass-production methods were practiced in the automobile factories of Hitlerite Germany and Stalinist Russia.

It is just as true that Düsseldorf under the Nazis and Pittsburgh or Wolverhampton under our system resembled each other *outwardly* and *economically* more than any of them resembled a village in the Scottish Western Isles or the Australian Outback. In fact, a sleight of hand has been performed, by which economic and material resemblances are taken, almost without argument, to imply (in fact, actually to *be*) cultural resemblances. Obviously, there is an important sense in which this assumption is unreal.

It is rather as if one should say that silver miners in the Nevada of 1900 were more like the silver-mining slaves of the Laurion mines in ancient Greece than they were like Middle Western farmers today because they both performed the same physical and economic functions. But even economically speaking, it was not the case that the workers or others in a town like

Sverdlovsk were living lives similar to those of citizens of Milan or Pittsburgh. The determining element seems to be the political culture (or culture in general) that soaks into one's bones rather than the question of whether one is riding a bicycle or not.

Again, Galbraith stated his position: "the two systems have a broadly convergent tendency" because "both communities are subject to the common imperatives of large-scale industrial production with advanced technology." In no fewer than four places in this declaration he tells us that we must, or might, "assume" some point about the USSR. But assumptions drawn from preconceptions are not the best way of describing a real polity. Galbraith also said, "The nature of technology, the nature of the large organizations that sustain technology, and the nature of the planning that technology requires—has an imperative of its own, and this is causing a convergence in all industrial societies" (*New York Times*, December 18, 1966).

To accept economic determinism, even to this degree, seems very peculiar in the late twentieth century. Marx and Engels were writing in a period when the economic forces were extremely powerful and the political ones comparatively weak. Even then, Engels could remark that "Force is itself an economic power."

Galbraith argued that those who disagreed with his views on "convergence" were such people as, on the one side, "right-wing members of the military and diplomatic bureaucracy in the United States" and, on the other, old-fashioned Communist dogmatists. By this ploy, he seems to have wished to say that all decent moderates and liberals everywhere must accept his line or lose their status. But the argument was a quite false one. In an exchange with Ota Šik, the minister in charge of the economy during Alexander Dubček's regime in Czechoslovakia, Galbraith put the view that in capitalist countries the monopolists impose prices and create fictitious necessities by brainwashing methods, and he implied that this was not the case in the East. Šik replied that in the Communist countries centralized and bureaucratized planners had, in fact, become the greatest monopolists in history, while the citizen had no possibility at all of choosing his purchases or discussing the prices. He added that in Czechoslovakia vast quantities of goods were produced which were often quite useless and simply rotted; that the price indices were often falsified; that 65 percent of Czech exports were made at a loss, having been produced simply to fulfill the production plans; that most machinery (tractors, for example) weighed two or three times more than elsewhere, because the execution of the plan depended on the quantity of raw materials used and not on the number of machines produced. Galbraith declared that he felt himself "a little more Marxist" than Šik. Šik, a reformist Communist if ever there was one, said that Galbraith knew nothing of the Communist countries and had little knowledge of what Marxism meant either. (This exchange took place at a conference held in Switzerland, of which the protocols have never been published in full.) But Šik's book *The Third Way* offers a cooler, though revealing, critique of the Galbraith position. Similarly, on our side of the line, the most effective demolition of Galbraithism came from that distinguished socialist thinker the late George Lichtheim, in his *A Short History of Socialism*.

As to the late Soviet standard of living, this was, in its essentials, lower than in 1914 not only for the peasant but even for the worker, as could be deduced from Soviet statistical manuals. Much else more impressionistically confirms this fact. For example, Stalin's daughter, Svetlana Alliluyeva, said in passing that her grandfather, a skilled worker in Petrograd in the second decade of this century, had a four-room apartment—she says, "as much as a Soviet professor could dream of today." Again, Khrushchev once mentioned in a speech that as a young miner during World War I (and of all workers, miners were allegedly the most exploited) he had a motorbike. Professor Richard Pipes of Harvard at this time summed up to another Senate subcommittee:

> *The Soviet citizen today is poor not only in comparison with his counterpart in other European countries, but also in comparison with his own grandfather. In terms of essentials—food, clothing and housing—the Soviet population as a whole is worse off than it was before the Revolution and in the 1920s. If one considers such intangibles as access to information and the right to travel as elements the Soviet citizen today is poor not only in comparison with his counterpart in other European countries, but also in comparison with his own grandfather. In terms of essentials—food, clothing, of the standard of living—as they should be—then the Soviet citizenry is positively destitute.*

Peter Drucker remarks in *The Age of Discontinuity* that a time-traveling economist from 1913, knowing nothing of intervening wars and revolutions, would, on arriving in the 1970s, find nothing not already included in his extrapolations for that time (apart from the industrial and commercial advances of Taiwan, Hong Kong, and Singapore), except perhaps the poverty of Russian farming. In fact, the last years of tsardom saw the beginning of the establishment, for the first time, of an independent and productive peasantry. In 1913, grain production ran at 820 kilograms per hectare. Fifty years later, after the Russian equivalent of the mechanization revolution on the farms, it had gone up (officially) to 950.

I have not made a public or other apology! Nor received one.

5.

## CNN's *Cold War*

The most highly publicized intrusion of myth and misapprehension met with lately has been Ted Turner's CNN production *Cold War*, which aired in 1998. The attitude can be checked in the companion book to the television documentary, *Cold War: An Illustrated History, 1945–1991*, by Jeremy Isaacs and Taylor Downing. We may start with its treatment of individuals. Its view of Lenin and others of his persuasion in fact contrasts markedly with its treatment of Western leaders. (We have already quoted it in Chapter VIII.)

What is wrong is not only the inadequacy of the book's assessment of a benign Lenin but its simplification of motive beyond the complexities and contradictions inherent in human character. It may, perhaps, also help us to gain a broader view of Lenin if we quote a comment of his (on religion, though in the same tone as his denunciations of other reprobates) in a letter of November 13–14, 1913:

> *Every religious idea, every idea of God, even flirting with the idea of God, is unutterable vileness . . . of the most dangerous kind, "contagion" of the most abominable kind. Millions of sins, filthy deeds, acts of violence and physical contagions . . . are far less dangerous than the subtle, spiritual idea of God decked out in the smartest "ideological" costumes. . . . Every defence or justification of God, even the most refined, the best intentioned, is a justification of reaction. (V. I. Lenin,* Polnoe sobranie sochinenii, *5th ed., vol. 48 [1964])*

When it comes to the Soviet spies Burgess, Maclean, and Philby, we are told in the book *Cold War* that "they acted from political conviction. They believed what they were doing was right." The same could be said of agents of Nazism like John Amery. But in any case, this is (again) a simplistic point.

On a different approach, but less simplistic, the poet Stephen Spender, who knew the three British spies (and to some extent sympathized with them), noted in his *Journals, 1939–1983,* "what they all had was the arrogance of manipulators. . . . Perhaps this was in part because they had voluntarily put themselves at the service of their Russian manipulators . . . their faith in a creed whose mixture of sanctity, bloodiness and snobbery gave them a sense of great personal superiority."

When the CNN book deals with Western political figures, we are on different ground. Richard Nixon is shown in the Hiss case as motivated solely by ambition. No doubt that played a role, but only a merely adversarial assessment could fail to consider that he might have had good motives too (but, as we shall see, "anti-Communism," unlike "anti-Westernism," would in any case have disqualified him morally).

Ronald Reagan is treated in less hostile, but still hostile, fashion, as a simpleton: "Reagan's world was like an old Hollywood movie: he saw things in simple terms of right and wrong, with the Communists as the bad guys." Now, regardless of party or political views, this is at the level of caricature, and would not be taken as adequate by any serious historian. The opinion of the Soviet ambassador to Washington at the time, Anatoly Dobrynin, is much more positive. And, which is more important, not only more positive, but more nuanced. And indeed, Reagan emerges from recent research on his papers (by Kiron Skinner, for instance) as incomparably less shallow than the more or less hostile caricature.

On a further point, whether Reagan was justified, in effect, in seeing the confrontation in "black and white," the CNN writers may disagree with the idea that when it came down to essentials, the Soviet system was fundamentally hostile to and concerned to procure the end of what is usually called the Western democratic culture. But in any case, agree or no, this is, give or take a nuance, the view not merely of simpletons but of major historians in the field. (To be fair, the book's view of Reagan's policies and of his effectiveness changes, indeed contradicts itself, as we proceed.) And, we should note, not only Reagan but also Truman and George Marshall are treated in the same uninformed, patronizing way.

The book begins its chapter on Cold War excesses in the United States with a photograph of a mob of three men carrying posters demanding the execution of the Rosenbergs. This is evidently intended to be a typical or defining illustration. No serious study of the period, left or right, would assent. The effect, and presumably the purpose, is to arouse emotional hostility not merely towards those photographed but also towards all the "anti-Communists" dealt with in the chapter. And indeed, the book continually speaks of "possessed with hating Communism," "witch hunt," "paranoia," "hysterical."

As Orwell wrote, critics of the Soviet system were called "rabidly anti-Communist." And, Orwell added, in his four-volume *Collected Essays*,

> *if from time to time you express a mild distaste for slave-labour camps or one-candidate elections, you are either insane or actuated by the worst motives. In the same way, when Henry Wallace is asked by a newspaper interviewer why he issues falsified versions of his speeches to the press, he replies: "So you are one of those people who are clamouring for war with Russia." There is the milder kind of ridicule that consists in pretending that a reasoned opinion is indistinguishable from an absurd out-of-date prejudice. If you do not like Communism, you are a Red-baiter.*

The execution of the Rosenbergs was indeed a major emotional and moral issue. It was, in fact, deplored by many who accepted that the Rosenbergs were guilty of espionage, as of course is no longer denied. But the CNN book prints a supposed psychological explanation–by a hostile defense attorney!–of the *judge's* decision.

As to the Rosenbergs' own motives, we are told that they were part of "a network of spies who felt uncomfortable that the United States was the sole owner of the key to atomic warfare." This gives an arguably acceptable motive for their espionage activity, though since they never confessed and thus never advanced such a motive, it is one constructed for them by sympathizers. It has the further disadvantage of being factually untenable. Julius Rosenberg's allegiance to Communism dates from before the war, and he entered a Soviet espionage ring in 1942 in connection with technical secrets (radar systems, bombsights, naval gunnery, etc.) and was not until later involved in nuclear matters at all.

The Rosenberg case was indeed highly divisive of American opinion. But its treatment here implies that anti-Communist suspicions were all of a knee-jerk nature. This distorts and destroys legitimate debate. In his memoirs, George Kennan tells us,

> *The penetration of American governmental services by members or agents (conscious or otherwise) of the American Communist Party in the late 1930s*

*was not a figment of the imagination of the hysterical right-wingers of a later decade. Stimulated and facilitated by the events of the Depression, particularly on the younger intelligentsia, it really existed, and it assumed proportions which, while never overwhelming, were also not trivial. . . . By the end of the war, so far as I can judge from the evidence I have seen, the penetration was quite extensive. (Quoted in Arnold Beichman, "A Tribute to George Kennan,"* Washington Times, *February 23, 2004)*

The other matter is that it is true that American executive and legislative institutions initiated not only the exposure of some members of the Communist espionage rings (many others remain unidentified to this day) but also a much-publicized persecution of members of the American Communist Party—a campaign we call McCarthyism. Senator Joseph McCarthy disgraced and distorted the real and legitimate public concern. But even in the United States, the attempt to equate anti-Communism with McCarthyism is a grave distortion. There were many strong opponents of McCarthyism among the famous American liberal anti-Communists, who waged a strong and powerful struggle against both. Moreover, McCarthyism was an American phenomenon only, and countries like Britain, where governments, political parties, and the public equally opposed the Communist threat, never went through such an experience. On the contrary, the hysteria in Britain—and even more in France—was almost entirely from the anti-anti-Communist side.

The details of the Hollywood persecutions are clearly laid out in the CNN book, but the use of the expression "torture by the Inquisition" may seem excessive, especially if we compare it with, say, a Moscow example from the field of drama. The great producer Vsevolod Meyerhold, then in his sixties, wrote to the prison authorities that he could fortunately put his complaint on paper, as the interrogator Boris Rodos had only broken his left arm (and urinated in his mouth); and later, on the further beating of his already much-bruised legs, he wrote that it felt as if they were being plunged into boiling water. After months of this, he was shot.

By the best Western standards, the Hollywood inquiry was nevertheless an excess. One of the factors in this and other cases that the book does not present is, however, the nature of the CPUSA. Not a political party in the ordinary sense, it was (with several million dollars and until the late 1980s) heavily financed by Moscow (as is now fully documented; see Chapter IX). Moreover, whatever else members of Communist parties did, they were required to give full and uncritical support to all Soviet actions.

During the earlier part of World War II, before the Nazi invasion of the Soviet Union, the CPUSA exerted its power in certain trade unions to prevent aid to Britain. And it urged the persecution of anti-Soviet left-wing groups, such as the Trotskyites, appealing to the U.S. authorities to arrest and suppress these other radicals. The CPUSA joined in the denunciations of the Yugoslav Communists when, in 1948, they threw off Moscow's control. And so on.

The major point is that the CPUSA was run on Leninist principles, with all decisions of the center automatically binding on its members, but also with the equally Leninist corollary that all methods of infiltrating and defeating enemies were legitimate. Many ordinary members of the party were people of goodwill with radical views, and most could not in the long run stomach its tactics. But active members often found themselves, as it were, trapped in takeover power plays within the larger groups to which they belonged, in Hollywood as elsewhere. Thus, though the House and other committees victimized American Communists, and are understandably reprobated, there is (as is now generally recognized) another aspect to all this.

At any rate, here again we find not the "black-and-white" picture presented by the book, but, in many cases, a real moral dilemma. Those disillusioned members of the CPUSA who thought that true accounts should be given and "named names" are simply presented as the equivalent of school snitches. But they too thought they were carrying out a moral duty and were themselves the subject of various persecutions over the years—though we can now record that this is largely forgotten and forgiven even in Hollywood. And as to the substance of the matter, Arthur Schlesinger Jr. has pointed out that such criteria would not have been applied to similar "betrayals" by former members of American Nazi movements. Much the same could be said of how, as the great physicist and democrat Andrey Sakharov put it, the American scientific community treated Edward Teller "meanly" and of the treatment of others in the intellectual world who had done what they felt to be their duty. Here again the old feuds seem to be dying out among the intellectual public—though they are still pursued by such productions as CNN's. Some of these points may indeed be arguable. But they are not treated as even arguable by CNN, which takes a simple and partisan view.

Another example: the Kent State killings of 1970 were certainly a tragedy and a blot on the record of the United States. To say this is to judge it, quite rightly, by American standards. But such events in other countries are judged by different standards, and this is precisely what makes nonsense of the theme that both the democratic and Communist countries sinned or erred. Four students were killed at Kent State by panicky National Guards, at once ordered by their officers to stop. CNN quotes a "commission's" report that "a nation driven to use the weapons of war upon its youth is a nation on the edge of chaos." This is, of course, misleading hyperbole: it was not a "nation" that was responsible, nor did it attack its "youth"—phrases that might be more applicable to Tiananmen Square. That the sponsor of the book and the film, Ted Turner, later said that Kent State and Tiananmen Square are comparable is enough of a comment on this point. But again, such attitudes are not compatible with any normal educational criteria of knowledge and judgment.

Among the reasons the CNN documentary and book give for the Cold War, the main omission is a vital one: that is, the conception that the Marxist-Leninist creed saw the world as a scene of essential antagonisms and insisted that the conflict must be pursued until the overthrow of the non-Communist order the world over. As we have said, this motivation has been confirmed by former Politburo members, post-Soviet foreign ministers, and others, and was only abandoned by the last Soviet foreign minister, Eduard Shevardnadze, in 1990.

*Cold War*'s presentation of what is, after all, its central theme is notably different from that advanced in its leading U.S. historical adviser's book on the subject, *We Now Know*, by John Lewis Gaddis, in which he describes the attempts by prominent Soviet officials to persuade Stalin to initiate at least a period of comparative cooperation with the West (see Chapter XIII). The book implies, and this in a shallow and superficial fashion, that all Stalin wanted was a buffer area between him and the West, contrary to Litvinov's clear understanding.

On a broader scale, the conflict is represented in *Cold War* as one between two "ideologies"—sometimes defined as capitalism versus Communism—that is, in a sort of balance. But this is to misuse the word "ideology" and thus to avoid the difference between the pluralist and total-itarian viewpoints. "Totalitarianism," to be sure, is a word largely avoided by the CNN book when it deals with Stalinism, though it was used of the Soviet order by both Gorbachev and Yeltsin, and found adequate by such famed scholars as Leszek Kolakowski and Giovanni Sartori, and by many others of major repute, such as the French historian François Furet.

The foreign policies of the West are also subjected by CNN to what can only be called misrepresentation from very early on, when Allied "intervention" in Russia in 1918–19 is presented as a major effort to overthrow the Soviet regime and one that had a permanent impact on Moscow's attitudes. Now, first of all, the American "intervention" was minimal, and American troops only had one minor skirmish with local Bolsheviks. The British intervention, employing a couple of brigades, was larger. Asked in by the Soviets to block German presence in the far north, the British were briefly in action against the Bolsheviks, but their total casualties were a few hundred, some of them against non-Bolshevik forces. It is true that history as taught under Stalin made much of this "intervention," though the American component was scarcely mentioned until it became politically suitable, in the 1940s. And no serious scholar accepts the view presented in the CNN book.

It is true, of course, that the Allies supported the anti-Bolshevik regimes in the Civil War, including those based on the majority of the elected Constituent Assembly that Lenin had forcibly dissolved. It is equally relevant that Lenin regarded the whole struggle as part of an international revolution to be exported as and where possible, with attempts to capture Warsaw, the crushing of the Social Democratic Georgian Republic, and so on.

The book is also simply ridiculous, even at its own level: (for example, a half page on Beria as Stalin's "evil genius".) As with a photograph of an American and a Soviet soldier meeting as the armies crushed the Nazis in 1945, with a note about the horse-drawn Soviet army beating the motorized Germans. The opposite, if anything, is true. The Germans had been largely horse-drawn, even in 1941. In 1945, the Soviets were incomparably more mechanized, mainly with American trucks—as I saw myself in the Balkans and as also emerges in Solzhenitsyn's poem of his own war experience in *Prussian Nights*. (Nor does the book mention that the Russians who then contacted the Americans were as a result later arrested.)

When it comes to the Cold War period, we continually find such expressions as, in reference to U.S. actions after the Communist seizure of power in Prague, "Washington deliberately fanned the flames of anti-Communism." Or, to put it another way, expressed opposition to the action. Intemperate remarks by Western politicians and others are prominently figured. The far more pervasive and continual Soviet denunciations of bloodthirsty Western imperialism, with endless cartoons of Uncle Sam and John Bull—Tito too—wallowing in blood and with teeth like bayonets, which persisted right into the 1980s, hardly figure. And as to revealing remarks, it is odd not to find Stalin's telling the Yugoslav leaders in April 1945, "The war will soon be over. We shall recover in fifteen to twenty years, and then we'll have another go at it."

More than once, the CNN book uses expressions like "left-leaning governments" as the targets of American policy. This is an evasion. Many left-leaning governments, such as the Socialist ones in Britain, Norway, Germany, and elsewhere, were among America's stoutest allies. "Left-leaning" is therefore a code word for "pro-Soviet"—quite a different thing.

Much space is devoted to American support for the anti-Communist parties and trade unions, left and right, in Italy, France, and elsewhere with, again, the Communists represented in a favorable light. We are told that though the Italian Communist leader Palmiro Togliatti had "spent the war years in Moscow, he was no stooge of the Kremlin," and sought to develop a form of Communism suited to Italy and opposed to tyranny, a program that appealed to many. This is followed by an account of the American financial and other assistance provided to the non-Communist democratic parties in Italy's 1947 election.

As to facts, Togliatti had been in Moscow not merely in the war but in the early 1930s as one of the half dozen top leaders of the Stalinist Communist International, and he sponsored many of its lethal purges. After Stalin's death in 1953, he occasionally developed a rather independent stance but remained generally committed to the Soviet Union. The program Togliatti put forward in 1947 did indeed appeal to a large public. So did the program of the Czechoslovak Communist Party before it took power, when it imposed one of the worst of the Stalinist dictatorships. The implication that Togliatti could simply be trusted is a strange one. And we may add to our view of the matter a detail that has recently emerged from Hungarian archives and has been published in *The First Domino,* by Johanna Granville. In Moscow on November 7, 1957, opinions of all the Communist leaders about executing Hungarian premier Imre Nagy were taken. Only Wladyslaw Gomulka, then head of the Polish United Workers' Party, disapproved, but Togliatti, while approving, asked that it be put off until after the Italian elections! The Americans are nevertheless presented as putting unfair pressure on or exerting unfair influence on the Italian electorate—mainly by financial means. It is not mentioned that the Italian Communist Party was itself heavily financed by the Soviets.

A further point is that after the elections, the Italian Communist Party remained free to operate, while in every country where a Communist regime had come to power, whether through elections or otherwise, the democratic parties had all been suppressed and their leaders killed or jailed. They too had promised liberty; indeed, liberty for all anti-Fascist parties was guaranteed in the Hungarian, Romanian, and Bulgarian peace treaties.

A constant theme is that Moscow had a legitimate fear of Western aggression. We are told, for example, that a million U.S. troops abroad were "all threatening the Soviet Union." They were, of course, much outnumbered by the Soviet army. More telling yet is the fact that right up to the end of the Cold War, the Communist armies in East Germany were on short notice to invade the West, while NATO troop deployment was wholly defensive.

There is notable inadequacy too on the issue of nuclear weapons. For example, it might have been thought evidential to include the fact that in 1948, although the United Nations Scientific and Technical Committee (to which the question of atomic development was referred and which included Russian and Polish scientists and the French Communist professor Frédéric Joliot-Curie) reported unanimously in September 1946 that inspection and control over the whole process of production was desirable and technically possible, the Soviet representatives rejected all plans incorporating this view as "an assault on State sovereignty" (Andrey Vyshinsky in the UN General Assembly, November 9, 1948). They also insisted on such limitations as were incompatible with the report of the Scientific Committee. As Vyshinsky put it in the Political Committee on November 10, 1949, "We are not obliged to subordinate ourselves or to render an account in this matter to any international organs."

More strikingly, on the development of the hydrogen bomb, we are told that Truman's decision to go ahead with it "fired the starter's pistol for the ultimate arms race." But as the USSR's leading nuclear physicist, Andrey Sakharov, pointed out, the USSR was going ahead with the development of the bomb regardless of American work on it, and the CNN book itself notes that in fact Moscow achieved a deliverable bomb before the United States did.

There is much more to be said on the distortions in this book, including on muddled or misleading passages on Soviet internal matters, but more especially on such issues as Cuba, where Turner personally tips the balance even further. It would be appropriate here to mention that the most dangerous attitudes to nuclear war, as Sergei Khrushchev, Nikita Khrushchev's son, puts it in his chapter on the Cuban missile crisis of 1962, were those of "Castro and Guevara," a point worth making when the latter is again being given high praise in the West. Turnerites would doubtless be with those who argue that at any rate Guevara "meant well." This defense has been, and still is, used of such figures, and their actions, from Lenin on—of the whole array of leaders and accomplices who carried out extreme physical coercion and mental constriction in the Communist states, and of the long Soviet effort to transform or subjugate the rest of the world. They demanded not merely absolution, but even approbation, on "long-term" moral grounds. As Vasily Grossman, the fine Soviet author and co-editor of *The Black Book*, on the Holocaust (suppressed in the USSR and only published in 1984), wrote of the Nazi genocide, "The sun has been extinguished by the smoke of the gas-ovens. And even these crimes, crimes never before seen in the universe, have been committed in the name of good."

## Chapter XV

# A Collapse of Unreality

---

### 1.

The speed of the Communist collapse above all shows how overdue it was. This can be seen not so much in the economic (and ecological) failure of the system as in the fact that the political and ideological superstructure had been so strong that it had been able to maintain itself, long after the objective conditions had rolled away, from inside this impressive-looking carapace.

The realities had made themselves unavoidably known to the lower, more awake levels of the apparat itself even in Russia over twenty years before they penetrated first the regime's own rank and file and then, after further delay, the leadership itself.

As Timothy Garton Ash noted in the 1980s, the condition for the final collapse was above all the crumbling of belief in the system. It was an irreversible failure of faith or belief, or nerve. Any analysis that misses this is superficial. In the West, however, there were still pockets of resistance to these realities, like the Japanese soldiers in World War II who fought on in isolated jungles unaware of the regime's collapse.

### 2.

But we can go further: the Soviet and East European Communists managed to deceive a number even of those who came into their countries from the West. The stupefying effect on Russia and the other Communist countries of the compulsory acceptance of Stalinist falsehood has had long-lasting and deleterious effects. For Westerners whose acceptance was not compulsory, the stupefaction still worked. And Westerners who came prepared to disbelieve their own eyes seem to have become increasingly addicted. And this in spite of the system's showing total incompetence even in falsifying the simplest and most obvious side of its public appearance, as any visitor to exhibitions designed as its show places for foreigners and as any visitors to the Intourist Hotel in Moscow were incessantly reminded. Moreover, as Garton Ash also noted, whole institutes in West Germany were based on investigating at firsthand and misunderstanding the East German economy. Anyone who went between Lübeck and Stettin, a distance of a few score miles, on the morrow of collapse, or even more between Helsinki and Vyborg, noticed the astonishing difference of mere day-to-day levels of civilization. The dreary, beggar-ridden, hopeless, unmaintained streets of Vyborg, part of the same country as Helsinki fifty years earlier, might have been from some medieval plague-and-rat-ridden scene.

3.

One has seen it argued that Russians were better off in the late Soviet period than earlier. It is clear that the basic economy was declining fast, and the ecology with it. The only thing to be said in support of the proposition is that, as Khrushchev put it, Stalin could enforce deprivation to a degree that even a slightly more relaxed government hardly could—though he could still largely prevent the population's knowledge of the West. Even so, the USSR only survived because of the export of oil.

Various conclusions are now put forward about the fall of the system. These boil down to a couple of propositions. The first is that living standards have been lower since the fall of the Soviet order. This is no more than to say, when the rations almost give out on a desert journey because of the incompetence and greed of the guides, that the feeding was better before their exposure.

The other approach, on a different but related matter, is to argue that the system would have collapsed in any case, so that there is no reason to give any weight to our huge investment in the pursuit of international peace and democracy. But, as Gorbachev himself put it, the Soviet economy was ruined by, above all, "insane militarisation," which is to say that the attempt to outstrip or otherwise destroy the resistance of the West was indeed economically suicidal (and not only economically).

A major factor in the academic and general dispute over the Soviet-Western relationship was in fact this notion (still around today!) that the Communist sphere was not doing badly in regard to its economy and ecology. As Alain Besançon wrote, direct observation and testimony gave a picture so different from that often found in Western academe that there seemed no way to reconcile them.

Even a whole series of days of food riots in half a dozen cities under the Khrushchev regime went unnoticed. If we imagine similar events here—food riots; strikes; nationalist demonstrations in Warrington, Bristol, Cardiff; scores shot; hundreds arrested—we may form some picture of the social and political pressures involved. The dispatch of two Politburo members (and very senior ones, Anastas Mikoyan and Frol Kozlov) to Novocherkassk during the riots there in 1962 was exactly on a par with the Soviet sending of two such representatives to Budapest in October 1956. Perhaps more remarkable still, the mutiny of the Soviet warship *Storozhevoy* in November 1975 aroused little comment. But if such a mutiny, and such an attempt to take a vessel into a neutral port, had taken place in the British or American navies, would we not have heard a terrific outcry about the collapse of morale? Indeed, it was an extraordinary event and a remarkable symptom.

## 4.

The social order of the USSR too, at its best, bore little resemblance to the official conception of it, to the party picture. Above all, it was both politically and economically class-ridden. Even members of the ruling elite had, in some respects, fewer political rights than ordinary members of the adult population in the West. For example, they had no right to suggest that the economic and political system itself was faulty. Below them, with privilege and a financial commitment to the status quo but with negligible power in a political sense, was the important stratum of members of lower committees, factory directors, and so on. And below those, the masses.

As to productivity, in what is now seen as its best period, under Brezhnev, the USSR used eight times as many workers as the United States, working on 30 percent more arable land per head, to produce less than 90 percent of the American grain total for a population 20 percent larger. American farmers were getting one pound of beef for every eight to nine pounds of feed; in the Soviet Union the proportion was one pound of beef per fifteen pounds of feed. The target for the Five-Year Plan was to raise milk output to three thousand kilograms per cow per year; an efficient British farm got about six thousand kilograms.

Even the record 1977 harvest was about 10 percent below what the country needed to feed its population and livestock. The USSR had to *import* not merely from the West but even from the not particularly efficient countries of the Soviet bloc itself. Yet when a Politburo member, Gennadiy

Voronov, suggested a measure of relaxation as the only way to improve agricultural production, he was dismissed.

Strictly speaking, the Soviet economy was not an economy at all, in the sense that its operations were in principle governed not by economic laws but by decisions taken preponderantly on a political-ideological basis. It was, that is to say, an economy only in the sense that distribution of goods in a barracks or a prison can be so considered. This naturally raises the point that barracks and prisons are notoriously susceptible to the development of a "real economy," in which supply sergeants and trusties are much involved. This was, of course, the case in the USSR too, and we may regard it as the lubricant without which the official economy could not work at all. Still, it was only a partial and inadequate lubricant, and the Soviet economy could only be kept going by the application, in the long run, of excessive force—which is to say that an economy organized on Soviet principles is inconceivable without strong administrative pressures. Thus, the mere structure of economic organization, determined by ideological creed, involved a command system of a very rigorous, though necessarily inefficient, type.

The first striking indication of radical change I myself came across was the first time I met Gorbachev, when he was still in power. We had a small seminar for him at Stanford University, during which a seismology professor noted that an Armenian earthquake that occurred at about the same time and was of the same intensity as the Californian one of 1989 had had a much higher casualty rate. Was this due to its largely hitting old villages, for in California more recent structures were held to anti-earthquake building laws? No, answered Gorbachev, we too had such laws in Soviet Armenia, but they were not enforced. Here was the country's leader emerging from the whole Soviet tradition of falsification. And, of course, he was also strongly presenting the point that the total state, which on paper was far more powerful than those of the West, was in fact less efficacious when it came to social realities.

Eric Hobsbawm writes that historians failed to predict the collapse of the Soviet Union. Not this historian (and others) who said, in effect, that the system was not viable and was heading towards a complete crisis. Nor did you have to be a historian to see that. It was clear to Orwell. The precise nature and timing of the breakdown could not have been predicted, of course (though certain elements in it seemed fairly probable). As Garton Ash points out in his *The Uses of Adversity*, on the issues raised by Orwell, only one view has survived—Orwell's.

### 5.

The confrontation with the West was, like the ruin of the economy, a product of the mental distortions of the Soviet order. The "insane militarisation" Gorbachev spoke of was a symptom of the mind-set that prevailed, which required an unceasing struggle with all other cultures. And, above all, it was a militarization the Soviet economy was unable to make decisive, even through ruining itself in the attempt. So the only way the West could have been put in an impossible position was if it could have been prevented from responding with adequate armament. And since this was not physically possible, it would have to have been secured by other means—that is, by inducing the West not to respond to the real threat. This could only be done by in some way destroying or radically weakening the West's will to respond adequately. And this was, of course, the aim of Soviet propaganda and diplomacy and the general effort to mislead the Western peoples and governments.

This was undertaken, with a long-drawn-out production of false claims of devotion to peace and, unbelievably, to freedom, goodwill, and all the other amicable evidence of progress and liberty. Though some elements in the West were sweetened, or silenced, by this ploy, it failed, just as the economy had failed to outmatch the West's response. The main reason for this failure was, of course, that the realities of Soviet actions and intentions could only be concealed by an enormous and, as it turned out, inadequate effort.

This big question remains. In the Soviet bloc itself, all who reached any reasonable level of knowledge or judgment were aware of and repelled by the actualities. It was outside that zone that the Soviets had a measure of success. And this is, above all, fearful evidence of the murky mental atmosphere we have tried to analyze and detoxify in these pages.

This was in part owing to the whole Stalinist heritage, but most of all to the brain-numbing atmosphere; in addition to being the product of an abnormal mental setup, the Soviet establishment was, or the larger part of it was (at the highest level), stupid. It was the product of a party that had well under ten thousand members in 1910 and over the postrevolutionary years had been purged of all tendencies to see reality in terms other than dull fantasy.

### 6.

It is not our purpose here to examine the current and future state of Russia. It is clear that the huge mental and physical distortions inflicted on the population, and the painful emergence from "Under the Rubble," have not been anything like fully overcome. And it has been reasonably argued that the mental regression of most of the last century has left in much of the nation's consciousness the remnants of earlier unprogressive cultural attitudes. Russia's history, and with it its habits of thought, are not those of the West. Or rather, the flowering of civilization in the country, from Pushkin on, was largely confined to a nondecisive urban stratum (and that not in all cities).

An example, odd though striking, from the Russian past was given by the physicist S. I. Vavilov in a collection of essays on the fiftieth anniversary of Karl Marx's death, in 1933 (see "The Old and the New Physics," in N. I. Bukharin and others, *Marxism and Modern Thought*, English edition published in 1935). He asks, "How are we to explain such an amazing fact as the lack of any science (even pseudoscience) in old pre-Peter-the-Great Russia? The 'history of science,' which has officially existed for thousands of years, is still not able to answer such questions."

Those eras are, indeed, hard to grasp without a clear imaginative feeling for the great differences between the Russian and Western experiences, a factor always threatened by the scarcely conscious habits of Western academic parochialism. Still, most historians would accept such cruxes as that the Magna Carta came in 1215, and the first Mongol invasion of Russia only a few years later; that the period of Mongol rule saw a regime of unprecedented tortuous intrigue; that the centuries that followed were of "absolutist" rule in a far more unrestrained way than what were called "absolutist" in Western Europe; that Peter the Great sought to "modernize" and "Europeanize" Russia by despotic methods; that in the nineteenth century a revolutionary intelligentsia with no experience of real politics emerged—to take a few of the necessary framework girders. Much useful work and valuable research on this past has been done, a great deal of it, in Russia over the past fifteen years.

To have destroyed an ideocracy is a great advance. But there are many states in the world that have reached that level and yet still have far to go.

7.

The current condition of Russia is deplorable in a number of ways. Yet we may note that a revolutionary transition took place without total disruption.

In 1991, Russia was not in the position that Germany—West Germany—was in in 1945, when a democratic or open society could be built almost from scratch. One result of the less complete and more gradual changes in Russia is that a huge burden of both physical and mental trappings and actualities of the past remain.

So we have a Russia with thousands of warheads and a chauvinistic tinge. We coped, the world coped, with a much worse Russia.

It has been, and will continue to be, a long hard slog.

# Part III

# Harp Song

## *of the* Humanities

…the selfish and foolish hope of *reasoning* him into an approbation…

–William Wordsworth

In all ages there is a great battle against intelligence, against the arts, but the attack takes different forms in different epochs.

–Anthony Powell

*Chapter XVI*

# The Whys of Art

———— ∞∞∞ ————

1.

So far, we have presented thoughts and facts about the political and social order but, as yet, little on those other major endeavors of the mind we call the arts or the humanities–though they too are affected by at least some of the mental, and also the organizational, inadequacies dealt with in our previous chapters. The issues we covered earlier are, on the face of it, more urgent, but the troubles that beset the arts, though perhaps less amenable to diagnosis, may be thought relevant to the whole question of civilization. And their particular phenomena often seem to be melded with the attitudes we have noted in those other fields.

Changes in art and culture history have never been easy to assimilate to political or economic changes. But perhaps we have enough evidence to show that particular subideologies, combined with or supported by a bureaucratic upsurge, have caused, or been associated with, what appear to be downhill trends. Different generations naturally engender different styles. No harm in that. Still, it can be argued that some fashions in the field are less troublesome than others.

In an analysis of this sort, one cannot exclude subjectivity, and to that extent, one must agree with Wordsworth. When a writer finds spokesmen of a new generation not susceptible to his or others' earlier work, several notions may occur to him. First, that tastes change, Francis T. Palgrave wrote, editing the second *Golden Treasury*, "nothing, it need scarcely to be said, is harder than to form an estimate, even remotely accurate, of one's own contemporary poets." So, to judge art and culture is indeed, in part, to make a more subjective assessment of the aesthetics, which is of taste. And if one asserts that a current trend or current trends are negative, one is, of course, open to the retort that in various epochs, changes of taste have emerged, deplored by the representatives of earlier trends but later seen as having their own value. True, but it is equally true that some striking and popular new art has soon proved no more than a regrettable and temporary fad–as with the once universally acclaimed Ossian or the German poet Friedrich Klopstock.

Moreover, our cultural people, in the sense of producers of the arts defined as creative, are now in a strong and unprecedented relationship with the bureaucratic or establishmentarian world discussed earlier. (This is, paradoxically, at a time when many of these cultural people have entered a period of what one might call ostentatious transgressiveness, something on which indeed both they and their state, official, and academic sponsors pride themselves.) Of course, there is no reason to think that sections of the intelligentsia are any sounder on the arts than they are on politics or history. And, here again, they, as a phenomenon, form a far larger social stratum than at any time in the past. It might be argued that, as with the personnel of the state apparatus proper, there is now such a superfluity of the artistically and literary "educated" class that their very number is part of the means of coping with, and employing part of, the product.

There comes to a point, hard to define specifically but more or less obvious, when a regrettable general impression is unarguably convincing–well, not "unarguably," yet beyond serious debate. Still, an organism, or a polity, may present faults seen as lethal that are in practice comfortably contained and do not require therapy. Nor would one want there to be any implied use of power from outside institutions or individuals.

## 2.

Even apart from analytics, a great deal of nonsense has been talked or written about art, or rather Art. Some reflections seem to be in order.

The question of what constitutes "art," and what distinguishes good from less good art, is an old one. We can be certain that humanity was creating what we call art long before the word, or the concept, existed. And–a further complication–how is it that we all accept that some Paleolithic paintings are among the best of their kind and excel by any standards? Well, not all; there are presumably those who are beyond such acceptance. And in considering the paintings of Lascaux, Altamira, and elsewhere, the question arises: What did their creators *think* they were doing?

Not decorating–they did not live in the caves. So why did these men go deep into them, too deep to see, and paint by the light of cedar wicks set in grease-filled hollow stones? Why are the hooves of many, but not all, the cattle shown in twisted perspective?

"Magic" is a word often used of all this. But it is indisputable that this was not the "hunting magic" found in later, and more distant, "primitive" depictions. "Religious" is also often applied. But magic or religious in what way? We simply don't know—but one thing seems obvious: they did not think of their painting as something called "art." This point was reinforced a few years ago by an interview with a Nigerian village sculptor of some fine formal statuettes, I suppose you would call them. Asked why he carved them, he could only reply that this is what he did.

3.

Thucydides tells us, quoting Pericles, that the Athenians "philo-kaloumen . . . kai philosophoumen," loved both beauty and wisdom. Can the modern age combine philosophy and philokaly?

One problem, nowadays, is the sort of art in which "beauty" is not merely abandoned but replaced by a positive addiction to the unbeautiful, or the antibeautiful. It is true that "beauty" became sentimentalized and cosmetic from the early nineteenth century. So it is possible that we have now broadened and deepened the idea. One can see today, for example, the view of Verdi as among the finest; a commentator in the *New Yorker* (September 24, 2001) saying of a performance of *Otello* that was astonishingly—and unanalyzably—moving, "stripped of directorial brainstorms and interpretive ego trips with no attempt to deconstruct or recontextualize." Or, as Joseph Brodsky noted (of Ezra Pound), "beauty" must arise of itself and cannot just be added from outside.

When a Greek used *kalos,* which we conventionally translate "beautiful," of a city, or a weapon, or a harbor, or a virtue, we feel that his judgment of the practical and the moral was essentially aesthetic. But this was not so. He did not differentiate the categories. *Kalos* meant, in effect, "admirable" or "fine." Similarly, *arete,* which we translate as "virtue," was used of everything from a racehorse's speed to the skills of a fighter or an orator and is better translated simply as "excellence." In the Renaissance, there was a natural attempt to revive this attitude with the concept of *virtù,* but the distinction between goodness and beauty was already so firmly established that reaction from it led mainly to a mere conscious amoralism.

We, or others, have used the word "art" of a wide range of human action (as in the Art of War, the Art of Love). All the same, we differentiate between various skills and the value we give to each. Even though we may speak of "trapeze art," its artistry depends wholly on a skill. If a practitioner regularly falls, he will not be admired. (One could argue—indeed, I would—that in our days there are "artists" who, in effect, do regularly fall into the arena and yet do not forfeit their prestige.) William Hazlitt, of course, wrote similarly of Indian jugglers. On a slightly different level, I remember in the mid-1970s watching no television but the odd opera and Joe Montana playing for the 49ers. I was not deeply interested in American football as such, but to see this combination of, I suppose, skill and judgment . . .

In the broader context, medieval Scandinavians can be cited as having had a wide range of skills, some of them "artistic" in the modern usage: the law, the accumulated skills and experience of brilliant shipbuilding and shipsailing, and the making and handling of weapons. It is not that the main arts—narrative prose and gnomic verse—required any less sophistication than those of the present day; there was simply less of them. Fewer people were doing fewer things. This was as true culturally as it was socially. We may feel that Earl Rognvald of Orkney, boasting eight hundred years ago of his nine skills—as draughts player, runner, reader, smith, skier, archer, oarsman, poet, and harper—set a standard towards which we should all strive. All the same, such comprehensive mastery was exceptional even then. And nowadays, with an immense range of skills to be mastered, an enormous spectrum of individuality seeking an ever-wider variety in the arts, and a huge and diversely specialized volume of knowledge, any oneness we can expect in our culture cannot possibly be that of the centralized and unitary.

A certain amount of scientific knowledge on the part of writers is desirable as a matter of mere literacy. We can go further and expect some of this knowledge actually to enter imaginative literature. When Quintilian says in the *Institutio oratoria* that knowledge of astronomy is essential to a proper understanding of poets, he is describing a culture in which some such merging of science and art applied. Yet even if that were regained, it would be an illusion to think that we could ever revive the full classical unity and interconnectedness of all the fields of knowledge, when a Greek geometer could put forward the proposition "I cannot demonstrate the properties of a triangle without the aid of Venus."

### 4.

The minds that produce and variegate our culture form part of a large spectrum. And when we speak of art, we should be wary of certain high-decibel voices ringing out with claims about it or about one or another contributor to its bulk. In particular, we should beware of some efforts to truly represent it, to stand as icons of its significance. Pretensions to, or perhaps better seen as projections of, high souldom, are, generally speaking, to be rejected. "Creativity" is a well-known dazzler. And as Anthony Powell put it in *A Writer's Notebook*, "It is a rule, almost without exception, that writers and painters who are always talking about being artists, break down at just that level." A heavy self-conscious solemnity is another symptom. In fact, low seriousness is a mark of every epoch. Apart from its role in silencing merited rejection, it is also to be seen as narrowing the grasp of the arts by blocking their lighter side. Proust noted (of Saint-Loup) that it is a philistinism to judge the arts by their intellectual content, "not perceiving the enchantments of its imagination that give me some things that he judges frivolous."

The more constrictive tendencies always start among a minority, an extremely small minority, even of the artistic or literary strata. Then, at some point, they spill over into intellectually or aesthetically more passive, though argumentatively even more active, personalities.

As for the art and literature-consuming public, it may be persuaded, or even deafened, by a small stratum. The difference between the way this has happened in the past and the way it is happening now is that this intermediate caste has increased in number and in power, and has to some extent adopted, or been penetrated by, the same sociopolitical ideologies whose mental estrangement from good sense we have already deplored.

### 5.

Constant Lambert, the eminent conductor and composer, is quoted as saying that even among what we would now call the high artistic intelligentsia, it was very rare to find one who was adept or interested in all of the arts. In what follows, we will concentrate on literature and, more specifically, verse. The examples given here could certainly be matched in other fields, but should suffice for our purpose.

Anthony Burgess said flatly that "Art begins with craft, and there is no art until craft has been mastered." There are several ways, in writing as in the other arts, in which the decoupling of craft and art may be accomplished. Explosively intended phrases tend to distract attention from any broader pattern. But a less sensational shift of direction may also serve, if a mood is created or titillated without concern for anything accomplished. As Dr. Johnson said of James Macpherson's supposed translation of the poetry of Ossian, "Sir, a man might write such stuff forever, if he would abandon his mind to it."

One new phenomenon of our time was the establishment of English schools and departments in the universities at about the same time as "modernism" arose. For the first time, we had a specific and separate group that was supposed to be exceptionally qualified to judge literature, as against that larger, more heterogeneous set of people constituting the cultural community. Literature was soon beset by theory, and in general by an excess of academicism and discussionising. As in other fields, many were and are simply misled by words. A local paper speaks of those "eating the menu instead of the meal." Academic critics claimed to be the only ones competent to discuss poetry properly and indeed to prescribe its forms, methods, and contents. This is as if a claim should be put forward that only professors of ballistics should discuss cricket or football. The American poet Karl Shapiro remarked that though he knew scores of poets, he almost never heard from them the adulation of Eliot found in the textbooks. Different worlds.

The past had dictatorial critics, but these have always been the more troublesome to the degree that they were systematic. No doubt, then and now, nondogmatic criticism contains a congeries of more or less unconscious assumptions. But that is not the same thing, just as those people are wrong who say that conscious and systematic political indoctrination is all right since in any case we are subject to unsystematic indoctrination in the set of assumptions implicit in our society.

The answer is that a supposedly full and conscious conceptualization is, even in so far as it may be successful at all, a narrower and shallower matter than the other; that it goes with an authoritarian attitude; that its products, because of the formality of their definition, are more solidified and less able to evolve. Just as it is those people who think they have discovered the laws of history who have, in our time, caused our major public catastrophes, so, in a lesser field, it is those who think they have discovered the laws of literature who have been the trouble.

But it should also be said that there is an element of illusion in these conceptualizations. Since it is impossible to achieve the pretended rigor, an element of unconscious prejudice after all remains; in fact, it is corrupted through repression and rationalization into something less, rather than more, rational. The more "rigor," the greater the belief that what is "rigorously" covered is the main and major matter, while in reality, it may simply be that part of the subject most susceptible to analysis. Obscurer but profounder aspects of a work then tend to be forgotten.

We may also feel that the bringing to the analytic consciousness of all one's attitudes to a piece of writing, even if it were possible, is not an unmixed advantage. A psyche that is entirely conscious (or with a subconscious component subject to instant recall) does not seem to be in accord with the present design of *Homo sapiens;* and even if an android with these characteristics could be produced, one suspects that it might not be wholly satisfactory. To put it in terms of the arts, we might consider A. E. Housman's view that poetry finds its way "to something in man which is obscure and latent, something older than the present organization of his nature, like the patches of fen which still linger here and there in the drained lands of Cambridgeshire." The rules of these profound and intricate unconscious activities are probably in practice unknowable. At any rate, if not unknowable, much of their working is at present unknown. If the vague, peripheral, and hypothetical knowledge we have is given the status of law, we are worse off than before.

Literature exists for the ordinary educated man, and any literature that actively requires enormous training can be at best of only peripheral value. Moreover, such a mood in literature produces the specialist who only knows about literature. The man who only knows about literature does not know even about literature.

6.

Common in all academic circles is the assumption that argument put forward with careful definition and meticulous analysis is automatically superior to more general argument in more ordinary language. The analyst is inclined to assume that anyone who is content to use such more general formulae does so because incapable of finding distinctions, untrained in the minutiae of new methods of analysis, and in general all thumbs. And he even feels perhaps that he has demolished a large-scale argument by dissecting, qualifying, and distinguishing, i.e., proving that there is more to be said. This is rather like a microscope trying to refute a telescope. It is basically an error about semantics. Language is capable of being used in either way, and neither is intrinsically superior to the other—as long as the operator is aware of what he is doing, and the method is suitable to the material. We find, in fact, that a general treatment, without pretense of finality but rather, as it were, open ended, is the preferable approach to literature.

One also sees it argued that the more one knows about a work of art, the better one is equipped to judge it aesthetically. In theory, this sounds all right. But even if we neglect the fact that much critical "knowledge" of a poem is in effect not knowledge at all but patterns imposed on the poem by the critic, a little common sense will tell us that things are not as easy as all that. Are we really to suppose that a modern expert on painting, able to analyze brushwork with a microscope and to identify the chemicals used, is a better judge of painting than were the great patrons of the Renaissance? Knowledge does not necessarily imply judgment. All truly critical, as against technical, argument is either intuitive or hypothetical or partial. This cannot be compensated for by a study of the raw material, however exhaustive.

The first great age of analytical criticism, the Alexandrian, produced among its frigidities some of the aberrations we have today—its brand of concrete poetry, for example, of which Henry Fuseli wrote: "The wing, the harp, the hatchet, the altar of Simmias were the dregs of a degraded nation's worn-out taste." But it is easy to see how the critical temper may promote meaningless drivel. One of superb Rimbaud's worst poems is the sonnet in which he allots various colors to the vowels. Critics were instantly found to give coherent interpretations (eight or ten were propounded in all), though, as Paul Verlaine tells us, Rimbaud "se foutait pas mal si A était rouge ou vert." But his "Sonnet des Voyelles," just because it was interpretation fodder, became the favorite and most quoted of the lot. That was in primitive times, when criticism had not yet reached its zenith. Still, even nowadays, the most ambiguous (or complicated-appearing) poetry often pleases the critic best. Whereas, in any reasonable sense, the more incomprehensible the poem, the worse it must be.

It also seems to be felt that emotionalism proves emotion, and that nonsense is aesthetically preferable to sense. Things have changed since Sophocles was able to establish his sanity in old age by reciting to a court the newly written lines on *Colonus*. I cannot feel that the point is irrelevant, any more than is Coleridge's unforgettable remark about Shakespeare that "his rhythm is so perfect, that you may be almost sure that you do not understand the real force of a line, if it does not run well as you read it."

It seems odd that a taste for involved intellectualism in literature should so often be accompanied, or succeeded, by a taste for the most extreme irrationalism. The writer A. G. MacDonell, reviewing novels in the mid-1920s, noted such a change in the titles: "Slashing" ones like *Rat-Ridden, Bilge-Bestank* gave way to a more "Shadowy" lot, like *And She Said So Too*. But on second thoughts, it will be seen that this is natural: the two approaches both involve, in most cases, contrivance, in its shallowest sense. We think of art from the intellect as clear, arid, formal. Obviously, this is not always so: *anything*, however emotionalist, which is devised to suit a conscious scheme is intellectual, in this bad sense. Hysteria is the product of frigidity, not of passion. Both extreme cases are often, it will be noted, missionary types: the one of a highly organized and ritualistic set of sacramental forms, the other of a theology of revivalist self-abandon. In either case, a sectarianism.

7.

One finds a political element, or at any rate a political tone, in these literary discussions—with an occasional lack of amenity. How George Orwell would have relished Anthony Hecht telling (in the introduction to his *Melodies Unheard*) of opponents of meter and rhyme that "one such radical has recently affirmed" that anyone that observes such constraints "is unambiguously a fascist."

One of the ways to give the impression of an aesthetic performance to those lacking the organ of taste is indeed to put into a work of art the political, religious, or other extraneous satisfactions popular with one or another audience. Particularly, of course, if strongly held. As Paul Valéry wrote, "Enthusiasm is not an artist's state of mind."

Few poets have had much experience of the political. They have generous impulses, no doubt, and concern for humanity. These can be expressed in various ways and are not sufficient for a poem involving facts. On political issues, it is extremely rare for the facts to be so clear, and the human involvement so direct and simple, as to approach the immediacy and undeniability of experience. Still, there can be few comments as inept as that of William Carlos Williams, in his introduction to Allen Ginsberg, that this Beat poet had gone "into his Golgotha, from that charnel house, similar in every way, to that of the Jews in the past war."

Not that even those few poets with some political knowledge and experience find it easy to produce political poems. Lawrence Durrell, one of those few, has dealt directly with political events in prose, in *Bitter Lemons*. But in the poem which concludes this book, as soon as he approaches the subject, he has the modesty, a sense of the subject's intractability, to write: "Better leave the rest unsaid." Excellent advice, for several reasons.

There is an idea that expressing any reputable sentiment or opinion on politics makes good verse. No. In particular, apart from satire, there is almost no good public verse in English (except for Andrew Marvell's "Horatian Ode"). J. C. Furnas in his book on—and against—slavery, *The Road to Harper's Ferry*, says, "Blake, Cowper, Wordsworth and Southey, when touching on slavery, wrote drivel." I have come across one good poem about the nuclear bomb—by the Irish poet Thomas Kinsella (not actually a "political" sort of poem). None of the hundreds on the death of Dylan Thomas is any good (and please don't let us speak of Princess Diana). On AIDS, there are a few good poems by Thom Gunn—a great exception.

Back in the first and second decades of this century, there was indeed a ferment of revolutionary-sounding attitudes, and these attracted precisely some of the *aesthetically* radical—Marinetti into Fascism, Mayakovsky into Bolshevism. Enmity of artists to "capitalism" and the "bourgeoisie" is a symptom of this radical temperament. Of course, the notion that capitalism is hostile to art is in itself absurd. In fact, capitalist or bourgeois patronage has often marked a great flowering of art: the Medicis, Venice, and Holland, or, to go further back, the great merchant republic of Athens.

The Mexican painters like Diego Rivera well illustrate one aspect of political modernism. And it is clear that an important part of the impact of their "new" art was due far more to the political type of content than to the quasi-cubism involved in the forms chosen. In the palace at Chapultepec, one may see romantic revolutionary paintings of generations ago, showing liberators like Benito Juárez and Porfirio Díaz cursing venomous foes, etc., to the applause and enthusiasm of romantically conceived peasants and of "the People" in general. The difference between these and the more modern Mexican paintings is not great, and indeed the later generation owes a good deal not merely to this political inheritance but also to an element of primitivism already to be seen in the work of their predecessors.

In fact, art with a revolutionary political component is very much a traditionalist form. The only exception I have come across, where a genuine new impulse seems visible, is in the strange statuary of Kemalist Turkey, with its earthy New Turks pushing up out of the soil. Here, perhaps, novelty may be due to a total lack of previous representational art. On a slightly different point, one of the truly remarkable things about the Mayan cities—Uxmal, in particular—is what one may (inadequately) call the elegance of the shapes and dispositions of the buildings (in a way like the Greek equivalent).

### 8.

L iterature is written in language. That language has a close relationship to common speech. To "heighten" speech is not in fact to depart from it more than very slightly. When poetry goes bad, from the point of view of language, it is invariably due to the creation of "poeticism"—a vocabulary, or diction, or general phraseology of an isolated type. This has usually in the past taken the form of certain words becoming traditional in poetry at the same time as they became obsolete in common speech. But it is also possible—and this is the form the vice took in the twentieth century—to depart from the true roots by *creating* linguistic forms equally separated from the natural language and equally to be regarded as poeticisms.

We distinguish poetry from prose. There are poetry magazines, poetry anthologies, and so on that may print the occasional confessedly "prose poem," but their contents and claims, generally speaking, differ from what is usually designated "prose." So it seems that poetry is a particular art. And, presumably, in some sense a particular craft. Traditionally, prosody sought, as Baudelaire put it, "the immortal needs of monotony, of symmetry and of surprise"; or, if we need an English equivalent, there is Dr. Johnson's "To write verse is to dispose syllables and sounds harmonically by some known and settled rule—a rule however lax enough to substitute similitude for identity, to admit change without breach of order, and to relieve the ear without disappointing it."

Of course, there has long been within or adjacent to such verse a subordinate or complementary tradition of something closer to prose, but this was always, until recently, peripheral to and dependent on the main tradition. Even in Johnson's time, his friend Christopher Smart, whose *Song to David* is a fine example of a long, wholly formal poem, also wrote that fine, free apostrophe to his cat Jeffrey. To some extent based on the psalms, or on a sort of loose or resolved hexameter, this genre was often not even that, but better seen as declamation. Clearly some of this what we might call declamatory verse is successful.

But after all, prose too may be typographically broken up into lines for some particular effect. We have the notes from which Churchill made his speech to a secret session of the House of Commons in 1940. After quoting a call to man Britain's defenses and resist the then threatened German landings, the notes go on:

> *That will play its part;*
> > *but essence of defence of Britain*
> > > *is to attack the landed enemy at once,*
> > *leap at his throat*
> > > *and keep the grip until the life is out of him.*

This might, in some sense, be called an art, perhaps of rhetoric. But in what sense is it prose? At any rate, it shows how the two arts meet at a not readily definable point.

It can be brilliantly used: for example, in the tenser and more dramatic passages of David Jones's magnificent *In Parenthesis*, the best book produced by World War I (though we may note that Jones did not call his work poetry but just a "writing"). It has produced terrible stuff too: Martin Tupper, highly respected in mid-Victorian times, is an example.

Freeish verse has been with us for some generations (when I was young, my sister's school magazine was full if it). Most poets of this century have written it, sometimes only rarely. Again, successes are possible, though uncommon—Robert Frost compared writing free verse to playing "tennis without a net"—and again, it depends for its effect on being under the protection of the guns of the main tradition.

## 9.

Modernism, in the broadest sense, was largely an import from France, starting with Impressionism. As Anthony Powell commented in *A Writer's Notebook*, it is extraordinary that "after Turner, Impressionism seemed altogether new; and 'modern poetry' after Browning." (Indeed, most of the tropes of symbolism, for example, are to be found in Shakespeare.) But the new artistic evolution seems to have been that French models impressed those who wrote in English. But the French had quite a different history.

Which may remind us that there was also an element, and often a very attractive one, of joking in the early Paris avant-garde. And further West, one finds the saving note of the comic in not only E. E. Cummings but also in Dylan Thomas, for example (even at his most portentous, he seems to fit Lautréamont's description of Byron, "L'hippotame des jungles infernales": more sympathetic, even as a monster, than the tyrannosaurs later infesting Bohemia).

10.

Stéphane Mallarmé, the true avatar of symbolism, wrote specifically of the new "dissonances" that the background of "strict" verse is needed to make them "profitable." This sensible rule was not (and is not) observed. And the "experimentation," as Mallarmé suggests, went beyond the technical into the whole approach, when every sort of grammatical, structural, and semantic novelty was tried out. Certain benefits resulted—acceptable variations in structure, half rhymes. It was no less a product of classicism than when Edward Gibbon himself spoke of the alternative aims of poetry being to "satisfy, or silence, our reason."

The crux, the main and major disjunction in all fields, was when the artist took the decision to abandon the laity. As Pasternak wrote later, "All this writing of the Twenties has terribly aged. They lacked universality. I have never understood these dreams of a new language, of a completely original form of expression. Because of this dream, much of the work of the Twenties which was stylistic experimentation has ceased to exist."

In fact, many writers classed as modernist were merely modern. Which is not to say that they were not affected by experimentalism proper, to various degrees. But with this notion of artistic alienation came the similar, but logically distinct, element of the existential human in his condition; and with the twentieth century, though deriving from earlier thought, came angst.

It may be argued that artistic alienation had been around for generations, ever since the "superfluous man" of Mikhail Lermontov, the Byron of Continental imagination, the romantic idea of the mad or maddish poet grandly isolated from the rest of mankind. As W. H. Auden put it, nearly two generations ago:

> *Chimeras mauled them, they wasted away with the spleen,*
> *Suicide picked them off, sunk off Cape Consumption,*

*Lost on the Tosspot Seas, wrecked on the Gibbering Isles*
*Or trapped in the ice of despair at the Soul's Pole.*

In any case, when we look back, we can surely say that the great revolution modernism thought it was bringing about simply failed.

Yet that is not the whole story. First of all, even if they were not as world-shaking as they imagined, they might still have left us some valuable, if peripheral, work. Such a modest contribution, after all, is all that Mallarmé claimed—that for him classical verse was "the great nave of that 'basilica' French poetry," while *verse libre* simply created special attractions on the side-lines.

Lionel Trilling noted how a demand excessively catered to in his time was for verse that advertised itself as being under high pressure. Some verse of that type may indeed be successful. But mere groaning and sweating and thrashing around, with adjectives to suit, simply begs for D. J. Enright's comment: "the effects may be striking but they don't strike very deep." And this is, or can easily become, bad taste—as Wordsworth put it, a "degrading thirst after outrageous stimulation." Nor will it do to attribute this sort of thing to a more "primitive"—and therefore more true and real—depth of feeling. Yet, as I write, I come across a poetry reviewer in the *Economist* praising "a raw vigorous celebration of instinctive animal energy." (The cave paintings, too, were subtle and civilized compared with what is now exhibited at the Royal Academy.)

Much has been published over the past decade or two that has something of the appearance of form, but relaxed, or dissolved, to the degree that it is really no more than an overextended type of free verse. We have indeed noted that this can also be said of verse reaching us from the other pole of arid academicism. There are, of course, many people on all sides who are in one way or another interested in poetry but not for poetical reasons.

Kingsley Amis once wrote me, "The trouble with chaps like that is that they have no taste—I don't mean bad taste, just the mental organ that makes you say This is bloody good or This is piss is simply missing, and they have to orientate themselves by things like 'importance' and 'seriousness' and 'depth' and 'originality' and 'consensus' (= 'trend')."

Even if its proponents did not say that all obscurity is profound—and some came near to saying that—they certainly implied that all profundity is obscure. But a muddy puddle may pretend to any depth; a clear pool cannot. Coleridge writes somewhere that he read one of Dante's shorter poems every year for ten years, always finding more in it. This did not mean that it lacked comprehensibility at first reading, merely that in this comprehensibility there were resonances that did not immediately declare themselves.

11.

This "death of the past" includes ignorance of the cultural knowledge that would have been taken for granted from Chaucer to Auden. One example: Byron's "The Isles of Greece" required some, though not much, background. The assumed historical knowledge in the lines "A king sate on the rocky brow / Which looks o'er sea-born Salamis"—not even knowledge, only literacy—is now largely forgotten (and the oddity of "Salamis" pronounced as if the plural of an Italian sausage might have been avoided by a parallel grip on scansion).

More generally, how widespread is this anticultural plague? I was talking to an aging and not in the least anti-intellectual Los Angeles businessman. He said that he had been schooled, and honed, in a certain ambience of the old anthologies (*The Golden Treasury, The Oxford Book of English Verse*) and other such inheritances, but that his children, still less his grandchildren, no longer seemed to have this access.

In the 1990s, television carried a replay of the 1940s Western movie *My Darling Clementine,* in the course of which a traveling actor playing Hamlet is terrorized by bad guys in a saloon, who make him stand on a table, shoot at bottles behind him, and order him to act something. He starts, "To be or not to be," but dries up. Doc Holiday comes in and finishes the speech for him. This shows that back then Hollywood producers thought that all this would be acceptable and comprehensible to the movie public. In the intervening years, generations have been miseducated, as we all know, in many different ways. And one of these is that there is (or so it seems) no longer a general memory not only of meter and rhyme but also even of their earlier existence. Craft, it might be said, has been painted into a corner.

There are indeed many voices, including young ones, that have called for and started a return to verse. The persistence of form and rhythm and rhyme in the general population, as in country music, is perhaps a sign of their ineradicability. And "light verse" has been, on the whole, a bastion of form.

It is true that a decline in the craft of verse has been noted before. Edmund Wilson's "Is Verse a Dying Technique?" appeared in the late 1920s.

Still, the then wave of free verse was only a peripheral fashion. We were not simultaneously untaught the older poets. And there were no creative-writing classes, and few experimental-academic versifiers, or, at any rate, far fewer and less obtrusive than today.

12.

Over the ages, the condition of the arts has been seen as a part—a striking and important part—of the exercise of the critical imagination, of the human mind, in their broader compass. And the record of those faculties has seen contractions and contortions as well as periods of progress.

Will the humanities nevertheless prosper? Such a view perhaps underestimates, as ever, the power of inertia and interests. In Anatole France's *Thaïs*, faced with the (to him) irrational spectacle of a Pillar Saint—up on his pillar—the Roman governor's secretary says, "There are forces, Lucius, infinitely more powerful than reason and science." "Which?" "Ignorance and madness"—and the saint was an "educated" man. Moreover, his views were to conquer. In Rudyard Kipling's words:

> *And they overlaid the teaching of Ionia*
> *And the Truth was choked at birth*

. . . to rise again many years later.

Let us hope for the best . . .

# Chapter XVII

# Bureaucracies and Barbarism

———— ∽∾∾∾ ————

1.

The expansion of corporationist, bureaucratic, and etatist trends that we have noted on the political side can also be seen, indeed scarcely are to be avoided, in the arts. Cyril Connolly once wrote, "better a state which can't read or write than one which begins to take a positive interest in literature." But it is not only a matter of the state. There is also a proliferation, well past the reasonable, of what we might call cultural nongovernmental organizations, especially in the United States. These last are, usually, Foundations, often created by millionaires but after a transition period end up promoting various social and other agendas alien to the intentions of their founders. In the case of the arts, many of the successor caste succumb to fashions emanating from art activists (and not affecting the economic or economic-social attitudes of millionairedom).

In the old days, there were indeed millionaires who finely collected and later made their collections public. One such patron gave us the Frick Collection in New York. But these were individuals following their own tastes. Now, a half-educated, or dis-educated, class puts vast wealth into purchasing objects that they believe to be "art." They are like the "savages" who in the old days would hand over large amounts of gold and ivory to gain possession of a few glass beads or a gimcrack mirror. The traders who, then as now, extolled the overwhelming value of these trashy gewgaws were on the whole not well regarded. And not only individuals but also corporations and foundations compete in this wastefulness. When people question money invested in modern scientific projects, one thought is that it would be interesting to find out how much money is wasted, in America in particular, but also in Britain, on artifacts that are totally valueless.

When it comes to illustrating how the state, or its nominees, can get into, or through, the arts in general, we turn to the British example. In

Britain, what may be called a specifically cultural bureaucracy has emerged. It finances, publicizes, and employs a penumbra of individuals and institutions. Its supposed purpose is the support and spread of culture. In practice, a narrow, state-creeping, parody of culture is propagated under this totally misleading phraseology.

The fate of the arts in Britain has been, or seems at first glance, or shock, to have been, more massively ludicrous than anywhere else. In 1990–that is, under a Conservative government–a request "to co-ordinate a national strategy for the arts" went to the Arts Council from the Minister for the Arts (they already had one!). This initiative and its results are best read of in the London *Times Literary Supplement* (June 5, 1992, and January 29, 1993) as they portentously unfold, covered in a fine spirit of ridicule. The *TLS* points out that the whole idea is, to put it mildly, dubious, and cites T. S. Eliot that culture cannot be planned "because it is also the unconscious background of all planning," and that "it is an essential condition of the preservation of the quality of the culture of the minority, that it should continue to be a minority culture."

As to the major arts project, we learn that in collaboration with regional arts associations and a variety of other organs, a National Arts and Media Strategic Unit was set up with a "Monitoring Group," which carried out a "major survey of public attitudes to the arts." Forty-odd discussion papers were published, of about ten thousand words each. These were then discussed at more than sixty "strategy seminars." The product was boiled down to a 172-page document which was circulated in twenty-seven thousand copies, as a draft. It is full of appeals to the richness and diversity required of national culture, and in a variety of other ways to challenge everyone, increase availability, and so on. The operation seems to have fallen into the hands of the National Heritage Department and to have been treated as a beneficiary of the national lottery. But here, our jaws having duly dropped, we must first concern ourselves with the mere size of the efforts, the mass employment given to a large bureaucratic intelligentsia or artistic bureaucracy, and also to numbers of parasitic "artists."

In an only too significant example, we learn of a small verse publisher, dependent on a grant from "East England Arts." This body urged him to publish work he did not care for and, when he refused, cut off this grant, giving it instead to a university press to bring out the work of "graduates of an Andrew Motion creative writing course." That is, a bureaucratic body instructed an independent publisher they were supposed to be funding to accept stuff he felt unacceptable (giving it to work from the interstices of the corporate-cultural apparat).

Meanwhile, there is a mass of art employees in the United States too. Doubtless many of these are worthwhile. But, equally doubtless, not all that many. I read a review in a local California newspaper by a contributor described as "one of the leading Bolinas Bay Poets"! (In 1998, we are told that there were already 1,671,000 people identifying themselves as artists in the United States, while some 1.3 million were in some form of art production.)

One of the implicit errors in all this is the idea that the more contributors to art, the better. But if the numbers are too large, the result is not so good. If a hundred qualified for the last round of a skiing event, it would be ruined, just as government would not run well if the membership of the House of Representatives or of the House of Commons went up to a thousand or two.

## 2.

A further trouble is that as the older institutions merge, we see a high degree of one-sidedness developing on the "intellectual" side (including the media). We spoke earlier of something like "feudalism" rather than fascism. Nor do we see overt suppression of the alternative ideas or movements so much as their relegation to something like irrelevance, their marginalization almost into impotence.

In Britain, we are told, in this context, there is a real efflorescence of "creativity." It is true that there is a vast expenditure of energy and money in procuring what are seen as the arts. The new development is the incorporation of the supposedly novel and transgressive into the establishment, whose connections and institutions finance and give venues to those most ready to parade themselves as scions of novelty and rebellion. A large swathe accepting all this is thus trained for the corporatist order.

The relationship of art and corporationism strikes one very much in looking at photographs of, for example, the newish Guggenheim Museum in Bilbao. In a modernized version, it strongly recalls the look-at-me-being-imposing efforts, or plans, of the Mussolini, Hitler, and Stalin regimes.

We have not dealt with the other, but parallel, state-funded downhill trend: more direct dumbing down on the part of the taxpayer-subsidized BBC. The Secretary for "Culture, Media and Sports," in September 2003, promoted a channel described by the press as an advance into deeper "soap, sex and swearing." But why should the taxpayer subsidize it?

The bureaucratization of culture is naturally accompanied by an implosion of taste. London's "Millennium Dome" was of course a bureaucratic and political fiasco, but it was also an artistic one. When a cultural bureaucracy of the modern type comes into being, by its very nature it primarily supports not what might be called the general cultural wellbeing but what are sometimes called the bureau-creepers. The fictional old-time Bradford City Tramways and Fine Arts Committee may have put up statues of their chairman Alderman Foodbotham, but at least they did not feel obliged or pressured into "nit-witted novelty."

Moreover, these bureaucrats give awards and positions and honors to people seen as providing corporatism with the perfume of patronage. The artists or writers themselves may perhaps feel that they are the jewels in the crown of the new culturalism (and similarly with the parallel selection from media-style academe). But in reality their role is to give employment and gratification to a cultural executive. The artist or writer is the subordinate; the bureaucrat, the superior.

Political totalitarians wish writers to follow rules laid down by Central Committees. Bureaucratically minded "liberals" do not go so far, but just the same, a wish to turn literature into a social service is implicit in much of what they say. Theologians wish to impress their conceptions upon literature. Moralists insist on its performing a role in accord with their systems (and we must consider as moralists those po-faced puritans who insist that the avoidance of obscene words and of explicit descriptions of sexual activity is a literary offense).

These do not necessarily achieve the powers of a Stalinist or Orwellian Ministry of Culture—Minicult—but they tend that way and do so in so far as it lies in their power. (The nonauthoritarians among us, in opposing this bullying, must of course defend the right to commit socialist realism or doctrinaire experimentalism.)

In addition to these political, religious, and moral prescriptions, there are those that supposedly arise within the art. These are often, in their various ways, formulae based on inadequate and superficial theories, prematurely rigorous in a field where rigor is impossible. One notes, indeed, a certain overlap. Experimentalist dogma is urged on us not on artistic grounds alone, but in combination with the idea that the condition of the world, or of Western society, demands disrupted art forms. But even the

Soviet view of the arts was, in theory, not just transmission of the orders of the Science and Culture Department of the Central Committee to the writers concerned on a purely political basis, but the putting into effect an allegedly aesthetic (or aesthetic-social) doctrine, socialist realism. In all these cases, it would be claimed that the theorist has the interests of the art at heart, even though he may sometimes admit to having other interests as well. Thus none of this, in a general sense, is a product of philistinism, as it has always been understood. We find not frank enmity but suffocating friendship.

These overall prescriptions for transforming culture, as against piecemeal advocacy on special points, end up in the stinking files of an agitprop department. Between the culture one regards as unsatisfactory and the culture that has been supposedly forced into satisfactory forms, it seems incredible that anyone could prefer the latter, even with himself in charge. All recent experience of state, and state-type, action in this field argues powerfully against it.

3.

I will now, in all fairness, relate two examples of aberrant excesses in the arts: the first produced by guardians of high aesthetics, the second by clumsy oafs.

The first might be called neo-Tatery at its most pretentious and most obviously subnormal. The London Tate has long suffered from some of its lapses, though, to be fair, other institutions have also crashed. (And, more recently, the worst has gone to the Saatchi people). Still, bottom seems to have been reached with the purchase and display by the Tate in 2002 of cans of his own excrement by (if "by" is the right word) the late Piero Manzoni. Manzoni himself had said he produced these artifacts with the express purpose of showing the gullibility of art buyers. But the Tate defended its purchase, at a higher price per gram than that of gold (with taxpayers' money), of Manzoni's product on the grounds that he was an "incredibly important international artist," and that his cans were "a seminal work" and a bargain— "nobody can deny that" (quoted in the *Daily Telegraph*, June 30, 2002, and July 2, 2002).

That this should be possible is not merely remarkable in itself. It may also remind us of the saying that the thirteenth stroke of a clock casts doubt on its earlier ones. The canned-crap scandal proved the existence of an art bureaucracy for which such an exhibit seemed admirable. The Tate, it is true, had been promoting poor stuff for years, but this time it delivered what may be seen as a signed and sealed confession.

The second example is from what I suppose is the other end of the spectrum. (I am grateful to John Julius Norwich for providing this only too revealing item in one of his annual Christmas selections.) The French Olympic swimming team in 1996 had a program in which they would goose-step in German military style to the side of the pool. Then, diving in, they would reenact the arrival of Jewish women in the death camps, their selection by Nazi doctors, and their march to the gas chambers. The team's technical director, Jean-Paul Clemencon, defended this, saying it had "great emotional value." (But in the end it was dropped.)

4.

These examples show what can be carried along on what might be seen as the side currents of the stream of art thought. If we return to a serious, or at least academic-type, level, we soon find less ostentatiously negative phenomena.

We see that a major change, if surprisingly seldom remarked on, has affected the whole educational system. Fifty years ago, or even more recently, it was taken for granted that anyone schooled to the age of eighteen had reached the level of being generally "educated," which included a reasonable capacity to communicate in English. He or she, going on to university, was then able to pursue special studies. Nowadays, many students of eighteen are not up to this level. One of the results is that we find people who become specialists, even highly qualified in their special field, without being educated in the broader sense (unless that has been picked up from their family or from other circumstances).

There are others of considerable learning whose minds lack proper balance or, of course, reject it when available. A Cambridge professor just tells me of a humanities graduate student there who could not find Athens on a globe. And of another (elsewhere) who could not locate Egypt. What do they learn instead?

As I write, the British ministry of education has been instructing academics in universities to produce more "publications." This is already a nuisance in the United States, where "publication" is high among the criteria for tenure and promotion. The result is an avalanche of highly researched but more often than not tedious and pointless articles advertised and printed in academic journals and then published by university presses in books, both of which are read by none except the writers themselves. And what is required of them is a thicket of footnotes, mainly not of a factual type but of the opinions of others.

Moreover, there is a Web site much used by university operators in which all academics are listed by name, along with a list of the number of their publications, a supposed useful aid to instant judgment. A friend of mine, himself an admirable writer on realities, tells me that there are two other academics with the same surname and first name as his, and that no distinction is made between them on this site, so that he and the others have an outstanding array of publications attributed to them.

The whole approach is deadening. How could it arise? It could arise only in the minds of those seeking a simplified method of judging, for the purpose of regulating and regimenting, their unfortunate victims. In his last book, my old and dear friend the late poet and critic D. J. Enright quotes a professor at the University of Wales, in a newsletter of the British Council's Literature Department: "we no longer ask as our first question how good a work is," as a result of which "a great many new texts" are available to "tell us about the cultures." As Enright puts it, "that's to say, literature doesn't matter."

Scores of similar cases could be registered, from the United States as much as from Britain. To prefer a given artist, or several of them, to others has been, in effect, reprobated as elitism. And as subjective. Yes, of course these differentiations are neither democratic nor objective. And what the point amounts to can be seen in the removal of Shakespeare from the compulsory curriculum at some universities. But what criterion is provided instead? Sometimes none, though the student cannot be realistically expected to read everything that has ever been written—and with equal attention. So some selectivity is always there. Don't ask.

5.

Research, the product of the inquiring mind, is a splendid employment of the intellect. Scholars with serious commitment are the pride of our, and our predecessors', culture. We should always remember that the humanities, and the minds embodying the humanities, have a variety of centers of concentration. There are those who truly follow language or mathematics or one or other of the arts. Even a very minor or limited subject can be the creative, deductive object of a fruitfully obsessive mind. There is so much to learn, and all of it, properly done, is a contribution to the general consciousness.

A striking, indeed breathtaking, example of the deployment of a scholarly language far beyond what most of us would regard as plausible is to be seen in the autobiography of Cyrus Gordon, the great Hittitologist. He tells of his first day, aged eighteen, at the great Hebrew Center at the University of Pennsylvania. It ends with the Chairman giving out tasks. Gordon is told to report on the Syriac version of the text in question. He says he doesn't know Syriac. "Where do you think you are? At kindergarten?" roars his teacher and tells him to go home and learn Syriac. Fortunately, Gordon's Aramaic sees him through (he already has French, German, other modern languages, and, of course, Latin, Greek, and Hebrew).

At a different level, I saw, passing through a university library and having chanced to pull it from a shelf, an issue of the organ of a Byzantological scholarly society. The contributions were in English, French, German, Italian, and (I think) Latin. This case is different. The subscriber would not be expected to have anything like a mastery of these, or even some of these, tongues, but would just need an ability to get the gist (and, of course, scholarly work limits the vocabulary in a helpful manner).

So, how much does a tolerable education require in the way of languages? Not as much as Cyrus Gordon, or even the browsers on Byzantium. Still, one comes across disquieting signs. At random: A university in Britain has for some time given degrees in classics to students who have studied the literatures in *English*. More striking, in a lead review in *Britannia* (2004), Professor S. E. Clearly complains that much of the crucial literature of late antiquity is not in English and therefore inadequately accessible to British archaeologists, who have "small Latin and less Greek," matched with a "faltering command of any foreign language."

A leading American university some years ago required two languages for its politics degree. This was reduced to one language and a mathematics apparatus, then to one language *or* the mathematics. Downhill all the way, and this last amounts to a removal of the humanities from a field of study.

Languages are harder for some than for others and, in any case, require a certain amount of real work. (It is usually said that one needs a vocabulary of about a thousand words to operate tolerably as well as practice in their use and syntax.)

But, as has been rightly commented, if you know no other language than your own, you don't really know your own. You have no perspective in which to see it. And any serious break out from monoculturalism requires it. I will sketch—no more than sketch—some direct background.

I recall an incident in 1940, when my battalion was in camp on Dartmoor. Our adjutant called, Did I know Czech? Two Czechoslovak officers had turned up. I said no, I didn't, but would try German with them. When I got to them, after a word or two in German, they asked, Could they use French? They spoke it very well: one could even detect a Midi accent. Yes, they had been training near Agen. They had been speaking in French to the adjutant, but he had been misled by their shoulder tabs—and he had been educated at Eton and Sandhurst and must have had scores of classes in the language, but, at some level, they hadn't taken.

I had many advantages over him: I had lived in France as a child and had later taken French at school at a fair literary level in England. Even so, when I went to a French university, it was more than a week before I was really managing. But over the years I caught up.

My father, though wholly Anglo-Celtic (Virginian and New England), except for a Swedish great-grandfather, spent much of his childhood in San Remo. As a result, he spoke Italian. French, and the dialects of the coast— San Remese, Niçois—but he resented having to take note of any other language, except a few words of German. (On a peripheral point, in that context, after marrying my English mother in Britain in 1915, he joined the American ambulance corps with the French army, where on arrival his comrades called him "Dook" because of the British accent he had picked up. But when he came back to Britain on leave, my mother could hardly understand his thick Americanisms.)

During World War II, I took a crash course of two or three months in Bulgarian. This had first-class results then and in peacetime. But, picking up Russian was more difficult; I never really mastered it: I still recall giving a talk in St. Petersburg and having a Russian friend quietly—and too late—correct my cases. Such experiences are given merely as firsthand illustrations of the nature of the problem.

On a different approach, it is strange to find, accompanying a general cultural disconnection from foreign languages, the quite common deployment of translations and reviews of translations of foreign poetry. Now, prose is one thing, and there are big problems even there—as with the successive translations of Proust (the last of which was done with the help of Dennis Enright). I read Proust originally in the C. K. Scott Moncrieff translation but once chanced to be stuck with the original of *Les jeunes filles en fleur* and instantly saw how vastly superior the French is. When it comes to French poetry, to which I am addicted, it would never occur to me to venture a critical opinion (remembering how Baudelaire and Mallarmé misevaluated Poe!). There are said to have been ten Frenchmen by the first decades of the nineteenth century who had perfect, as against excellent, English (including the poet Valéry Larbaud)—that is, were qualified to judge English poetry.

At any rate, it is truly astonishing to find long and complex reviews of verse translated from (or even in) a language unknown to the reviewer. (There is, indeed, an international genre that invites a simple verbal transmittal and has not much to lose in the process—Pablo Neruda, for example, or with modes like ballad meter). And yet—the occasional triumph;

All this notwithstanding, it need hardly be said that knowledge of non-English languages is in itself no guarantee against folly.

6.

More generally, at the highest levels, academic writing—in English—is stupefying in two different, though often complementary, ways. First, we everywhere find a grotesque vocabulary held together by a tangled syntax, if such it can be called. But second, going a long leap further, we get theory. To illustrate the first, let me quote Geoffrey Grigson, in *The Private Art* (published in 1982!); he describes a book about Byron by a professor of English at a great university in which in "a few minutes" he had found "behaviourly," "factive," "reportorial," "factiveness," "attitudinal," "suppositional," "contextualised," "interiorised," "postcivilised," "episodically," "audience problem," "postpubescent," "postmythic," "iconograph," "variant phase." These are just untenable words. We go from there to worthless word conglomerates. Clive James, reviewing an otherwise deplorable book, comments that it looks as if it started as a dissertation; he quotes such clues as phrases like "non-cognitive structural features," "universalistic social psychological processes," "a cognitive model of ontology," "ideational, formations."

Then, as to theoretical approaches to literature, I will again avoid naming the offenders and merely quote a paragraph from a review by the great Bernard Knox of some academic work on the classics. The specimens he gives are from recent publications on Homer:

*For readers unfamiliar with the esoteric language produced by classical scholars of recent decades, the book provides some typical specimens. They include the neo-Freudian: "Developmentally the Achilles complex is like a running spiral arrested after its first circuit, where, having doubled back upon itself, it dissects itself at a point only slightly in advance of its origin." There is feminist doubletalk: "The Bride [Penelope] transmits her desire to the suitors through a triple network of 'ciphers' which are set in a nebulous cloud of 'blossoming,' and which sort the alphabetic units emitted by a 'letter box.'" The reader also received a sample of the narratological: "[T]his chapter is devoted to the narrative situation of complex narrator-text or embedded, focalization, NF1 [F2Cx]. There is embedded (or secondary) focalization when the NF1 represents in the narrator-text the focalization of one of the characters." Believe it or not, this is part of a discussion of the story of Achilles in the "Iliad." (*Los Angeles Times Book Review, *April 5, 1998)*

And this is in the classics! So that the reservations we may have about literacy in less rigorous fields must be even stronger. A waste, in fact, of the often promising minds sucked into this circling Sargasso.

The state of the human mind today is not to be registered merely in the historical or political or similar spheres, or from the record of our public ideas and actions. For that would be to neglect the arts and the humanities—a traditionally important area of thought and feeling. The humanities are not divided from the rest of human experience by an insuperable barrier. The challenges are everywhere.

# Chapter XVIII

# Awake to Affirmation

———⌘———

## 1.

Finally, or almost finally, let us look briefly, but in a fuller perspective, at a human activity that is both an art and a branch of knowledge. History, known from antiquity as a Muse, is of course to be seen both as a search for, and as a depiction of, certain realities. It can also, perhaps, be thought of as a philosophy of the mind addressed to not the least of the problems facing humanity. Its craft has been the extracting of truth from the accumulated data of the past; its art, the presentation of its findings in acceptable form. Thus, the drives of the historian are those of form, tone, and balance—that is, the aesthetic—and the will to discovery, a different, if complementary, urge.

It is impossible for a history to be exhaustive. The human past is inhabited by millions of individuals, in myriads of contexts, themselves in a process of change. To some degree, history's themes may be compared with the way fractals are applied to, say, a coastline: at first, there is a general view of what is seen as a thousand-mile stretch, a view that, however, can be developed by using each inlet, and eventually each rock, to produce a vastly more complicated array. The historian's subject may be the big general picture, but there is also room for the researcher of detail, even the equivalent of the expert on shellfish. The only mind for which there is no place is the one that insists that the manatees are mermaids.

The past has endless data, and whoever researches it, or any of it, must have some principle of selectivity—that is to say, a viewpoint. But this is not the same as an ideology (nothing could be more stultifying). As Bertrand Russell wrote of Hegel, "Like other historical theories it required, if it was to be made plausible, some distortion of facts and considerable ignorance."

As has been clear from our earlier chapters, the historian who seeks to extend the frontiers of knowledge is always, in part, motivated by sheer curiosity. In my own case this may be shown by (for example) my having a few years ago published a paper, in an organ of the Society for the Promotion of Roman Studies, on the place-names of Roman Scotland (a controversial subject, but one which has not led to any charge of ideological or other prejudice).

Anyone who is not genuinely addicted to the search for knowledge is unlikely to have the psychological energy to be a true scholar in any field. But in history this work clearly resembles more that of a detective than that of a scientist—a search for and judgment of particular evidence rather than of repeatable experiment. This detective side of historical research needs skill, background, and intuition. As Jacques Barzun has put it, historical verification is "conducted on many planes, and its technique is not fixed. It relies on attention to detail, on common-sense reasoning, on a developed 'feel' for history and chronology, on familiarity with human behavior, and on ever enlarging stores of information." And, "No interesting or important question . . . can be settled without detailed knowledge, solid judgment, lively imagination, and the ability to think straight. What to do and how to go about it come with practice; to enumerate rules would be endless and of little use." This is, in fact, the crux: that judgment is needed, that it is a delicate matter, and that no mechanical criteria for validating or rejecting evidence exist.

One direction into which some have been led was and perhaps still is an excessive reliance on "documents." As Macaulay wrote, "It is perfectly possible, as all who have made any historical researches can attest, to read bale after bale of dispatches and protocols without catching one glimpse of light about the relations of governments." On a slightly different note, Arnold Toynbee thought that our knowledge of the classical world was helped by not having an excess of material.

To move into "social" history—though all histories, except on very specialized subjects, have a social component. And numbers of general historians—Trevelyan and Halévy, for example—have covered undeniably social themes. But nowadays the term is mainly used, as John Lukacs has said, of the application of academic sociology to history. Thus it is not that we should avoid social studies research. But when it comes accompanied by formalist notions, it becomes distortive. Locke warned us, three centuries ago, against the temptation to be "misled by similitude, and by affinity, to take one thing for another." And though we may hope in principle to get as much knowledge of past humans as possible, it nevertheless remains true that millions of lives are lost into total, or almost total, darkness.

As Trevelyan wrote in another context, "An historical event cannot be isolated from its circumstances, any more than the onion from its skins, because an event is itself nothing but a set of circumstances, none of which will ever recur."

Generalizations are nevertheless possible; lessons can be learned. And if the events are viewed from various viewpoints, that is no more than is true of a set of photographs viewed from various angles and in different lights, which will give pictures that differ in many ways, without any one of them being false or misleading if interpreted with a modicum of common sense. But there are, of course, distorted or falsified pictures.

The human past is, as we noted earlier, full of highly improbable data, so that an appeal to the commonsense likelihood of events which the Westerner finds implausible will not do. Many of the facts are so extraordinary that there is a natural, if sometimes unconscious, bias against accepting them. Richard Whatley, in a paper written a few years after the Battle of Waterloo, argued that the evidence for the career of Napoleon was so extraordinary that it would certainly not have been accepted if attributed to some Israelite or other king in ancient times. He was also able to show that contradictory accounts existed of most of the major events of the Napoleonic period. And he concluded ironically that there was thus no reason even to believe in the emperor's existence.

It is indeed the case that where history, and particularly recent history, is concerned, we are often in a position in which a great many important facts (possibly most of them) are, taken individually, very hard to substantiate beyond reasonable doubt. Nevertheless, paradoxically, it remains true that from an assembly of facts, few of them absolutely certain, a clear account of a full series of events, an account that is defective only in a certain fuzziness at the edges, can yet be established.

One must not take anything for granted. The past, perhaps especially the last six or seven generations, has been replete with the astonishing and the unpredictable.

## 2.

There is still as much, or almost as much, good scholarship around as ever. Of course, there is a great deal more bad scholarship these days than perhaps for half a millennium, and, equally of course, much energy has to be spent on rebutting it. But, I would suggest, this is not energy wasted, energy that would otherwise be employed in research. On the contrary, it sharpens one's wits. That is to say, it keeps our critical faculties exercised and our powers of dupe-detection up to scratch. And I think we can add, more broadly, that even the Thermopylaes have, if not yet decisively, slowed down the barbarian hordes.

3.

Human history has only been with us for a few thousand years. Humanity's future (short of a cosmic disaster) presents an unimaginably long prospect, with as yet hardly thinkable technological—and doubtless other—surprises.

In a couple of centuries, let alone a couple of millennia, the world will be looking back on us in a historical mode. What will their research and assessment show? One thing seems fairly certain: our assorted idea-driven credos will appear to be primitive delusions, and much of our cultures' output of sophisticated argument will seem absurd.

Thomas Jefferson told us at some length how education should be "primarily historical." He added that our people would thus be enabled to "judge of the future." This careful phrasing does not, I think, imply any claim to predictability, but it certainly implies its contrary—that those ignorant of history will be incompetent to consider the possibilities.

Jefferson saw historical education as vital to the citizens of a free society—if they are to remain free in the longer run. History is, in fact, that part of the humanities which enables us to look back with a real perspective and so, also, to look forward as well-briefed as we can be. We need the whole accessible past to give us a deep perspective. We need the history of the twentieth century because it contains, if sometimes in vestigial form, the elements of the present—and the future.

No, we cannot predict. The near future teems with urgent problems, with as yet irresoluble balances of force and thought. The law-and-liberty cultures may flourish; and as yet unpromising regions may over a period bring not merely the forms but the habits of consensuality to their populations. Let us hope.

But all this depends to an extent on whether the dragons of expectation can be cleared out of our mental skies. For unlike with the other arts, major errors in history entering much or any, of the public mind, can be dangerous. Everywhere we always find the human urges to preserve at least a measure of personal autonomy, on the one hand, and to form communal relationships, on the other. It is the latter that tends to get out of hand. To form a national or other such grouping without forfeiting liberties and without generating venom against other such groupings—such is the problem before the world. To cope with it we need careful thinking, balanced understanding, open yet unservile minds.

# Epilogue

R ather than summarize or concentrate this book, which has broadened as it has progressed rather than been brought to focus, it seems best to note what it is and what is not. Clearly, it is about certain aspects of the relations between and within human groups, written by an observer in, and of, the last decades of the twentieth century and the first years of the twenty-first, and this is to say that it takes little account of the long perspectives of the human future into which it, and its author, will fade.

Nor is that the only sphere it fails to cover, or even more than touch upon. The immensities of the universe that frightened Pascal, all the questions of cosmology and philosophy, the deeper questions of human love and death—these are not susceptible to the sort of general arguments presented so far. On them, one can only speak as an individual, carrying out what might be called a . . .

Reconnaissance.

1.

*On a clear night, we may look up at the All*
*As if standing at the central*
*Point of a huge flash-freaked black opal.*

*Then, past our vision, the mind supplies*
*Metagalaxies, immensities*
*For those impressible by mere size.*

*Well, we're nearing technologies that could scan*
*Cities on planets of Aldebaran,*
*Oceans as far off as M31,*

*And the forward edge of the far future's*
*Wave'll sweep right over those frontiers*
*For our heirs' almost endless voyages and ventures.*

*"Almost" because the very universe*
*Must in the end darken and disperse,*
*Or so say our current cosmographers.*

*They plumb near the big bang's first nanosecond*
*—Though that may be only scraping the rind*
*If the full fruit's forever beyond.*

## 2.

*We've always trolled for implicit patterns,*
*Lucretius interwove a sleet of atoms,*
*Some Greeks stamped number on reality's phantoms,*

*Random stars fell into constellations*
*Imposed on the celestial regions*
*By the ancient craving for aggregations.*

*And centuries later, the Hereford Map*
*Gave the world strict, but spurious, shape,*
*Jerusalem at the center, a mental warp.*

*Now: seething quanta, dimensions, a spate*
*Of force fields round which the intricate*
*Equations weave their dazzling net.*

*But unobserved arrhythmias thresh*
*Around and soon break out of the mesh,*
*The massive computing starts afresh,*

*And, as the phenomena froth and foam,*
*From their polders they toil to divert and dam*
*The oceans of the continuum.*

## 3.

*William James once wrote of how temperament*
*Determined each philosopher's bent.*
*With the data so weak, we can only assent;*

*Though surely only the most rigid doctrine*
*Solely depends on (say) the endocrine*
*Balance of what's in the brain-dead groin?*

*There are, of course, many scenarios,*
*Quite a collector's cellar of curios.*
*We can only go where our thoughts will carry us,*

*Which mayn't be far—the point's Robert Heinlein's—*
*Any more than a collie has much of a chance*
*To grasp how its dog food gets into cans.*

4.

*Some ache for those worlds beyond the voids*
*With appropriate orbits, the needed fluids,*
*To commune with minds of non-anthropoids.*

*But, above all, there's the heavy artillery*
*Of instruments, the tempestuous flurry*
*Of equations tearing through thickets of theory,*

*And why shouldn't sages with minds like prisms*
*Probe the intergalactic chasms*
*Enjoying their new-knowledge orgasms?*

*Still, tracking the trail of the big bang*
*Is a waste for those happy with yin and yang*
*Or leaning back into the Allfühlung.*

5.

*If to peter out is the lot of the All,*
*Its tenure is longer than ours. But still*
*We may find some sort of parallel.*

*As wavelengths flatten to infinite*
*(Or are crushed to minima less than nought),*
*Existence fades into total night.*

*Meanwhile minds bred up from matter*
*—At once their prey and their predator—*
*Are faced with various ultimata.*

*Of the whole, we've only the thinnest slice,*
*Just a brief tangle till we're torn loose*
*From the thorns of time, the weeds of space.*

*Does that last wrench, as the body link goes,*
*Or almost so, fill a timeless pause*
*Where the unflake falls and the unstream flows?*

6.

*Research hounds, trained to be untranscendental,*
*In two different packs hot on the scent'il*
*Flush out the mood-modes, material, mental.*

*Some trace the intense billion-neuron torque*
*That the crimped folds of the cortex spark;*
*Others strip the viewed psyche stark.*

*But concept cantilevers somehow don't solve*
*The bridging of the spidery gulf*
*Between the nerved senses and the self.*

7.

*Half free of the clumsy cosmos grope,*
*As if not quite woken from non-REM sleep,*
*Wisps of totality may take shape,*

*Mist-moments smooth as chiseled stone,*
*Sweet Agnosis, sculptor Anon,*
*With all of the undivine withdrawn,*

*And, faintly felt through the near alive,*
*The softest touch of a tendril of love*
*Too light for leaf or belief . . .*

*Appendix A*

# "No One Foresaw the Collapse
# of the Soviet System"

————⊛————

There is a common misperception that writers on the Soviet Union did not foresee its fall. Assertions to this effect in fact pervade the literature and usually go unanswered.

It seems worth looking back at my own record, if only to show how a proper feeling for and judgment of history and politics could indeed lead to the right conclusion. Naturally, there could be no prediction of the detail of events, though even there certain general probabilities could be and were adumbrated.

The by no means exhaustive excerpts from books and articles given here are consistent over the whole period of Soviet decline and are put forward as a reasonable example for those considering long-term trends the world over and their probable outcomes. Of course, I am not the only one to foresee, and give reasons for, the downfall of the Soviet system: indeed, in these pages, I cite others, and in particular George Orwell. But the record here is alone sufficient to rebut a too widely accepted chimera.

> *Human nature being what it is, the power of the Party to impose conformity is in practice a highly qualified one. This failure is a radical one, and relevant to both the strength and the permanence of the grip of the regime's ideas upon the population. (*Common Sense about Russia, *1960)*

> *The Soviet Union is ruled by party officials who have certain fixed ideas about the nature of the desirable organization of society. Changes will not come about without considerable resistance from them. But one thing seems certain: the regime will either evolve peacefully or it will perish.*

>   *For thinking people even in Russia have understood that ideological formulae are not an adequate substitute for examination of the facts; that a regime is*

*best judged by its acts rather than its slogans; and, above all, that those who rise to the top under the present Communist system are not likely to be the best judges of realities, let alone ideas, in spite of their skill at manipulating the political machine. This new understanding on the part of Russians of good will and good sense is bound in the long run to be fatal to any who may attempt to go against "the iron laws of history" with which they have so often threatened others.* (Common Sense about Russia, 1960)

*The relevant forces within and without the Soviet Union are anything but static, and I would expect, barring a war, that another decade or two may see enormous changes. The cycle cannot go on indefinitely amid circumstances that ensure that the regime must evolve or perish.* (Power and Policy in the USSR, 1961)

*The potentials for great change therefore exist. The Soviet Union is on the verge of becoming, in most respects, an advanced country. Meanwhile, these economic and social forces are held back by a political integument suitable to earlier times. It is actually, in a sense, the classical Marxist situation: "From forces favoring development the conditions of production now turn into fetters on these forces. . . . Then a period of social revolution sets in. . . . Owing to the alteration of the economic basis, the whole immense superstructure is, gradually or suddenly, subverted."*

*These dilemmas of the regime have expressed themselves over the last few years, equally classically, in a series of economic crises, as the political leadership has attempted to make some adaptation of the system of rule to the real problems. For it is old experience that ruling classes and castes cannot easily adapt themselves to new conditions.*

*No system of human thought, or of human organization, is immutable. The Communist movement, arising out of Lenin's interpretation of Marxism, has seen radical changes. . . . At the end of 1964, we see the Communist movement beset with heresy and schism. We see within it tendencies toward freedom of thought, toward liberation from the various anti-humanist dogmas that have poisoned it for more than a generation. The progress that libertarian ideas have so far made should not be exaggerated. But the fact that they are there, ready to emerge, even after the long years of Stalinism, is heartening proof that they are ineradicable.* (Russia after Khrushchev, 1965)

*Liberal feeling exists as a powerful aspiration among the intelligentsia and other classes excluded from effective political life, just as it did under the autocracies of the nineteenth century. It then formed the seedbed for change, but the actual changes did not come until the ruling groups were at the very least highly disorganized.*

*Such disorganization in the apparat is quite conceivable. But it could only follow a whole series of crises and power grabs that would shake both its self-confidence and its solidarity to the degree that a faction within it might feel bound to attempt alliance with something in the nature of a genuine democratic force. This cannot be excluded. For, even when we go on to deal with day-to-day politics, we need not lose sight of the fact that they are ephemeral, transitional. We are all liable to exaggerate the stability of that which exists. In spite of the great and obvious weaknesses besetting it, the Austro-Hungarian Empire was not thought to be facing disintegration at the beginning of this century. With all the signs of change visible in 1780, the idea of the collapse of Bourbon rule in France would have been thought laughable.*

*But when the stability of a regime depends on the formal power of the government in being, when it is evident that the social, economic, and intellectual tides have set in firmly against the system, then, in the long run, the apparent and visible stability is misleading. The Soviet Union must now be regarded as being in a most unstable condition and subject to extreme change over perhaps quite a short period.* (Russia after Khrushchev, *1965)*

*Meanwhile, we may note that if the Soviet Union is to deal with its colonial problem in even the most superficially adequate way, it has no real choice but to turn itself into a genuine federation. But if the unity so created were voluntary, it might be temporary and precarious. The present rulers would certainly make no move in such a direction if they could possibly help it. But they may yet find themselves constrained by forces outside their control to make concessions—which could only lead to bigger demands, put forward from positions of increased strength. The question is critical, and not only is it unsolved, but it is probably insoluble under the present system. That is to say, it is one of the elements in the present general crisis of the Soviet system, and one that could lead to future changes which may now appear remote and extravagant. Here, again, we should remember that the Soviet future is unlikely to comprise an easy and evolutionary development, and that any too cautious or conservative view of its potentialities is certain to be wrong.* (Russia after Khrushchev, *1965)*

*Russia, that sleeping giant, is already straining half consciously at the bonds that hold her.*

*But whether, and to what degree, the new forces find expression through*

*Party and Soviet channels, we may at least expect a tough political struggle. At some stage, in any case, the power of the bureaucratic integument which at present prevents development to sanity must be eroded or broken. . . . We might conclude that some such development—and in the fairly near future—is not too unlikely. (*Russia after Khrushchev, *1965)*

*Although it would be going too far to say that this is irreversible, it seems probable that the Soviet system has thereby entered into a general crisis from which it can only emerge, if it emerges at all, transformed out of all recognition.*

*Russia faces issues which can scarcely be settled without the genuine involvement of the public. For the problems before the country can hardly be solved under the monopolistic rule of an elite of narrow, ideology-bound machine bureaucrats. As George Orwell could write flatly, as long ago as 1946 (in his "Second Thoughts on James Burnham"), "The Russian regime will either democratise itself or it will perish." (*Russia after Khrushchev, *1965)*

*The USSR is, in principle, in the classic prerevolutionary situation foreseen by Marx—of an obsolete political integument holding in all the living social, intellectual and economic forces. The recourse of the present rulers is further to strengthen the integument, rather than to understand and come to terms with the vital forces involved. In the short term, we cannot say what will happen. In the long term the policy cannot work. (*Studies in International Communism, *July 1968)*

*The first thing to emphasize is that there is nothing exceptional or accidental about the Czechoslovak development. It is simply one further example which shows, as did those in East Germany in 1953 and Poland and Hungary in 1956, that traditional Communism—involving monopolistic control of all the media of information and education—is a dead end and invariably produces a political system radically inappropriate to its society and economy.*

*Back in the mid-forties, George Orwell remarked (in his "Second Thoughts on James Burnham") that, though he could not see how it would happen, it was clear that Communist regimes must democratize or perish. The "great slave empire" of which certain intellectuals dreamed would not, he said, come to pass. . . .*

*Rulers who operate on the formula of the old poker player—"You can fool all the people some of the time and some of the people all the time, and them's pretty good odds"—are forgetting that the third element—"You can't fool all of*

*the people all of the time"—is likely to prove decisive sooner or later. And the
reasons are to be sought not simply in the "indomitability of the human spirit"
but also in the simple logic of the whole Communist position.*

*Totalitarianism is, of course, capable of certain economic and other
achievements. But sooner or later, to put it briefly, its methods ossify into dogma
and its rulers degenerate into a blinkered incompetence so that necessary change
cannot be undertaken or even conceived. It is not so much the ethical superiority
as the sheer practical advantage of political liberty which needs stressing. . . .*

*In a modern changing economy, when everything in the "line" becomes a
matter of doctrine, when subordinates are not permitted to dispute the main
policies, sooner or later trouble must arise. In the long run the system is not only
inhuman but also unsuccessful, and crisis is not an accidental but a necessary
result. . . .*

*All the same, Russia, like the other Communist states, is now, in principle,
in the pre-revolutionary position foreseen by Marx—an obsolete political shell
seeking to contain genuine social and economic trends. . . .*

*In fact, the social, economic and intellectual forces all tend with increasing
pressure against the political system. . . . It is naturally impossible to make rigorous predictions. But opinion among serious students is increasingly coming
to the conclusion that the present system has no great chance for surviving
long. . . .*

*There are forces at work in the Communist states which are bound to pro-
duce crisis and change, and no policy which ignores this will be viable. There
might be something to say for such an attitude on the part of the West if it genuinely amounted to* Realpolitik. *But, except possibly in the very shortest run,
there is nothing realistic in a policy which ignores the inevitable dynamics of the
situation. . . .*

*More broadly, greater readiness to cope with the unexpected and a large
extension of diplomatic contingency planning seem to be indicated.*

*In time, the Communist world is faced with a fundamental crisis. We cannot
say for certain that it will democratize itself. But every indication is that it will, as
Orwell said, either democratize itself or perish. . . . We must also, though, be prepared to cope with cataclysmic changes, for the death throes of the more backward
apparatus may be destructive and dangerous. ("Communism Has to
Democratize or Perish,"* New York Times Magazine, *August 18, 1969)*

*The country is now stuck in a situation in which revolutionary change is called
for by all the social, economic and intellectual forces, and opposed and aborted*

*only by a political machine specially constructed for the purpose. It is a highly artificial situation, resembling that of Mr. Waldemar in Poe's story. (Review of Michel Tatu's* Power in the Kremlin, *1969)*

*The current regime has learned one lesson from Khrushchev—that random reforms within the system have not done any good. But the* immobilisme *to which they have instead retreated equally provides no solution. It therefore appears inevitable that the pressures will continue to build up. The question that remains to be answered is whether the political integument will be destroyed explosively or will erode away gently. ("Immobilism and Decay," in* Dilemmas of Change in Soviet Politics, *ed. Zbigniew Brzezinski, 1969)*

*All the thought in Russia has long been in intellectual opposition; and most of the feeling too. By most standards, the regime has long since lost the mantle of heaven. It is not merely ripe, but greatly over-ripe, for major change. Basically the trouble seems to be that the technical and administrative organization possible in the modern epoch enables regimes quite obsolete from the point of view of their citizenry and of their countries' international interests to persist long past what would once have been a breaking-point. (Review of* The Chronicle of Current Events, *1972)*

*Perhaps the most realistic attitude for the West, barring total and unforeseeable change in the Kremlin, is to understand the dangers and revert to a sensible policy of unprovocatively matching the USSR in armament, and blocking Soviet expansionism. This would, however intransigent their ideological mood, divert them into a period of watching and waiting for an opportunity—as happened after the defeat in Poland in 1920, until 1939. Such a "temporary" suspension of expansionism would allow the positive forces in the USSR time to develop: even perhaps produce an evolution towards sanity, a gradual crumbling of the ideological foundations in the ruling group itself.*

*Apart from a catastrophic breakdown, which is by no means impossible, slow and firm pressures and inducements from our side might eventually lead first to the abandonment in practice of the Soviet struggle to the knife with the West, and later to its abandonment even in principle. (*Present Danger, *1979)*

*The weaknesses at home nevertheless imply a point beyond which the USSR could not match the West in armaments, simply from over-strain of the economic base. There can be no need for panic about a limitless arms race. Once* *the West committed itself to reasonable strategic and conventional parity, and to firm diplomatic action, the USSR would have little choice—whatever its longer-term intentions—but to accept the situation. (*Present Danger, *1979)*

*As far as we can tell at present, then, the probability is that political developments over the coming period are likely to be within the regime, and that it is only when pressures become so strong that concessions are made by the regime (even if not granted in good faith) that visible progress may occur. . . .*

*We should be prepared for surprises over the next decade and should not fall into the temptation of believing the* status quo *to be as stable as it may appear to the superficial glance. . . . The machinery Stalin built is organizationally effective and ideologically disciplined to the extent that it can (in principle at least) keep the political integument in being long past the stage at which other political forms would fail. And this implies that the pressures, when they reach a critical point, will be very high indeed. (*We and They, *1980)*

*If the crisis of the communist regime is to begin under the present leaders or their probable successors, I would expect it to come about not as the result of any of their specific policies, but rather through unforeseen catastrophes with which their methods, and indeed their personalities, are not fitted to cope. They will soon have to face, in some form or other, a major dislocation which their present small-scale economies and conservation measures will not go very far to avert. The Soviet economy is, in principle, overextended.*

*It will be obvious that this whole question must bedevil relations between the Soviet ideologists, military men and administrators in various fashions, even to the point of shaking the entire structure of the state.*

*Without elaborating the details of the forces concerned (and it should be noted that this is even more a crisis of ideas than of economics), we can at least see that we are faced by an economy and a society whose inextinguishable tendencies run counter to the political integument at present hemming them in, thus creating conditions of a classical Marxist pre-revolutionary situation. It therefore appears inevitable that the pressures will continue to build up.*

*Apart from general political considerations, there is a further major obstacle to the coming into being of a "liberal" USSR, in any sense of the word whatever. And this is that in anything recognizable as a liberalization, even in the narrowest sense, the major non-Russian republics would almost certainly opt for independence. (*We and They, *1980)*

In an article in *Foreign Affairs* ("Stalin's Successors," April 1970), I developed all this on a broader scale. But I refer to it here for my tributes to others who took much the same view—in particular, Michel Tatu (Moscow correspondent of *Le Monde*), Hugh Seton-Watson, Ronald Hingley, Roger Garaudy, Andrei Amalrik, Anatole Shub, and K. S. Karol (*New Statesman* correspondent). What they had in common was a clear view of, above all, the motivations and mentalities of the Soviet leadership cadres.

*Appendix B*

# An Anglosphere in the Neosphere
# (A Political Exercise)

———— ⣿ ————

1.

In this sketch, we have limited ourselves to the evolution of what has been called the Anglosphere.

The world as a whole carries such a wide range of actual and potential data that it is hardly possible to attempt to present it with any plausibility. The "outside world" will continue to smolder; and if we confine ourselves to the law-and-liberty culture, it is mainly because it contains an accessible present and, to some degree, future. And, moreover, it contains the possibility of global evolution. It is this, rather than any clear predictability, to which we give our attention.

Our perspective cannot give a full condition or context of what may be our future in ten or twelve years time, if only because technology will bring about unforeseeable change. And, for example, developments in the undeveloped world and in Western policies towards it may shift critically. We are here assuming that the current crises, if not "settled," have at least been brought under control, and in that context, we present a direction rather than a "program."

2.

Though we are not here concerned with world politics as such, the Anglosphere, by its very nature, is non-isolationist, and must be involved in institutions such as the United Nations, especially to the degree that rhetoric is replaced by reality. And with other compatible and comparable comunities, such as the projected Hispanosphere, and such welcome areas as India, Japan—and perhaps a future civic and liberal EU, a genuine Europe of communities.

For meanwhile, there is, however, one international matter that is unavoidably relevant to what follows. And as to our present concerns, it is plain that we assume that the EU will either decline or, in the longer run, be assimilated into and even transcend the Anglosphere.

The tide there, for the moment, is still running against the law-and-liberty order in favor of a denationalizing European corporatist superstate. But as anyone who has looked at the twentieth century knows, changes dismissed as improbable or impossible have often come about. And ideas and policies that appeared to embody the future have faded away. Is there any prospect of a change in Europe, of a retreat from the organizational and ideological overstretching of today (putting it mildly)?

Yes, and this is of course desirable not only in our Anglo-American context. There are many signs of erosion of the superstate idea. Even Jacques Delors has gone on record urging a retreat. The euro—designed admittedly for political and not economic reasons—has been given only a decade or so, if that, by leading economists. More important is the recognition of the decay of democratic or communal feeling in the citizenries, who have to accept laws in whose making they have no part. This was, if hesitantly, dealt with in the officially sponsored and heavily documented *Norwegian Study of Power and Democracy* (Oslo, 2004).

It is clear that the perspective that follows is not compatible with the EU in its present form—and even less so in some of the forms currently being discussed. Only a very much looser, less unreal, variant will do. One, that is, which among other things provides for membership of other bodies, not merely international or military, but political and cultural. Such arrangements have existed in past cultures.

What follows is what might be called an exercise in political and cultural science fiction. It assumes that, perhaps sooner rather than later, the European Union will run out of excuses, and especially in Britain—though also elsewhere—major rethinking will ensue.

This is a science fiction without monsters, dealing with a coming (we hope) period in which they have lumbered off, or been corralled. I have elsewhere written of the substance—of the how and why—of the Anglosphere. Here we go into the sort of structural evolution it might go through.

With that in mind, let us embark on what is no more than a sketch, or dramatization, of how when the time is right an Anglosphere may develop.

3.

S o, some years hence, after a *long* political campaign, after preliminary negotiations, the representatives of the interested states assemble for more substantive consultation. We can envisage them meeting to coordinate their foreign policy and their military policy, with some intention of also beginning to coordinate economic arrangements, and exploring their political unity as well.

They would set up a permanent Consultative Council, which at this stage would simply consist of a representative or so from each state. In the Council, to which considerations of representativeness do not apply as strongly as they must in an assembly, a suitable proportion of representation might be as follows:

| **For a Council of 25** | | **For a Council of 12** | |
|---|---|---|---|
| United States | 12 | United States | 5 |
| United Kingdom | 5 | United Kingdom | 2 |
| Canada | 2 | Canada | 1 |
| New Zealand | 1 | Australia | 1 |
| Australia | 2 | New Zealand and Pacific Islands | 1 |
| Pacific Islands | 1 | Caribbean | 1 |
| Caribbean | 1 | Ireland | 1 |
| Ireland | 1 | | |

The Pacific, Caribbean, and Irish memberships might not necessarily come into existence as early or as completely as those of the others.

Under the Council would be a permanent Committee set up to coordinate foreign policy, whose area of competence would cover the entire world scene. (In this field, as in others, coordination might be regarded as a first step to a closer integration.) At the same time, a permanent Military Committee would be appointed, with competence (unlike NATO) over the whole world. Equally important, these two committees would also provide a unified approach to political warfare—concentrating information and expertise and insisting on the major role of this side of the struggle. And in addition to having its equivalent of our chiefs of staff, the Association might eventually (or early, come to that) raise or sponsor its own forces on a limited scale—for example, ones designed to prevent coups by pro-totalitarian elements in specific areas. At the appropriate time, after adequate consultation, the Committee could recommend stronger and more permanent institutions.

Without detailing the steps and discussions that would take place, we may think that in a still longer run, as the Association idea prevailed in the homelands, the Council would call into being a larger Assembly, the two bodies together forming an Intercontinental Congress. It would then debate and issue a Declaration of Interdependence, on something like the following lines:

### Declaration of Interdependence

*We, the peoples of [the founding members], sharing the same aspirations, holding the same views of human liberty and progress, and wishing to defend and develop these ideals;*

*And considering, the better to achieve this, that a greater unity of purpose between us, with closer consultation and mutual assistance in all fields, has become increasingly desirable among the dangers and difficulties of the modern world;*

Declare *us an Association whose aims shall be:*

*• to become a center and bastion in all parts of the world round which states sharing in any degree our aims, or needing support against our mutual enemies, may rally; and an exemplar of that world community which does not at present exist;*

*• to coordinate the lessons and, to such degree as may be practicable, to forward institutional coordination in matters of law, of economics, and of social and other spheres;*

*• to bring to our citizens all the benefits of mutuality and cooperation and in general to take all possible measures for the strengthening, encouraging, and rejuvenating of the principles of which we speak.*

Such is a possible draft. Or, if a more philosophical type were thought appropriate, it might run more on the following lines:

*We, the representatives of the United States of America, the United Kingdom, Canada, the Commonwealth of Australia, New Zealand, [and such others as may agree],*

Considering *the state of the world today,*

Believing

*1. that the enemies of our tradition are still threatening;*

*2. that among many nations not hostile to us, the influence of ideas and policies antagonistic to the development of a peaceable and democratic world order is nevertheless disturbing;*

*3. that disarray and disunity in the politics and defense arrangements of our countries contribute both to strategic danger and to political disintegration.*

Affirming

*1. that the solving of political and social problems is only to be arrived at by free discussion of alternative solutions unfettered by dogma and with the practical possibility of peacefully replacing governments;*

*2. that dictatorship, the planned society, is less human, less efficient, and (contrary to its claims) less scientific than our own; and that utopianism is everywhere shallow, impractical, and oppressive;*

*And* Holding *that our countries, subscribing to a common political tradition, economically and otherwise, form the strongest force of humanity;*

With the aim *of providing a present center of hope in the world, and for the future a center round which peace, cooperation, and democracy can develop;*

*Now declare our interdependence.*

The precise scope of such a Congress would have to be determined by negotiations and they would, in any case, be subject to change. The most important thing is not so much the detail of any initial agreement, which can only be broadly foreseen and not precisely prescribed, but the fact that such an agreement, whatever its form, would in itself constitute the first step in the direction of creating a new and decisive political force in the world.

The Consultative Council, as we have suggested, should number not more than around twenty, and the assembly no more than around a hundred. (The Continental Congress in 1776 numbered fifty-six; the Constitutional Convention in 1787, thirty-nine.)

Any original founding meeting might, of course, be simply of representatives of the founding parties, without any special attention to the relative size of delegations—as indeed was the case with the Continental Congress: like the latter, even after the formation of the Association, delegates would presumably, at least at first, speak as representatives of states rather than parties. All the same, it seems right to lay down from the start some sort of proportion in the representation, partly to emphasize that this would be something devised to be or to develop into something stronger than a merely temporary congeries of states.

Such long-term representation would have to take several points into account. First, the United States, with its great preponderance of population and responsibility, would have to be given, if not a majority of seats, at least something close to that, even though numerical voting as such would not play much part, at least until a much later stage than the one we are contemplating. No delegation should have less than three members, for practical reasons. And while the United States, and to a lesser extent the United Kingdom, as largest and second-largest partner, should be weightily represented, this should not be to the extent of their population.

A scheme of representation should be devised to ensure:

1. that every state or unit be represented;

2. that the larger and more powerful states be given greater representation, but not in proportion to their strength;

3. that the United States, providing two-thirds of the population and an even greater proportion of the economic and military strength, should be represented in numbers ensuring that it could not be easily outvoted; and yet be short of an absolute majority. That is to say, it would be in a position in which it could secure a majority by the adherence of a limited number of other delegates. The sort of proportions that might be suitable could be of the following type:

| | |
|---|---:|
| United States | 49 |
| United Kingdom | 18 |
| Canada | 9 |
| Australia | 7 |
| New Zealand | 3 |
| **Subtotal** | **86** |
| Ireland | 3 |
| Jamaica | 3 |
| Trinidad | 2 |
| Caribbean (other) | 2 |
| Pacific | 4 |
| **Total** | **100** |

There are various ways in which such a result can be given formal definition—by weighting in one sense or another the populations, the federal or nonfederal structure, and so forth of the states concerned. This particular numbering was obtained by the following formula: (a) two members for each unit; (b) one additional member from federal-multiple states for each unit larger than one million and a half inhabitants, or unitary states if that state has such a population; (c) one member for each state passing each multiple of ten million; but ten members for each state passing fifty million; and (d) one member for each "region" exceeding fifty million inhabitants for a state of over one hundred million. This, like alternative methods, is of course very arbitrary. But a rule or definition even of this sort is always useful.

The last provision (d) would, of course, apply only to the United States, which falls naturally into four such cases:

- A Southern region, made up of the Old Confederacy less Texas, and with the addition of Kentucky and Missouri.
- A Midwestern Region, including the twelve states usually so designated, plus Oklahoma.
- A North Eastern Region, consisting of New England, New York, New Jersey, Pennsylvania and Delaware, Maryland, West Virginia and the District of Columbia (and the commonwealth of Puerto Rico, if so willing).
- A Western Region, including the Pacific and Mountain states, plus Texas, with Hawaii and Alaska.

The second-biggest population is that of the United Kingdom. The country is already divided into recognizable national regions, plus three small areas that do not even come under, nor are represented in, the Westminster parliament—the Isle of Man, with its own parliament and laws, and the two bailiwicks of the Channel Islands. Northern Ireland, though represented in Westminster, also has its own parliament, although it is sometimes suspended. There are also representative bodies in Scotland, a country with, in any case, a totally different legal system from that of England, and in Wales, where numbers of English laws do not apply, or apply differently (from those on drink to those on the establishment of the church). Which will remind us that although the election or selection of the delegates rests with the member state, a declaration of intent to the effect that all the components of the nonunitary members should be represented is desirable—so that, in the United Kingdom, for example, not only the units of England, Scotland, Wales, and Northern

Ireland should be represented but also, if only in one delegate in alternate years, the Channel Islands, and the Isle of Man, while Bermuda, the St. Helena and the Falkland groups, and Gibraltar also need consideration. The Caribbean Islands still dependent on the United Kingdom have been omitted in this sketch as probably better represented in a general Caribbean vote, but if the independent states of the area are not to participate in the first forming of the association, then the Cayman Islands, the Turks and Caicos Islands, Montserrat and the British Virgin Islands (in association with the U.S. Virgin Islands) might, if they chose, constitute a preliminary local grouping; and a similar group could emerge in the Pacific. Thus, at least at first, a portion of the votes of the British area might be nominated by the central government, and others by its competent areas (just as similar arguments might be appropriate for the United States). For example, the nominees of Scotland would be selected by the Scottish assembly, and the nonfederal American nominees either appointed by the state legislatures or by the "regions" of states through a committee of their governors. There are various conceivable methods. The important thing would be to encourage the springing up of alignments cutting across the original national boundaries. The transfer of as much of this representation as possible to a state and regional basis would tend to prevent, in particular, any impression of a monolithic imposition of American will or, more to the point, of the misuse of it.

One would hope and expect, in any case, that the delegations would soon, if not immediately, cease to form monolithic blocs but be divided on "party" lines—at any rate, one would hope this would happen with the delegations from larger states. Such "parties" would at first be no more than ad hoc alliances, but out of them something stronger might eventually develop, paving the way for a further consolidation of the Congress. For certain votes, however, a majority might be required within each delegation. In a longer run, direct electoral processes would doubtless be demanded, but all that is for the further future. If possible, the representatives should not be, or not long be, simply government appointees and spokesmen.

The Congress could, at first, have little power. It would be above all a great public forum and symbol of the unity of the Association, and a venue of high debate. The main work of the Association would probably be done by the congress's committees.

One may envisage the following committees:

a Foreign Affairs Committee
a Military Committee
an Economic Committee
a Social Committee
a Legal and Constitutional Committee

The two first named would conduct the main immediate policies of the association. The Economic Committee would concern itself with means of conducting agreed economic policies and providing greater economic unity among the member nations, and at the same time be a consulting chamber for the exchange of and study of economic experience. The Social Committee would concern itself generally with making experience and discussion in its field directly available to the constituent nations. The Legal and Constitutional Committee would devise and maintain the mechanisms and principles of the Association; at the same time, it would be concerned gradually to advance the legal and constitutional rapprochement of the constituent nations and to transmit the lessons of experience.

There might also be a Tribunal to adjudicate on such matters as the members wish to refer to it. It would have the advantage, for them, over the World Court that it would not contain any judges primarily responsible to party machines; and it would have the advantage over the European courts that it would be within an accepted idea of law.

When it comes to permanent staff, we can only say that after the experience of the EU, but also on general grounds, every effort must be made from the start to ensure not merely an absence of bureaucratic distortion but active work to prevent and combat the bureaucratic attitude. The permanent staff should be as small as possible, and both it and the representation in congress and its committees should be as far as possible not recruited from the bureaucracies of the home countries. It is likely that governments will find themselves even so making some appointments from their permanent civil services; but at least this should be kept to a minimum, and above all the antibureaucratic principles should be institutionalized as far as possible.

As, and to the extent that, the Association becomes involved in economic, judicial, and political processes, we can envisage the beginnings of a common citizenship. Again, it is largely a question of phraseology. If the meaning implied by "common citizenship" is too broad, some other phrase might be found implying fewer, though still substantial, rights.

The President of the Association must be the President of the United

States, the largest and strongest member. It seems logical that the Queen, as head of state of so many component nations (she is, we may note, sovereign of a dozen independent states besides the United Kingdom—of Canada, Australia, and New Zealand and countries in the Caribbean, the Pacific, and the Indian Ocean), should have a titular precedence, with some such title as "Queen in the Association."

As to the capital, there may be arguments in favor of Jamaica or the Cayman Islands, as being nearer to the Pacific elements of the Association. But on the whole, Bermuda (should the Bermudans be agreeable) would seem to be both a small and a suitable place, both racially and geographically—and probably not far from the point of balance when the confederation's populations are taken into account too. The hideous old American base there might be reconstructed and enlarged (not much) for the purpose, at least as a first step.

The embryonic structure here suggested for the Association marks the state of its beginnings, but also taken into account is its eventual evolution in some very long term into a greater unity. Such evolution should go more easily if the right direction is built in from the start.

In addition to those we have named, it is perfectly conceivable that other countries particularly close to our condition might also accede—for example, Norway and Gambia, in each of which English is widely understood and in each of which the political and civic structure is close to that of the rest of the states.

The new Association's flexibility could comprehend varieties of membership. For example, on defense, there are some of the smaller states which while wishing for the other benefits of the Association, might not want a direct military commitment. This could no doubt be solved by some such arrangement as their delegates not voting on defense issues. But membership of the Association, however partial and limited, must give full rights of representation in the larger Assembly.

For propounding what may seem to be too formal and schematic a plan for the Association, I am far from putting forward any single form of connection or membership as the only one possible. Since there are states in this worldwide category whose political, social, and geographical position varies so much, flexibility seems to be advisable. While the larger countries forming the core of the Association must be committed to its strategic and political unity, some smaller states may find it more suitable to accept, at least at first, only the less specific benefits of a general unity, consultation, and moral support. Flexibility in this certainly implies a variety of particular negotiations. The notion that in politics things can be imposed to suit the tidy schematisms of the theorist is the stigma of tidy-minded academics or of etatist bureaucrats or of dogmatic revolutionaries. It is by argument, by example, by all the untidy methods of real politics that our friends may be persuaded. And their own conditions of political life, their own particular circumstances, must be allowed for at every point.

Our Association should, in fact, emerge from a series of not interlocking so much as complementary, or supplementary, agreements. The scheme presented above should be regarded as no more than an imaginative exercise in envisaging the sort of result that might arise after some years of balanced negotiations.

As we have said, this can only emerge from, and may be regarded as a proper accompaniment of, a world that has been dealing effectively with its other huge array of problems.

Meanwhile, a Europe emerging from its present catatonia would have had a lot of trouble evolving, a subject we will not pursue. But, as I have argued elsewhere, a settled cooperation, including joint membership of various organizations, should *in the long run* bring the West, though not only the West, to agreement and adjustment—to the benefit of all sides.

# Select Bibliography

———⊶⊷———

Abramovich, Raphael. *The Soviet Revolution, 1917–1939*. New York: International Universities Press, 1962.

Almond, Mark. *Revolution*. London: De Agostine Editions, 1996.

Andreski, Stanislav. *Social Sciences as Sorcery*. New York: St. Martin's Press, 1973.

Applebaum, Anne. *Gulag: A History*. New York: Doubleday, 2003.

Aristotle. *The Ethics*. Baltimore: Penguin, 1955.

Aron, Raymond. *Democracy and Totalitarianism*. London: Weidenfeld & Nicolson, 1968.

———. *The Opium of the Intellectuals*. Garden City, N.Y.: Doubleday, 1957.

Ash, Timothy Garton. *The Polish Revolution: Solidarity*. 3rd edition. New Haven, Conn.: Yale University Press, 2002.

Bauer, Peter. *From Subsistence to Exchange and Other Essays*. Princeton, N.J.: Princeton University Press, 2000.

Bede, the Venerable. *A History of the English Church and People*. Harmondsworth: Penguin, 1968.

Beevor, Anthony. *Berlin: The Downfall, 1945*. London: Viking, 2002.

———. *Stalingrad*. New York: Viking, 1998.

Beichman, Arnold, ed. *CNN's Cold War Documentary: Issues and Controversy*. Stanford, Calif.: Hoover Institution Press, 2000.

Besançon, Alain. *La falsification du bien*. Paris: Julliard, 1984.

———. *The Intellectual Origins of Leninism*. Oxford: Basil Blackwell, 1981.

Bhagwati, Jagdish. *In Defense of Globalization*. New York: Oxford University Press, 2004.

Brovkin, Vladimir. *Behind the Front Lines of the Civil War: Political Parties and Social Movement in Russia, 1918–1922*. Princeton, N.J.: Princeton University Press, 1994.

——. *The Mensheviks after October.* Ithaca, N.Y.: Cornell University Press, 1987.

Bukharin, Nikolai, et al. *Marxism and Modern Thought.* New York: Harcourt, Brace, 1935.

Burckhardt, Jacob. *The Greeks and Greek Civilization.* London: HarperCollins, 1991.

Burnham, James. *The Managerial Revolution.* New York: The John Day Company, 1941.

Cherniaev, V. Iu., ed. *Piterskie rabochie i "diktatura proletariata," oktiabr' 1917–1929.* St. Petersburg: BLITS, 2000.

Churchill, Winston. *Winston Churchill's Secret Session Speeches.* New York: Simon & Schuster, 1946.

Cohn, Norman. *The Pursuit of the Millennium,* rev. and expanded ed. New York: Oxford University Press, 1970.

——. *Warrant for Genocide.* New York: Harper & Row, 1967.

Conquest, Robert. *The Great Terror: A Reassessment.* New York: Oxford University Press, 1990.

——. *Present Danger: Towards a Foreign Policy.* Stanford, Calif.: Hoover Institution Press, 1979.

——. *Russia after Khrushchev.* New York: Praeger, 1965.

Crankshaw, Edward. *Putting Up with the Russians.* London: Macmillan, 1984.

Djilas, Milovan. *Conversations with Stalin.* New York: Harcourt, Brace & World, 1962.

——. *The New Class.* New York: Praeger, 1957.

Dostoyevsky, Fyodor. *The Possessed.* London: Dent; New York: Dutton, 1931.

Enright, D. J. *Injury Time.* London: Pimlico, 2003.

——. *Interplay: A Kind of Commonplace Book.* Oxford; London: Oxford University Press, 1995.

——. *Play Resumed: A Journal.* Oxford; New York: Oxford University Press, 1999.

Ferrero, Leo. *Leonard de Vinci, ou L'oeuvre d'art.* Paris: Editions Kra, 1929.

Feshbach, Murray. *Ecocide in the USSR: Health and Nature under Siege.* New York: Basic Books, 1992.

Feuer, Lewis. *Ideology and the Ideologists.* New York: Harper & Row, 1975.

Frankel, Charles. *Human Rights and Foreign Policy.* New York: Foreign Policy Association, 1978.

Furet, Francois. *The Passing of an Illusion: The Idea of Communism in the Twentieth Century.* Chicago: University of Chicago Press, 1999.

Gellner, Ernest. *Encounters with Nationalism*. Oxford: Blackwell, 1994.

Gibbon, Edward. *The Decline and Fall of the Roman Empire*. London: D. Campbell, 1993–94.

"G. K. Zhukov: neizvestnye stranitsy biografii." *Voennye Arkhivy Rossii*, #1 1993.

Gottlieb, Anthony. *The Dream of Reason: A History of Western Philosophy from the Greeks to the Renaissance*. London: Allen Lane, The Penguin Press, 2000.

Graham, Loren R. *The Ghost of the Executed Engineer: Technology and the Fall of the Soviet Union*. Cambridge, Mass.: Harvard University Press, 1993.

Grossman, Vasilii. *Forever Flowing*. New York: Harper & Row, 1972.

——. *Life and Fate*. London: Harvill Press, 1995.

Haskel, Francis. *History and Its Images: Art and the Interpretation of the Past*. New Haven, Conn.: Yale University Press, 1993.

Haslam, Jonathan. *The Vices of Integrity: E. H. Carr, 1892–1982*. London; New York: Verso, 1999.

Haynes, John, and Harvey Klehr. *Venona: Soviet Espionage in America in the Stalin Era*. New Haven, Conn.: Yale University Press, 1999.

Himmelfarb, Gertrude. *The New History and the Old*. Cambridge, Mass.: Harvard University Press, Belknap Press, 1987.

Hingley, Ronald. *The Russian Mind*. New York: Scribner, 1977.

Hitchens, Christopher. *Orwell's Victory*. London: A. Lane, Penguin Press, 2002.

Hobsbawm, Eric J. *On History*. London: Weidenfeld & Nicolson, 1997.

Hollander, Paul. *Anti-Americanism: Critiques at Home and Abroad, 1965–1990*. New York: Oxford University Press, 1992.

——. *Political Pilgrims*. New York: Oxford University Press, 1981.

Holloway, David. *Stalin and the Bomb*. New Haven, Conn.: Yale University Press, 1994.

Ivanov, Iu. "Polozhenie rabochikh Rossii v 20-30 gg." *Voprosy Istorii*, #5 1998.

Jackson, Henry M. *Henry M. Jackson and World Affairs: Selected Speeches, 1953–1983*. Seattle: University of Washington Press, 1990.

James, Clive. *As of This Writing: The Essential Essays, 1968–2002*. New York: W. W. Norton, 2003.

Junge, Mark, and R. Blinner. *Kak Terror Stal "Bolshim."* Moscow: AIRO-XX, 2003.

Kedourie, Elie. *Nationalism*. London: Hutchinson University Library, 1961.

Kennan, George. *Memoirs, 1925–1950.* Boston: Little, Brown, 1967.

Khilnani, Sunil. *Arguing Revolution.* New Haven, Conn.: Yale University Press, 1993.

Khlevniuk, Oleg. *Politbiuro: mekhanizmy politicheskoi vlasti v 1930-e gg.* Moscow: ROSSPEN, 1996.

Khlevniuk, Oleg, ed. *Stalinskoe Politbiuro v 30-e gody: sbornik dokumentov.* Moscow: AIRO-XX, 1995.

King, David. *The Commissar Vanishes: The Falsification of Photographs and Art in Stalin's Russia.* New York: Henry Holt & Co., 1997.

Koestler, Arthur. *Arrow in the Blue, An Autobiography.* London: Collins, with H. Hamilton, 1952–54.

——. *Darkness at Noon.* New York: Macmillan, 1941.

Kolakowski, Leszek. *Main Currents of Marxism.* Oxford: Clarendon Press, 1978.

Kotek, Joël, and Pierre Rigoulot. *Le siècle des camps: detention, concentration, extermination.* Paris: Lattès, 2000.

Kramer, Hilton, and Roger Kimball, eds. *The Future of the European Past.* Chicago: Ivan R. Dee, 1997.

Kudryashov, Sergei. "Stalin and the Allies: Who Deceived Whom?" *History Today,* v. 45 #5, 1995.

Lal, Deepak. *Unintended Consequences: The Impact of Factor Endowments, Culture, and Politics on Long Run Economic Performance.* Cambridge, Mass.: MIT Press, 1998.

Lambert, Constant. *Music Ho! A Study of Music in Decline.* London: Faber and Faber, 1934.

Laqueur, Walter. *Fascism.* New York: Oxford University Press, 1996.

——. "What to Read (and not to Read) about Terrorism," *Parisian Review,* #3 2002.

Lenin, Vladimir. *Collected Works.* Moscow: Foreign Languages Publishing House, 1960–70.

Levashov, Viktor. *Ubiistvo Mikhoelsa.* Moscow: Olimp, 2002.

Lichtheim, George. *A Short Story of Socialism.* New York: Praeger Publishers, 1970.

Macaulay, Thomas. *Critical and Historical Essays.* London: J. M. Dent, 2001.

Macfarlane, Alan. *The Origins of English Individualism: The Family, Property and Social Transition.* Oxford: Blackwell, 1978.

Mandelshtam, Nadezhda. *Hope Abandoned.* New York: Atheneum, 1974.

——. *Hope Against Hope.* New York: Atheneum, 1970.

Marx, Karl. *Karl Marx, Frederick Engels: Collected Works*. London: Lawrence & Wishart, 1975–.

Matthews, Mervyn. *Privilege in the Soviet Union: A Study of Elite Life-Styles under Communism*. London: G. Allen & Unwin, 1978.

Medvedev, Roy. *Let History Judge*, rev. and expanded ed. New York: Columbia University Press, 1989.

——. "Pisateli Evropy na prieme u Stalina." *Moskovskie novosti*, 23 July 2002.

Moynihan, Daniel P. *Pandemonium: Ethnicity in the International Politics*. Oxford; New York: Oxford University Press, 1993.

Naimark, Norman. "Cold War Studies and New Archival Materials on Stalin," *Russian Review* 61 (January 2002): 1–15.

Nakhapetov, B. A. "K istorii sanitarnoi sluzhby GULAGa," *Voprosy istorii*, Moscow, #6 2001.

Oakeshott, Michael. *Rationalism in Politics and Other Essays*. London: Methuen, 1981.

Orwell, George. *Animal Farm*. New York: Harcourt, Brace & Company, 1946.

——. *The Collected Essays, Journalism, and Letters of George Orwell*. New York: Harcourt, Brace & World, 1968.

——. *Homage to Catalonia*. London: Secker & Warburg, 1938.

——. *1984*. Harmondsworth: Penguin Books, 1954.

Oskolkov, E. N. *Golod 1932/1933*. Rostov-na-Donu, 1991.

Pasternak, Boris. *Doctor Zhivago*. New York: Pantheon, 1958.

Pavlenko, Iurii and Raniuk, Iurii. *"Delo" UFTI, 1935–1938*. Kiev: Izd-vo Feniks UANNP, 1998.

Pechatnov, Vladimir. *The Allies are Pressing on You to Break Your Will*. Washington, D. C.: Cold War International History Project, Woodrow Wilson International Center for Scholars, 1999.

Petrov, N. V., and A. I. Kokurin. *Lubianka: Organy VChK-OGPU-NKVD-NKGB-MGB-MVD-KBG, 1917–1991: spravochnik*. Moscow: Mezhdunarodnyi fond "Demokratiia," 2003.

Pipes, Richard. *A Concise History of the Russian Revolution*. New York: Knopf, 1995.

——. *Russia under the Bolshevik Regime*. New York: Knopf, 1993.

Plumb, John Harold. *The Origins of Political Stability, England, 1675–1725*. Boston: Houghton Mifflin, 1967.

Powell, Anthony. *Messengers of Day*. New York: Holt, Rinehart, and Winston, 1978.

——. *Miscellaneous Verdicts; Writings on Writers, 1946–1989.* London: Heinemann, 1990.

——. *Under Review: Further Writings on Writers, 1946–1990.* London: Heinemann, 1991.

——. *A Writer's Notebook.* London: Heinemann, 2000.

Procacci, Giuliano, ed. *The Cominform: Minutes of the Three Conferences, 1947/1948/1949.* Milano: Fondazione Giangiacomo Feltrinelli, 1994.

Pryce-Jones, David. *The Strange Death of the Soviet Empire.* New York: Metropolitan Books, 1995.

Putnam, Robert D. *Making Democracy Work: Civic Traditions in Modern Italy.* Princeton, N.J.: Princeton University Press, 1993.

Rauschning, Hermann. *Germany's Revolution of Destruction.* London: W. Heinemann, 1939.

Remnick, David. *Lenin's Tomb: The Last Days of the Soviet Empire.* New York: Random House, 1993.

——. *Resurrection: The Struggle for a New Russia.* New York: Random House, 1997.

Rieff, David. *A Bed for the Night: Humanitarianism in Crisis.* New York: Simon & Schuster, 2002.

Riva, Valerio. *Oro da Mosca: i finanziamenti sovietici al PCI dalla Rivoluzione d'ottobre al crollo dell'URSS.* Milano: Mondadori, 1999.

Roberts, Paul Craig. *Alienation and the Soviet Economy.* Albuquerque: University of New Mexico Press, 1971.

Russell, Bertrand. *Portraits from Memory: And Other Essays.* New York: Simon & Schuster, 1956.

Sakharov, Andrei. *Alarm and Hope.* New York: Knopf, 1978.

——. *Memoirs.* Translated by Richard Lourie. New York: Knopf, 1990.

Sartori, Giovanni. *The Theory of Democracy Revisited.* Chatham, N.J.: Chatham House Publishers, 1987.

Schapiro, Leonard. *The Origin of the Communist Autocracy.* New York: Praeger, 1965.

——. *Totalitarianism.* New York: Praeger, 1972.

Seton-Watson, Hugh. *Neither War nor Peace: The Struggle for Power in the Postwar World.* New York: Praeger, 1966.

Slanska, Josefa. *Report on My Husband.* New York: Atheneum, 1969.

Solzhenitsyn, Aleksandr Isaevich. *The Cancer Ward.* New York: Dial Press, 1968.

——. *The First Circle.* New York: Harper & Row, 1968.

——. *The Gulag Archipelago.* New York: Harper & Row, 1973.

"The Spanish Civil War: The View from the Left." *Revolutionary History* 4, no. 1/2 (1998).

Spender, Stephen. *Journals 1939–1983*. London; Boston: Faber and Faber, 1985.

Stoppard, Tom. *The Coast of Utopia*. London: Faber, 2002.

Swianiewicz, Stanislaw. *Forced Labour and Economic Development: An Enquiry into the Experience of Soviet Industrialization*. London: Oxford University Press, 1965.

Symons, Julian. *The Thirties*. London: Cresset Press, 1960.

Szamuely, Tibor. *The Russian Tradition*. New York: McGraw-Hill, 1974.

Taubman, William. *Khrushchev: The Man and His Era*. New York: W. W. Norton, 2003.

Thompson, Edward Palmer. *The Making of the English Working Class*. Harmondsworth: Penquin, 1968.

——. *The Poverty of Theory and Other Essays*. New York: Monthly Review Press, 1978.

Tocqueville, Alexis de. *Democracy in America*. New York: Vintage Books, 1990.

Todd, Emmanuel. *The Final Fall [La chute finale]*. New York: Karz Publishers, 1979.

Trevelyan, G. M. *Clio, A Muse, And Other Essays*. London: Longmans, Green and Co., 1931.

Ulam, Adam. *The Communists*. New York: Scribner, 1992.

——. *Russia's Failed Revolutions*. New York: Basic Books, 1981.

Vaksberg, Arkady. *Stalin's Prosecutor: The Life of Andrei Vyshinsky*. New York: Grove Weidenfeld, 1991.

Vasil'ev, Valerii, and Shapoval, Iurii, eds. *Komandyry velikoho holodu [Commanders of the Great Famine]*. Kyiv: Heneza, 2001.

Weissberg, Alexander. *Conspiracy of Silence*. London: Hamilton, 1952.

Winslow, Charles-Edward Amory. *The Conquest of Epidemic Disease: A Chapter in the History of Ideas*. Princeton, N.J.: Princeton University Press, 1943.

Wolfe, Alan. "Paths of Dependence." *New Republic*, 14 October 2002.

Zhelev, Zheliu. *Fashizmut*. Boulder, Colo.: Social Science Monographs, 1990.

Zirkle, Conway. *Death of a Science in Russia*. Philadelphia: University of Pennsylvania Press, 1949.

Zubok, Vladislav, and Constantine Pleshakov. *Inside the Kremlin's Cold War: From Stalin to Khrushchev*. Cambridge, Mass.: Harvard University Press, 1996.

# Index

Abakumov, Viktor, 112
absolutism, 38, 170
academe, 9, 37, 39, 40, 44, 49, 66, 112, 122,
   135, 166, 170, 204
   in arts bureaucracies, 196–201
   being morally "nonjudgmental" in, 107
   counterfactual agendas of, 124
   dumbing down of, 124
   humanities in, 175, 190, 196, 197–201, 206
   language requirements in, 198–200
   poetry analysis of, 180–83, 188
   political theory vs. reality in, 51–56
   publication demands in, 196–97
   radicalized, 140–41
   vocabulary and syntax favored by, 200–201
activism, 27, 38, 40, 50, 72, 191
   positive alternatives not offered by, 46
   student, 7, 9, 31, 54
   terrorism vs., 12
*Age of Discontinuity, The* (Drucker), 154–55
*Age of Extremes, The* (Hobsbawm), 88, 126
AIDS, 184
Albigensian Crusade, 64
Albright, Madeleine, 59
Alcibiades, 24
Alexandrian age, 182
Algeria, 82
   election in, 25–26
Alliluyeva, Svetlana, 154
Alter, Victor, 128–29
Amalrik, Andrei, 220
American Nazi Party, 12
American Socialist Party, 32
Amery, John, 155
Amis, Kingsley, 188
Anglosphere, 221–31
   capital of, 230
   committees of, 228–29

Declaration of Interdependence of, 224–25
   permanent staff of, 229
   representation in, 226–28
   structural evolution of, 222–30
   tribunal of, 229
*Animal Farm* (Orwell), 18
anti-Americanism, 7, 80, 140
*Anti-Americanism* (Hollander), 7
antipatriotism, 19–20
*Anti-Semite and Jew* (Sartre), 36
anti-Semitism, 36, 112
Applebaum, Anne, 109
*arete*, 177
Argentina, 83
Aristotle, 25, 52, 72, 82
Armenia, 168
Aron, Raymond, 61–62
art buyers, gullibility of, 195
arts, 175–201
   aesthetic judgment of, 175, 182
   artistic alienation and, 187–88
   "beauty" in, 177
   capitalist patronage of, 184, 191
   changes of taste in, 175–76
   craft in, 180, 189–90
   creators of, 176, 194
   downhill trends in, 175
   educational decline and, 189
   Impressionism, 186
   involved intellectualism in, 182–83
   literature, 178, 179–90, 191, 194, 197; *see also*
      poetry
   Mayan, 185
   Mexican, 184
   modernism in, 180, 184, 186–88
   Nigerian, 177
   Paleolithic, 63, 176–77, 188
   political elements in, 183–85

*241*

arts (*continued*)
  sciences and, 178
  skills and, 178–79
  Soviet, socialist realism in, 194–95
  stylistic experimentation in, 187, 190
  Turkish, 184–85
  unconscious elements of, 181
  valueless artifacts as, 191
arts bureaucracies, 175, 176, 191–201
  aberrant excesses produced by, 195–96
  activism and, 191
  alternative ideas marginalized by, 193
  art employees in, 192–93, 194
  bad taste of, 194
  BBC dumbed down by, 193–94
  canned-excrement scandal and, 195–96
  educational decline and, 191, 196–201
  literary influence of, 194
  prescriptive formulae imposed by, 194–95
Ash, Timothy Garton, 165, 166, 168
asylum seekers, 82
Athenians, 177
  Academy of, 72
  democracy of, 23–24, 37, 184
Atlee, Clement, 19
Auden, W. H., 36, 187–88, 189
*Ausgleich,* 66
Austria, 66
Averroës, 64
Avicenna, 64

Baader-Meinhof Gang, 12
Babeuf, Gracchus, 15
Bakunin, Mikhail, 91
Baltic-White Sea Canal, 108–9, 121
bank robberies, by Bolsheviks, 95
barbarism, 64, 68
  *see also* arts bureaucracies
Barents Sea, battle of, 132–33
Barzun, Jacques, 204
Baudelaire, Charles, 85, 185, 200
Bauer, Peter, 67
BBC, 193–94
Beauvoir, Simone de, 148–51
Bede, Venerable, 28
*Bed for the Night, A* (Rieff), 68
Beevor, Anthony, 128
Beichman, Arnold, 157–58
Belgium, 69
Beria, Lavrenti, 112, 118, 128, 161
Berlin Wall, 141
Bernal, J. D., 146
Besançon, Alain, 44, 166
Bevin, Ernest, 19

Bhagwati, Jagdish, 67
bin Laden, Osama, 69
Bismarck, Otto von, 39
*Bitter Lemons* (Durrell), 184
Blackshirts (British Union of Fascists), 32
Blakeway, John, 34
Bohemia, 66
Bolsheviks, 14, 42, 87–94, 102, 161
  administrative machinery destroyed by,
    27–28
  Central Committee of, 89
  Communist Party and, 93–94
  funding of, 95–97
  "masses" and, 88, 89, 90, 91
  misevaluations of, 87–88, 91, 92–93
  as Nazi agents, 51, 111, 120, 121–22
  peasants and, 92–93
  political terror policy of, 89
  proletariat and, 88, 89, 90–94
  Russian army destroyed by, 27, 28
  worker opposition to, 89, 90–91
Booker, Christopher, 81
Bosnia, 58
Bradford City Tramways and Fine Arts
    Committee, 194
Brett, Simon, 48
Brezhnev, Leonid, 167
*Britannia,* 198
Brittan, Samuel, 72
Brodsky, Joseph, 177
Browder, Earl, 137
Brzezinski, Zbigniew, 218
Budenny, Semyon, 127
Bukharin, Nikolay, 33, 91, 106, 108, 116, 122,
    170
Bulgaria, 11, 130
  opposition parties in, 137
  Stalinist takeover in, 142
bureaucracies, 10, 12, 49, 50, 62, 71–83, 175
  British, 43, 78, 191–94
  capitalism and, 74
  centralizing of, 71–72
  decline caused by, 71, 72, 75, 76–77, 83
  executive power and, 72, 80
  expansion of, 78
  individualism and, 71–72
  peripheral institutions of, 79
  power seekers in, 77
  Russian, 77–78
  transcendent justifications of, 78–89
  of universities, 77
  *see also* arts bureaucracies; corporatism;
    European Union
bureausophy, 78

Burgess, Anthony, 180
Burgess, Guy, 155–56
Burnham, James, 72, 216
Bush, George W., 80
Byron, George Gordon, Lord, 187, 189, 200
Byzantium, 79, 198
    iconoclasts vs. iconodules in, 73
    synodic records of, 47, 72

California, 168, 193
    counties of, 75
Cambodia, 17
Cambridge Five, 15
Camus, Albert, 45, 151
canned-excrement scandal, 195–96
Čapek, Karel, 63
capital account liberalization, 67
capitalism, 11, 17, 20, 50, 62, 73, 74, 160, 184,
    191
Carlisle, Donald, 123
Carlyle, Thomas, 38
Carr, E. H., 87–88, 104–8
Castro, Fidel, 76, 163–64
cave paintings, Paleolithic, 63, 176–77, 188
Ceres, 40
Chamberlain, Neville, 53
Charles II, King of England, 122
Chartism, 41
Chénier, André, 1
Chen Yi, 150
Chernayev, V. Ju., 90
Chiaromonte, Nicola, 53
children, Soviet purges of, 115–16
children's rights, 80
*China Youth*, 150
Chinese Communism, 146
    Beauvoir and, 148–51
    familial denunciation in, 150–51
    Great Leap Forward of, 107
Chinese Eastern Railway, 117
Christian Right, 46
churches, 7–8
Churchill, Winston, 53, 133, 136, 186
city governments, 73
city mobs, 25, 92
class war, 17
Clearly, S. E., 198
Clemencon, Jean-Paul, 196
Cloak Makers Union, 32
Clootz, Anacharsis, 38–39
CNN, *Cold War* documentary of, 93, 135,
    155–64
*Coast of Utopia, The* (Stoppard), 37
Cohen, Stephen, 106

Cohn, Norman, 107
Cold War, 133, 135–43
    mentality of, 141
    misevaluations of, 135, 139–43
    moral equivalence idea of, 139–41
    radicalized academic view of, 140–41
    in Soviet propaganda, 138
    triumphalism and, 142–43
*Cold War*, 93, 135, 155–64
*Cold War: An Illustrated History, 1945–1991*
    (Isaacs and Downing), 93, 155–64
Coleridge, Samuel Taylor, 182–83, 188
*Collected Essays, Journalism, and Letters of George
    Orwell, The* (Orwell), 157
*Cominform, The: Minutes of the Three Conferences,
    1947/1948/1949* (Procacci, ed.), 33
*Commissar Vanishes, The* (King), 121
*Common Sense about Russia* (Conquest), 213–14
communes, 15
Communism, 20, 32, 36, 77, 78–79, 82, 95, 107,
    160
    Chinese, 146, 148–51
    failure of, 12
Communist countries, 7–9, 19, 162–64, 165,
    167
    free holidays for foreign communists in, 98
    "left" and "right" in, 11–12
Communist International, 162
Communist Party:
    British, 88, 97, 98, 139
    Czech, 25
    democratic centralism of, 97
    French, 98, 115, 138
    Greek, 105
    Italian, 98, 162
    Soviet, proletariat in, 93–94
    U.S., 98, 137
    world's, Soviet funding of, 96–98, 158
concentration camps, 30, 31–32
Condorcet, Marie Jean Antoine Nicolas
    Caritat, Marquis de, 38
conformism, 10, 12, 45, 49, 72, 79, 147
Confucius, 37
Connolly, Cyril, 191
*Conquest of Epidemic Disease, The* (Winthrop), 41
Conrad, Joseph, 63
consensuality, 8, 11–12, 18, 24, 25, 27, 28, 29,
    46, 72, 75–76, 206
conservatism, 12, 13, 18, 20
"conspiracy of equals," 15
Constantine V, 73
Constitution, U.S., 38
Continental Congress, 225
Ćopić, Vladmir, 139

Cornford, Morris, 98
corporatism, 9, 72–79, 82, 83, 193, 194, 222
  of city governments, 73
  declining educational system and, 75–76
  intellectual rebels and, 76
  new bureaucracy of, 76–79
  as "pink Fascism," 73, 78
  progressive ideology in, 78–79
  similar political parties in, 73
  small business vs., 74, 75
Council of People's Commissars, 89
Cranston, Maurice, 3
Creevey, Thomas, 46
*Crime and Punishment* (Dostoyevsky), 78
Cromwell, Richard, 122
Cuba, 103, 163–64
Cummings, E. E., 187
Czechoslovakia, 11, 34, 66, 153–54, 162, 199
  Communist coup in, 25
  free holidays for foreign Communists in, 98
  1968 liberalization of, 53–54
  Slánský's execution in, 139

Dada, 76
Damaskinos, Archbishop, 32
Dante, Alighieri, 188–89
Davie, Donald, 132–33
Davies, Joseph, 99, 116
Davies, R. W., 113
*Decline of the West?* (Seton-Watson), 39
Defense Department, U.S., 49–50
Delors, Jacques, 222
democracy, 8, 12, 18, 23–30, 162–63, 166
  Athenian, 23–24, 37, 184
  characteristics of, 26
  city mobs and, 25
  civic order in, 28–30
  concept of, 24, 29
  Fascist, 25
  free elections in, 25–26
  habituation in, 26, 27
  "people's," 25
  political apathy and, 27
  political culture of, 29
  self-defense as duty of, 29
  stability required by, 27
  undemocratizable institutions and, 27–28
democratic centralization, 65, 97
Denmark, 81
Derrida, Jacques, 40, 44
Deutsch, Arnold, 15
de Valera, Eamon, 66
Diana, Princess, 184

Djilas, Milovan, 18
Dobrynin, Anatoly, 156
*Doctor Zhivago* (Pasternak), 92
Donskoi Cemetery, 109–10
Dostoyevsky, Fyodor, 37, 77–78
Downing, Taylor, 93, 155
*Dream of Reason, The* (Gottlieb), 40
Drucker, Peter, 154–55
Dubček, Alexander, 153
Dubinsky, David, 129
Duclos, Jacques, 137, 138
Durrell, Lawrence, 184

East Germany, 137, 163, 166
*Economist*, 74, 188
"educated" class, 9, 15, 18, 20, 47–48, 49, 54,
  72, 74, 176, 190, 196
educational system, 79
  decline of, 75–76, 191, 196–201
  history in, 87, 206
Edwin, King of Northumbria, 28
Egyptians, ancient, 122
Ehrlich, Henrik, 128–29
Eikhe, Robert, 113
*Elder Edda*, vii, xi
Eliot, T. S., 180, 192
Elizabethan era, 42
Engels, Friedrich, 14, 17, 41, 42, 43, 50, 153
engineers, Soviet purges of, 108, 109–10, 117,
  119, 123
Enlightenment, 24, 37–44, 61
  British, 38, 40–42
  French, 38–39
  German, 39, 40
Enright, D. J., 1, 145, 188, 197, 199
Enron, 17
environmental issues, 62–63, 67
Epicureans, 73
equality, social, 19, 61–62
Erasmus, Desiderius, 37, 47, 55
Eratosthenes, 55
establishmentarianism, 73, 108, 176
euro, 222
European Children's Rights agreement, 80
European countries, 10, 12, 58, 67–70
  military strength of, 68–69
  obstructive mode of, 69
European Union (EU), 61, 79–83, 221, 229
  administrative structure of, 81–82
  concealed maneuvers in, 81
  corruption in, 82
  downhill trend exemplified by, 83
  English common law subordinated by, 80

mob rule in, 82
objections to, 79–81
regulationism of, 79, 80, 82
xenophobia as illegal in, 80
Evdokimov, E. G., 112–13

Fabian Society, 15–17, 79, 104
fanaticism, 7, 8, 27, 42, 64
Fascism, 11, 23, 30–33, 36, 82, 97, 125
characteristics of, 30, 34
as democracy, 25
in domestic context, 30–31
Marxist application of, 33
pink, 73, 78
racism in, 31–32
"right-wing" as, 31
*Fashizmut* (Zhelev), 11, 30
*Federalist Papers, The* (Hamilton), 29–30
Ferrero, Leo, 23
*First Circle, The* (Solzhenitsyn), 103
*First Domino, The* (Granville), 162
Fischer, Ernst, 120
Foot, Dingle, 65
*Foreign Affairs,* 220
*Foreign Policy of the Soviet Union, The* (Gromyko), 135
Foucault, Michel, 40
France, 34, 44, 45, 47, 68, 69, 149–51, 162, 186, 199
asylum seekers in, 82
Communist Party of, 98, 115, 138
Constitutional Court of, 82
corruption in, 75
democracy and, 24, 25
Enlightenment of, 38–39
health services in, 16
Holocaust reenacted by Olympic swimming team of, 196
intelligentsia of, 44, 61–62
left-wing humanism in, 151
modernism in, 186–87
navy of, 27
Paris mob experience of, 25, 92
Second Empire of, 24
and Soviet purges of children, 115
France, Anatole, 190
free elections, 25–26
free verse, 186, 188, 190
French Revolution, 38
"the people" in, 92
Frick Collection, 191
Frinovsky, Mikhail, 118
Frost, Robert, 186

Furet, François, 160
Furnas, J. C., 184
Fuseli, Henry, 182

Gaddis, John Lewis, 160
Galbraith, John Kenneth, 151–55
Gamarnik, Jan, 114–15
Garaudy, Roger, 220
Garfield, James, 66
Georgian Republic, 161
Germany, 31, 41, 69, 82, 83, 96, 106, 117, 162, 171
Enlightenment of, 39, 40
foreign visitors and, 34
horse-drawn army of, 161
philosophers of, 43–44
in WWI, 43, 126–27
*see also* Nazis
germ warfare, alleged, 146, 149
*Ghost of the Executed Engineer, The* (Graham), 108
Gibbon, Edward, 72, 85, 187
on historical evidence, 112
Ginsberg, Allen, 183
globalization, 63
benefits of, 67
nineteenth century, 64–65
global warming, 62–63
Goebbels, Joseph, 25
Goethe, Johann Wolfgang von, 43
*Golod 1932–1933* (Oskolkov), 102
Gomulka, Wladyslaw, 162
Gorbachev, Mikhail, 60, 106, 141, 160, 166, 168, 169
Gordon, Cyrus, 198
Gordon riots, 25
Gordov, General, 131
Gorky, Maxim, 32, 34
on Lenin's unhumanitarian views, 93
Gorky Pedagogical Institute, 114
Gottlieb, Anthony, 40
Gottwald, Klement, 98
Graham, Loren R., 108
grain production, 102, 154–55
Gramsci, Antonio, 17, 78–79
Granville, Johanna, 162
Great Britain:
academic publication demands in, 196–97
Admiralty of, 43, 78
agricultural productivity of, 167
asylum seekers in, 82
bureaucracy of, 43, 78, 191–94
city mob experience of, 25, 92
civil service staffing methods in, 76

Great Britain (*continued*)
  Colonial Office of, 78
  Communist Party of, 88, 97, 98, 139
  Conservative Party of, 16, 43, 192
  1832 Reform Bill of, 46
  empire of, 63–64, 68, 69
  English common law of, 80
  Enlightenment of, 38, 40–42
  Fascists in, 32, 82
  fox hunting in, 42
  immigrants in, 82–83
  Industrial Revolution in, 40–41
  Labour Party of, 16, 19, 97
  leftist thought in, 14
  "liberal" as term in, 13
  Liberal Party of, 16
  military aid to Soviets from, 132–33
  National Health Service of, 16–17
  1926 General Strike of, 43
  Parliament of, 40–41
  as signatory of treaties, 58, 80, 81
  socialism in, 13, 15–17, 42, 44, 104, 162
  Soviet espionage in, 15, 155–56
  undefeated navy of, 42–43
  U.N. delegation of, 57–58
  working class of, 41, 43
  *see also* Anglosphere
*Great Deception, The* (Booker), 81
Great Sanitary Awakening, 41
*Great Terror, The* (Conquest), 111, 118, 142
Greece, 32, 189
  attempted Communist takeover of, 105
Greeks, ancient, 52, 64, 177, 185
  science of, 178
  *see also* Athenians
*Greeks, The* (Kitto), 52
Grigson, Geoffrey, 200
Gromyko, Andrey, 135
Grossman, Vasily, 130, 164
"ground nut" scheme, 65
Guevara, Che, 7, 163–64
Guggenheim Museum, 193
Guild Socialists, 50
Gunn, Thom, 184

habeas corpus, 26, 38, 80
Haiti, 27
Halévy, Elie, 41, 204
Hamilton, Alexander, 29–30
Hapsburgs, 66
Harbintsy, 117
Harriman, Averell, 130, 137
*Harvest of Sorrow, The* (Conquest), 101, 104

Haskell, Francis, 122
Haslam, Jonathan, 105
Hastings, Warren, 112
Havel, Vaclav, 11–12, 13
Hazlitt, William, 178
Hecht, Anthony, 183
Hegel, Georg Wilhelm Friedrich, 40, 203
Heidegger, Martin, 40
Helsinki Agreement, 61
Herbert, A. P., 16
Herzen, Alexander, 37
Himmelfarb, Gertrude, 41
Hingley, Ronald, 48–49, 220
Hiss, Alger, 156
history, 5, 13–14, 111–12, 170, 180, 203–7
  ancient, 111
  documents and, 204
  in education, 87, 206
  improbable data in, 205, 222
  rebutting bad scholarship in, 205–6
  social, 204
  Soviet falsification of, 121–22
  of twentieth century, 206–7
*History and Its Images* (Haskell), 122
*History of Soviet Russia, A* (Carr), 105–6
*History of the English People in the Nineteenth
  Century* (Halévy), 41
Hitler, Adolf, 31, 34, 36, 42, 65, 66, 82, 107,
  130, 133, 136, 193
  appeasement of, 104–5
  election of, 25
  July 1944 plotters against, 25
  Trotsky as agent of, 51
Hobhouse, L. T., 19
Hobsbawm, Eric, 14, 87–88, 126, 168
Hodgkin, Dorothy, 48
Hollander, Paul, 7
Holocaust, 164
  French Olympic swimming team's reenact-
    ment of, 196
Homer, 200–201
homophobia, 36
Hook, Sidney, 59
Hoover, Herbert, 96
Hoover Institution Archives, 97
Hopkins, Harry, 123
"Horatian Ode" (Marvell), 184
Housman, A. E., 25, 181
Howard, John, 40
humanitarian aid, 67, 68, 96, 132
humanitarian laws, 13
humanities, 175, 190, 196, 197–201, 206
human rights, 57, 58, 61–62, 128–29

Hungary, 162
  1848 revolution in, 66
  1956 revolution in, 53
hydrogen bomb, 163

Ibn Batuta, 37
Ibn Khaldun, 64
iconoclasts vs. iconodules, 73
ideologies, 3, 11, 42, 73, 78–79, 160, 168, 175, 179, 203
  distortions in, 4–5
  generalities in, 87
  psychological thirst for, 79, 87
  uncritical acceptance of, 77, 87
Ignatieff, Michael, 58, 68, 69
immigration, 82–83
imperialism, 36, 63–66, 67, 138
  benefits of, 63–64, 68
  liberal, 68
  necessary military intervention and, 68–70
Impressionism, 186
India, 9, 107, 221
  Penal Code of, 63–64
  Second Five-Year Plan of, 67
Indian Ocean, smoked skies of, 62
individualism, 71–72
Industrial Revolution, 40–41
Inkpin, Albert, 97
Innocent III, Pope, 148
*In Parenthesis* (Jones), 186
Inquisition, 64, 158
*Institutio oratoria* (Quintilian), 178
intellectuals, 9, 19, 20, 47, 81, 87, 91, 97, 107, 159, 193
intelligentsia, 17, 20, 65, 66, 67, 120, 176, 179
  French, 44, 61–62
  ideological, 42
  Russian, 45
  Soviet falsification believed by, 51, 120
interest groups, 7, 81
  pressure brought by, 49–50, 72
International Brigade, 139
International Criminal Court, 59, 61
internationalism, 57–70
  and cultural attitudes to law, 58–59
  humanitarian aid in, 67, 68
  idealism in, 59
  law-and-liberty cultures in, 58–59, 61–62
  new Western alliance in, 69–70
  tribunals of, 59–61
  *see also* globalization; imperialism; treaties
International Monetary Fund (IMF), 67
international tribunals, 59–61, 229

Iran, 92
Iraq, 8, 58
Ireland, 81
Irish Fascists, 32
Irish Republican Army (IRA), 9, 66
Isaacs, Jeremy, 93, 155
Islamic countries, 64
Islamists, 26
"Isles of Greece, The" (Byron), 189
isolationism, 62, 69
Israel, 57
"Is Verse a Dying Technique?" (Wilson), 189–90
Italy, 9, 34
  Communist Party of, 98, 162
  differing attitudes to law in, 59
  Fascist Party of, 31
  Red Brigades of, 12
  sixteenth-century despotism of, 14
Ivinskaya, Olga, 147

Jacobins, 27, 92
James, Clive, 23, 200
Japan, 103, 149, 165, 221
  Meiji, agricultural productivity in, 102
Jefferson, Thomas, 87, 206
Jesuits, 55
*jeunes filles en fleur, Les* (Proust), 200
Jewish Anti-Fascist Committee, 118, 129, 139–40
Jewish Social Democratic Bund, 128–29
Johnson, Samuel, 19–20, 180, 185
Joliot-Curie, Frédéric, 163
Jones, David, 186
Jones, John Paul, 27
Jones, W. H. S., 52
*Journals* (Powell), 48
*Journals, 1939–1983* (Spender), 156
Jowett, Kenneth, 45

Kaganovich, Lazar, 113, 114
Kalmykova, Mrs. A. M., 95
*kalos*, 177
Kamenev, Lev, 89, 114, 121
Kant, Immanuel, 43
Karol, K. S., 220
Katyn massacre, 60, 125, 129–30, 149
Kennan, George, 123, 157–58
Kent State killings, 159–60
Kharkov Physics Institute, 120
Khatayevich, Mikhail, 102
Khlevniuk, Oleg V., 109, 112, 113, 114
Khmer Rouge, 17

Khodzhayev, Faizulla, 122–23
Khrushchev, Nikita, 51, 118, 120, 132, 154,
    163, 166, 167
Khrushchev, Sergei, 163
Kiev Medical Inspectorate, 102
King, David, 121
Kinsella, Thomas, 184
Kipling, Rudyard, 42–43, 190
Kirov, Sergey, assassination of, 112–14
*K istorii revoliutsii v Bukhare i natsional'nogo*
    *razmezhevaniia Srednei Azii*
    (Khodzhayev), 123
Kitto, H. D. F., 52
Klopstock, Friedrich, 176
Knox, Bernard, 200–201
Kodatsky, I. F., 113
Kolakowski, Leszek, 160
Koltsov, Mikhail, 119
Kosior, Stanislav, 113
Kostov, Traicho, 142
Kotek, Joel, 31–32
Kozlov, Frol, 167
*Kritika*, 123
Kuibyshev, Valerian, 113
kulaks, 33, 65, 101, 102, 117
Kulik, Grigory, 127, 131
Kulik, Mrs. Grigory, execution of, 131
Kyoto Protocol, 62

Lal, Deepak, 67
Lambert, Constant, 179
Landau, Lev, 120
Langlois, Maurice, 44
Laqueur, Walter, 12
Larbaud, Válery, 200
Larkin, Philip, 48, 146
Lascaux Cave, 63, 176–77
Latvia, 90, 117
Lautréamont, 187
law-and-liberty cultures, 9, 26, 29, 38, 44, 65,
    72, 79, 83, 206, 221, 222
  current attacks on, 46
  internationalism and, 58–59, 61–62
  mental threats to evolution of, 50
*Law and the Profits, The* (Parkinson), 76
League of Nations, 60
Leavis, F. R., 146
Lebanon, 64
leftism, left wing, 7, 11–21, 31, 33, 47, 48, 69,
    97, 151, 162
Lenin, Vladimir, 14, 32, 35, 42, 65, 111, 161,
    164
  church valuables seized by, 96

in CNN's *Cold War,* 155
  death of, 93
  faked photograph of, 121
  funding methods of, 95, 96
  inhumanity of, 93
  massacres ordered by, 93
  on religion, 155
  scoundrels utilized by, 92
  U.S. humanitarian aid allowed by, 96
  workers and, 89, 90–91
  world revolution and, 137
Leninism, 8, 17, 45, 65, 89, 97, 159
*Lenin's Tomb* (Remnick), 131
*Léonard de Vinci* (Ferrero), 23
Lermontov, Mikhail, 187
Levashov, Victor, 112
*levée en masse,* 24, 39
Levine, Léon, 44
*L'Humanité,* 115
liberal imperialism, 68
*Liberalism* (Hobhouse), 19
liberalism, liberals, 7, 18–20
  anti-patriotism in, 19–20
  Bolshevik, 28
  coining of term, 13
  definition of, 18
  equality as politically imposed by, 19
  "renegade," 18–19, 20
liberty, 11, 18, 19, 23, 57, 108, 163
  equality vs., 19, 61–62
Libya, 57
Lichtheim, George, 65, 154
Likachev, M. T., 60
*Lion and the Unicorn, The* (Orwell), 149
literature, 147, 178, 179–90, 191, 194, 197
  *see also* poetry
Litvinov, Maxim, 136, 137, 160
Liverpool, 73
Locke, John, 204
Lominadze, V. V., 114
London School of Economics, 16, 104, 142
London *Times,* 105
London *Times Literary Supplement,* 67, 140, 192
*Long March, The* (Beauvoir), 148
Los Angeles, small businesses in, 75
Lukacs, John, 204
Luxemburg, Rosa, 108
Lyubchenko, Panas, 33

Maastricht Treaty, 58–59
Macaulay, Thomas, 5, 20, 112, 204
McCarthy, Joseph, 158
McCarthyism, 158–59

MacDonell, A. G., 183
Machiavelli, Niccolò, 52
McIlroy, John, 97
MacLean, Donald, 155–56
Macpherson, James, 180
Madison, James, 74
Mafia, 77
Magnitogorsk, 108, 109
Mahler, Horst, 12
Maisky, Ivan, 133, 136
Makashov, A. V., 123
*Making Democracy Work* (Putnam), 58–59
Malaya, 75
Malenkov, Georgy, 138
Mallarmé, Stéphane, 187, 188, 200
Manchuria, 149
Manzoni, Piero, 195
Marshall, George, 156
Martov, L., 91
Marvell, Andrew, 184
Marx, Karl, 24, 50, 53, 74, 153, 170
Marxism, 8, 17, 33, 36, 39, 40, 41, 44, 47,
   50–51, 65, 88, 91, 117
*Marxism and Modern Thought* (Bukharin, et al.),
   170
Marxism-Leninism, 8, 95, 160
massacres, 68
   Katyn, 60, 125, 129–30, 149
   by Lenin, 93
mass demonstrations, 25, 41, 67, 82, 139
"masses," 35–36, 41–42, 88
   Bolsheviks and, 88, 89, 90, 91
*Masters, The* (Snow), 145
Mayan art, 185
media, 49, 79, 88
Medvedev, Roy, 115
Mekhlis, Lev, 127
*Melodies Unheard* (Hecht), 183
Mensheviks, 42, 90, 91
Meretskov, Kirill, 127
Merkulov, Vsevolod, 127
Mexican art, 184
Meyerhold, Vsevolod, 158
Mezzogiorno, 14
Michnik, Adam, 11–12
Middle Ages, 38, 55, 178
Mikhoels, Solomon, 112
Mikolajczyk, Stanislaw, 137
Mikoyan, Anastas, 114, 167
military:
   defense technologies of, 75
   necessary intervention by, 68–70
   Russian, 27, 28

Soviet, 114–15, 117, 119, 126, 127–28,
   130–31, 166, 169
Soviet, Allies' aid to, 132–33, 161
women in, 49–50
Millennium Dome, 194
Milosevic, Slobodan, 8–9, 59
Milosz, Czeslaw, 46
Minogue, Kenneth, 45
minorities, 7, 8
Mironov, Vasili, 117
Missouri Militia, 12
mob rule, 25, 82, 92
modernism, 180, 184, 186–88
Molotov, V. M., 101–2, 113, 114, 136–37
monarchism, 14
Monarcho-Fascism, 32
Moncrieff, C. K. Scott, 199–200
Montaigne, Michel Eyquem, Seigneur de, 37,
   55
moralists, 194
More, Thomas, 14
Moscow Metro, 108
*Moscow News,* 115
Moscow-Volga Canal, 121
Mosley, Oswald, 32
Moynihan, Daniel Patrick, 62
Mussolini, Benito, 25, 31, 34, 193
*My Darling Clementine,* 189
Mytilene, 24

Nagy, Imre, 162
Napoleon I, Emperor of the French, 25, 80,
   122
   improbable career of, 205
Napoleon III, Emperor of France, 24
National Alliance, 12
National Arts and Media Strategic Unit, 192
National-Fascism, 33
National Health Service, 16–17
National Heritage Department, 192
nationalism, 19, 31, 32, 39, 65–67, 69–70
   containment of, 66
   regulationism and, 66–67
   terrorism and, 66
   unmoderated, 65–66
nationalization, 16, 53–54
National Socialist parties, 31, 65, 77, 82
   *see also* Nazis
NATO, 69, 70, 163
Naxalities, 9
Nazis, 25, 31, 53, 107, 149, 152, 155, 161
   Bolsheviks as agents of, 51, 111, 120, 121–22
   Gestapo of, 34, 125

Nazis (*continued*)
  Holocaust of, 164, 196
  IRA's support of, 66
  Nuremberg trials of, 59–61
  "people's" as term of, 35–36
  Poland invaded by, 60, 125, 129, 136
  totalitarianism of, 33–34
  in U.S., 12, 159
Nazi-Soviet Pact, 125
Needham, Joseph, 146
Neruda, Pablo, 200
New England town meetings, 24
New Party, 32
*New Republic,* 52
*New Yorker,* 177
*New York Times,* 153
Nicholson, Harold, 32
Nietzsche, Friedrich, 43–44
Nigerian art, 177
Nikitchenko, Iona, 60
*1984* (Orwell), 17, 35, 122, 146
Nisbet, Robert, 71
Nixon, Richard, 156
North Korea, 8, 17
Norway, 31, 32, 162
  in WWII, 132–33
*Norwegian Study of Power and Democracy,*
  222
Norwich, John Julius, 196
nuclear weapons, 65, 163–64, 184
Nuremberg trials, 59–61

ochlocracy, 25, 82
"Old and the New Physics, The" (Vavilov),
  170
old regimes, 14
Olympic Games, abolition of, 72
Olympic swimming team, French, 196
*Ora da Mosca* (Riva), 97–98
Ordzhonikidze, Grigory, 114
Orwell, George, 30, 47, 138, 146, 149, 183, 194,
  213, 216
  on anti-Semitism, 36
  on falsification, 122
  on future corporate state, 72–73
  on hostility toward anti-Communists, 157
  on renegade Liberals, 18–19
  socialism as defined by, 17
  Soviet collapse and, 168
Oskolkov, E. N., 102
Ossian, 176, 180
*Otello* (Verdi), 177
Owen, Robert, 15

Pakistan, 26
Palchinsky, Peter, 108, 109
Paleolithic art, 63, 176–77, 188
Palgrave, Francis T., 175
Pantisocracy, 15
pantomime horse, 73
Papkov, S. A., 118
*Paradise Lost* (Milton), 1
Parkinson, C. Northcote, 75, 76, 78
*Partiinaia organizatsiia Tadzhikistana v*
  *1924–1926 godakh* (Makashov), 123
*Partisan Review,* 12
Pascal, Blaise, 55
*Passagers Clandestins, Les* (Langlois), 44
Pasternak, Boris, 92, 119, 130, 147, 187
path dependence, 52
patriotism, 19–20
Pechatnov, Vladimir, 136
"Peculiarities of the English, The" (Thompson),
  41–42
Pedro the Cruel, King of Castile and León, 64
Pennsylvania, University of, 198
"people," 25, 35–36, 92
"People's Will" terrorists, Russian, 66
Pericles, 23, 24, 177
Peter I "the Great," Tzar of Russia, 170
Petkov, Nikolai, 142
*Petrograd Workers and the Dictatorship of the*
  *Proletariat, October 1917–1923*
  (Chernayev, et al.), 90
Philby, Kim, 155–56
philistinism, 179, 195
pink Fascism, 73, 78
Pipes, Richard, 154
planned economy, Soviet, 88, 101–10, 123
  collectivization in, 101–2, 103, 120
  crash industrialization in, 103, 126–27
  "cultural revolution" and, 103, 109
  execution of professional economists in, 106
  falsification of, 103
  Five-Year Plans of, 100
  grain requisition in, 102
  human costs of, 101–2, 109
  industrial increase in, 106
  misconceived giant projects in, 108–9, 110
  misevaluations of, 101, 104–8, 110
  1932–33 terror-famine in, 101–2, 120
  population estimates in, 104
  realities of, 108–10
  short-term goals of, 103
  steel production in, 103, 108, 109
  underqualified specialists of, 103, 109–10
Plato, 14

*Play Resumed* (Enright), 1
pluralism, 5, 6, 7, 8, 26, 27, 42, 45, 49, 64, 74, 77, 160
Poe, Edgar Allan, 200
*Poems* (Conquest), 44
poetry, 179–90
  academic analysis of, 180–83, 188
  classical, 188
  comic elements in, 186–87
  declamatory, 185
  decline in craft of, 189–90
  educational decline and, 189
  emotionalism in, 182–83
  form in, 189
  free verse, 186, 188, 190
  incomprehensible, 182, 188–89
  language and, 185
  light verse, 189
  old anthologies of, 189
  poeticisms in, 185
  political elements in, 183–84
  prose, 185–86
  stylistic experimentation in, 187, 190
  symbolism in, 186, 187
  translations of, 199–200
  typography of, 186
Poland, 11, 26, 101, 117, 137, 138, 162
  Jewish Social Democratic Bund in, 128–29
  Katyn massacre in, 60, 125, 129–30, 149
  Nazi invasion of, 60, 125, 129, 136
*Polemic,* 146
police forces, 54
*Politburo* (Khlevniuk), 112
Pollitt, Harry, 98, 139
polygamy, defense of, 16
Pound, Ezra, 177
poverty, 19, 63, 67, 68, 109
*Poverty of Theory and Other Essays, The*
  (Thompson), 41–42
Powell, Anthony, 48, 173, 179, 186
power, drive to, 77
*Power and Policy in the USSR* (Conquest), 214
*Power in the Kremlin* (Tatu), 217–18
Praed, Winthrop Mackworth, 19–20
*Present Danger* (Conquest), 141, 218–19
"Prevention of Literature, The" (Orwell), 18–19
primitivism, 52, 184
*Private Art, The* (Grigson), 200
Procacci, Giuliano, 33
progressivism, 12, 13, 14, 15, 23, 47, 45, 78–79
proletariat, 88, 89, 90–94
  modern conceptions of, 91–92
  Roman definitions of, 91

  in Soviet Communist Party, 93–94
  and "the people," in French Revolution, 92
Proust, Marcel, 179
  translations of, 199–200
*Prussian Nights* (Solzhenitsyn), 161
Pryce-Jones, David, 81
Ptolemy, 55
Punic War, Second, 111
Putnam, Robert D., 58–59
Pyatakov trial, 109, 118

Quintilian, 178

racism, 31–32
radicalism, 13, 140–41
Rajk, Laszlo, 138
Rakovsky, Khristian, 94
Rankovic, Aleksandar, 18
rational choice theory, 52
Reagan, Ronald, 156
"Reconnaissance" (Conquest), 209–12
Red Brigades, Italian, 12
Red Scare, 96
Reed, John, 97
referenda, 13, 81
*Reflections on a Ravaged Century* (Conquest), 80, 135
regulationism, 58, 66–67, 72
  of EU, 79, 80, 82
"Rehabilitating Communist History" (McIlroy), 97
Remnick, David, 131
Renaissance, 37, 177, 182
*Report on my Husband* (Slánská), 139
Revel, Jean-François, 46
*Revenge,* 42
revisionism, 124
revolutionary movements, 5, 15, 24, 87, 184
  South American, 74
  worldwide, as Soviet goal, 135–37, 141, 160, 161, 164
  *see also* Bolsheviks
Rhodesia, 31
Rieff, David, 68
righteousness, 7–8, 21, 46
right wing, 7, 11–13, 31, 33, 46, 48, 69
Rigoulet, Pierre, 31–32
Rimbaud, Arthur, 44, 182
Riva, Valerio, 97–98
Rivera, Diego, 184
*Road to Harper's Ferry, The* (Furnas), 184
Rodos, Boris, 158
Rolland, Romain, 115

Romans, ancient, 91
  emperors unpersoned by, 122
  in Scotland, 204
Roosevelt, Eleanor, 123
Rosenberg, Julius and Ethel, 139–40, 156–57
Ross, Alan, 132
Rousseau, Jean-Jacques, 38, 71
Russell, Bertrand, 93, 203
Russia, 37, 42, 77–78, 87, 95, 103
  administrative machinery in, 27–28
  army of, 27, 28
  bureaucracy of, 77–78
  1891–92 famine in, 93
  foreign travelers in, 34–35
  future of, 169–71
  grain production of, 102, 154–55
  history of, 170
  Mongol rule of, 170
  "People's Will" terrorists of, 66
  in WWI, 126–27
  *see also* Bolsheviks; Soviet Union
*Russia after Khrushchev* (Conquest), 214–16
Russian Federation, 97
Rwanda, 58, 69
Rybalchenko, General, 131
Rykov, Aleksey, 89

Sakharov, Andrey, 130, 159, 163
Salerno, 14
Sandinistas, 91
Sartori, Giovanni, 160
Sartre, Jean-Paul, 36, 44, 148
Scandinavians, medieval, 178
Schlesinger, Arthur, Jr., 159
Schopenhauer, Arthur, 40
Scotland, 204
Searle, John, 40
Sebag-Montefiore, Simon, 113–14
Secchia, Pietro, 98
Second Punic War, 111
"Second Thoughts on James Burnham"
    (Orwell), 216
Seferis, George, 32
Senate, U.S., 152, 154
September 11, 2001, terrorist attacks, 6
  Arab bombers in, 9, 12
  extreme right wing groups' view of, 12
Seton-Watson, Hugh, 39, 220
sexism, 36
Shakespeare, William, 182–83, 186, 197
Shakhty trial, 109
Shapiro, Karl, 180
Sheinin, Lev, 60

Shenoy, B. R., 67
Shevardnadze, Eduard, 135, 141, 160
Shining Path, 9
*Short History of Socialism, A* (Lichtheim), 154
Shub, Anatole, 220
*siécle des camps, Le* (Kotek and Rigoulet), 31–32
Sierra Leone, 58, 68
Šik, Ota, 153–54
Simonov, Konstantin, 131
*Singled Out* (Brett), 48
Skinner, Kiron, 156
Slánská, Josefa, 139
Slánský, Rudolf, 139
Slutsky, Avram, 118
small businesses, 74, 75
Smart, Christopher, 185
Smith, Ian, 31
Snow, C. P., 145–48
social animals, 28
Social Democratic Party, 42, 95, 161
Social-Fascism, 32
socialism, 11, 13–18, 36, 45, 65, 72, 73, 77, 79,
    89, 115, 138
  British, 13, 15–17, 42, 44, 104, 162
  cranks attracted to, 14, 17, 20
  "democratic," 26
  dogmatic, 15
  origin of, 14
  state-controlled economy in, 17, 20
  statist version of, 13–14, 20
  working class and, 15, 16
socialist realism, 194–95
Social Revolutionaries, 90, 101
social workers, 54
Society for the Promotion of Roman Studies,
    204
sociology, 71, 204
Socrates, 24
Solzhenitsyn, Aleksandr, 103, 161
Somalia, 69
*Song to David* (Smart), 185
"Sonnet des Voyelles" (Rimbaud), 182
Sophocles, 182
South America, 74
*Soviet Communism: A New Civilisation?* (Webb
    and Webb), 17, 104
Soviet Union, 17–18, 31, 33–35, 51, 69, 87–171
  agricultural productivity of, 167–68
  air force of, 75
  census figures of, 51
  Central Committee of, 133
  collapse of, 11, 94, 108, 142, 165–71, 213–20
  Cominform, 33, 138

Comintern of, 32, 96, 139
conformist writers of, 147
decent hotels lacked by, 18
earthquake casualties in, 168
ecology of, 166
English espionage of, 15, 155–56
failed economy of, 166–68, 169
falsification in, 35, 50–51, 87, 97, 103, 111, 116, 119, 120–23, 168, 169
finances of, 95–99
food riots in, 167
foreign book royalties paid by, 98
Foreign Commissariat of, 97
Foreign Ministry of, 136–37
foreign revolutionary activity funded by, 96
gulags of, 109, 115–16, 117, 128
horse-drawn army of, 161
infant mortality in, 116
internal passport system of, 35
Jewish Anti-Fascist Committee trial in, 118, 139–40
Kharkov Physics Institute of, 120
literature as political weapon in, 147
Manchuria looted by, 149
mental control in, 35, 120–23
mental distortions in, 169–70
militarization of, 166, 169
misevaluations of, 12, 50–51, 89, 99, 111, 120, 122, 145–64, 166
and Nazi invasion of Poland, 60
New Class of, 94
1920s famine in, 96–97, 132
Nuremberg trials and, 60–61
oil exports of, 165
People's Commissar of Health of, 114
Politburo of, 101–2, 112–14, 118, 119, 132, 136, 167–68
propaganda of, 96, 97, 119, 138, 161, 169
Sanitary Department of the Gulag of, 116
scientists in, 119–20
as self-described proletarian, 94
socialist realism in arts of, 194–95
social order of, 167
treaties signed by, 61
U.S. ambassadors to, 99, 116, 130
U.S. humanitarian aid to, 96, 132
workers' pay in, 53–54
world revolution as goal of, 135–37, 141, 160, 161, 164
world's Communist parties funded by, 96–98, 158, 162
*see also* Bolsheviks; Cold War; planned economy, Soviet; Stalin, Joseph

Soviet Union, purges in, 94, 111–24, 126, 139, 142, 162
army officers in, 114–15, 117, 119, 127–28, 131
children in, 115–16
disabled people in, 117
economy as negatively affected by, 123
engineers in, 108, 109–10, 117, 119, 123
faked photographs in, 121, 122–23
fake trials in, 60, 111, 116, 119, 122, 138
mass operations in, 116–17
misevaluations of, 112, 122, 123, 124
national category in, 117
NKVD in, 112–13, 116, 117, 118, 119, 122
physicists in, 120
poets and writers in, 119–20
prescribed numbers in, 117
professional economists in, 106
rehabilitated victims of, 122–23
revisionism and, 124
suicides in, 114–15, 118, 119
torture in, 114, 118, 119, 127, 158
unassimilable elements in, 117
visual images amended in, 121–23
"Wives of Enemies of People" as penal category in, 115–16
Soviet Union, in World War II, 115, 125–33
army officer purges and, 127–28
basic military supplies lacked by, 132
British military aid to, 132–33
crash industrialization as justified by, 126–27
Gulag prisoners in army of, 128
heavy cruisers of, 126
human rights and, 128–29
Katyn massacre and, 60, 125, 129–30
losses of, 126, 127, 133
misevaluations of, 125, 126, 128
soldiers of, 126, 128, 130–31
Stalingrad campaign of, 128, 130
Stalin's military errors in, 127–28
Third Ukrainian Front of, 130–31
T-34 tank of, 126
U.S. military aid to, 132, 133, 161
Sowell, Thomas, 19
Spain, 13, 30
Muslim culture of, 64
Spanish Civil War, 139
spanking, banning of, 80
Spender, Stephen, 156
Stalin, Joseph, 8, 31, 33, 34, 77, 98–99, 105, 106, 107, 133, 135, 160, 161–62, 166, 193
altered portrait of, 121

Stalin, Joseph (*continued*)
  bank robberies of, 95
  death of, 110, 162
  evidence of disagreement with, 113–14
  faked photographs of, 121
  Katyn massacre ordered by, 129–30
  Kirov assassination and, 112–13
  1932–33 "terror-famine" and, 101
  postwar foreign policy of, 101, 135–37,
      141
  purges and, 112, 113–14, 115, 116, 117, 118,
      119, 139
  Rolland's conversations with, 115
  torture approved by, 118
  WWII military errors of, 127–28
*Stalin: The Court of the Red Tsar* (Sebag-
    Montefiore), 113–14
*Stalingrad* (Beevor), 128
Stalinism, 17, 18–19, 35, 45, 88, 108, 114, 136,
    142, 160, 162, 165, 169, 194
  characteristics of, 18
  postwar repression in, 131
  and soldiers' independent spirit, 130–31
*Stalin-Kaganovich Correspondence, 1931–36, The*
    (Davies, ed.), 113
*Stalinski terror v Sibiri* (Papkov), 118
"Stalin's Successors" (Conquest), 220
Stanford University, 168
State Department, U.S., 62
  East European Department disbanded by,
      123
steel production, 16, 103, 108, 109
stereotype labels, 36
Stevenson, Robert Louis, 4
Stoics, 73
Stoppard, Tom, 37
*Storozhevoy*, mutiny of, 167
Strachey, John, 32
Strachey, Lytton, 46
Street, Peter, 122
Streicher, Julius, 61
student activism, 7, 9, 31, 54
*Studies in International Communism* (Conquest),
    216
Sudan, 68
"surplus value," 53
Sweden, 7
Swianiewicz, Stanislaw, 106
Switzerland, 39
  rural cantons of, 24
syndicalism, 13
synodic records, 47, 72
Syracuse, 24

Syria, 57, 64
systems analysis, 51–52

Taliban, 48
Tate, Allen, 36
Tate Gallery, 195–96
Tatu, Michel, 217–18, 220
Teller, Edward, 159
Tenn, William, 83
terror-famine, 101–2, 120
terrorism, 8
  activism vs., 12
  Bolshevik, 89
  of French Revolution, 92
  moral deterioration in, 66
  *see also* September 11, 2001, terrorist attacks
Texas, counties of, 75
*Thaïs* (France), 190
*Third Way, The* (Šik), 154
Third World, 96
  poverty in, 67
  unmoderated nationalism in, 65
Thomas, Dylan, 184, 187
Thompson, E. P., 41–42, 88
Thucydides, 5, 177
Tiananmen Square, 160
Tikhon, Patriarch, 96
Ting Ling, 148
Titoism, 138–39
Tocqueville, Alexis de, 71
Togliatti, Palmiro, 162
Tomskii, Mikhail, 119
Tories, 19–20, 46
totalitarianism, 30, 33–36, 69–70, 73, 151, 160,
    194
  "left" and "right" in, 11, 31, 33
  mental control in, 35
  "people" and "masses" in, 35–36
Toynbee, Arnold, 204
trade unions, 16, 41, 159
Trafalgar, battle of, 122
treaties, 58–59, 61–63, 80
  public approval needed for, 59, 80, 81
Tretyakov Gallery, 99
Trevelyan, G. M., 204, 205
tribunals, international, 59–61, 229
"Tribute to George Kennan, A" (Beichman),
    157–58
Trilling, Lionel, 188
triumphalism, 142–43
Trotsky, Leon, 51, 89
  as Nazi agent, 51, 120, 121–22
Trotskyites, 159

Truman, Harry S., 156, 163
Tukhachevsky, Nina, 115
Tupper, Martin, 186
Turkish art, 184–85
Turner, Ted, 76, 135, 155, 160, 163–64
*Twenty Years' Crisis, The* (Carr), 104–5

*Ubiystvo Mikhoels* (Levashov), 112
Ukraine, 33, 101–2, 112, 119, 128
UNESCO, 62
United Nations, 221
  British delegation to, 57–58
  Commission on Human Rights of, 57
  composition of, 57
  Declaration on Human Rights of, 61–62
  ineffectiveness of, 58, 68
  Moynihan at, 62
  Scientific and Technical Committee of, 163
  Security Council of, 57–58
  supranationalizing of, 69
United States:
  academic publication demands in, 196–97
  agricultural productivity of, 167
  ambassadors of, 99, 116, 130
  anti-Communists in, 157–59
  art employees in, 193
  Communist Party of, 98, 137
  Constitution of, 38
  Defense Department of, 49–50
  downhill trend in, 72
  extreme right groups in, 12
  isolationism in, 62, 69
  military interventions by, 68–70
  naval aircraft of, 43
  Nazis in, 12, 159
  progressivism in, 15
  public image of, 62
  Senate of, 152, 154
  Soviet humanitarian aid from, 96, 132
  Soviet military aid from, 132, 133, 161
  State Department of, 62, 123
  technological lead of, 42
  as treaty signatory, 58–59
  *see also* Anglosphere
universities, 14, 15
  bureaucratization of, 77
  English departments of, 180
  publication demands in, 196–97
  student activism at, 7, 9, 31, 54
  *see also* academe
urban mobs, 25, 92
*Uses of Adversity, The* (Ash), 168
Utah, 16

utopianism, 14–15, 27, 92
  negative, 46
Uxmal, 185

Valéry, Paul, 23, 183
Vavilov, S. I., 170
Verdi, Giuseppe, 177
Verlaine, Paul, 182
Vilmorin, Elizabeth de, 44
*virtù*, 177
Voltaire, 38
von Kotzebue, August, 66
*Voprosy istorii*, 90, 116
Voronov, Gennadiy, 167–68
Voroshilov, Kliment, 114, 127
Vyshinsky, Andrey, 33, 60, 163

Wales, University of, 197
Wallace, Henry, 157
Walpole, Horace, 20
war crimes trials, 59–61
Warsaw Ghetto, 32
*We and They* (Conquest), 219
Webb, Sidney and Beatrice, 15–17, 51, 79, 104, 124, 145
Weissberg, Alexander, 120
welfare state, 82
*We Now Know* (Gaddis), 160
Whatley, Richard, 205
"What to Read (and Not to Read) about Terrorism" (Laqueur), 12
"When the Russian tanks roll westward" (Larkin), 48
Whigs, 19–20, 46
White Aryan Resistance, 12
Wiles, Peter, 53
Wilkes, John, 38
Willett, John, 34
Williams, William Carlos, 183
Wilson, Edmund, 189–90
Wilson, Harold, 146
Winthrop, C. E. A., 41
Wolfe, Alan, 52
Wordsworth, William, 173, 175, 184, 188
World Council of Churches Central Committee, 7–8
World War I, 16, 19, 43, 102, 104, 126–27, 186, 199
World War II, 16, 25, 34, 44, 60, 66, 78, 104–5, 124, 159, 165, 183, 199
  *see also* Soviet Union, in World War II
*World without War* (Bernal), 146
Wright, Thomas, vii

*Writer's Notebook, A* (Powell), 179, 186

xenophobia, 80, 83

Yagoda, Genrikh, 101, 116, 118, 121
Yaroslavsky, Yemelian, 89
Yeltsin, Boris, 160
Yezhov, Nikolay, 114, 116, 117, 118, 121

Yugoslavia, 8–9, 18, 33, 59, 130, 138–39, 159, 161–62

Zhdanov, Andrey, 138
Zhdanov, Yuri, 146–47
Zhelev, Zhelyu, 11–12, 30, 34, 35
Zhukov, Marshal Georgy, 132
Zinoviev trial, 60, 114, 118